BRINGING
UP KIDS
WITHOUT
TEARING
THEM
DOWN

Books by Dr. Kevin Leman

LIVING IN A STEPFAMILY WITHOUT GETTING STEPPED ON

PARENT TALK

UNLOCKING THE SECRETS OF YOUR CHILDHOOD MEMORIES

MAKING CHILDREN MIND WITHOUT LOSING YOURS

THE BIRTH ORDER BOOK

BONKERS

MEASURING UP

SEX BEGINS IN THE KITCHEN

GROWING UP FIRSTBORN

WERE YOU BORN FOR EACH OTHER?

KEEPING YOUR FAMILY TOGETHER
WHEN THE WORLD IS FALLING APART

BRINGING UP KIDS WITHOUT TEARING THEM DOWN

Dr. Kevin Leman

A JANET THOMA BOOK

THOMAS NELSON PUBLISHERS
Nashville • Atlanta • London • Vancouver

Published in Nashville, Tennessee, by Thomas Nelson, Inc.

The Bible version used in this publication is THE NEW KING JAMES VERSION. Copyright © 1979,1980, 1982, 1990, Thomas Nelson, Inc., Publishers.

Leman, Devin.
    Bringing up kids without tearing them down / Kevin Leman.
        p. cm.
    "Original publisher: Delocorte Press, 1993" —CIP data sheet.
    Includes bibliographical references and index.
    ISBN 0-7852-7806-0
    1. Child rearing—United States. 2. Self-esteem in children. 3. Parent and child—United States. I. Title.
HQ769.L37 1995b
649'1—dc20   95-12288
                                                           CIP

Printed in the United States of America
10 11 12 13 — 00 99

This book is affectionately dedicated to our daughter Lauren Beth Leman, born August 22, 1992. Although almost everyone thinks we're your grandparents, we take a great deal of pride and joy in being your mom and dad. Don't think of us as "old parents," just wiser and more experienced!

Love, your dad, and mom too.

CONTENTS

PART III
What to Do When Reality Discipline
Runs Smack into Reality

"I REALLY MISS YOU, DAD. . . ."

■

The greeting card came in the mail and, as he opened it, an eager father could see it was from his daughter who had just gone away to college.

"Does she need money already?" he mused as he took out the card. But there was no request for money. Instead the cover said, "Thanks, Dad, your strength helped me to grow . . ." And on the inside it continued: ". . . And your belief in me allowed me to be myself."

If the card had stopped there with just a signature from his daughter, the father would have been touched, but a rather lengthy note followed:

Dad, I hated saying good-bye to you. I didn't think it'd be that hard for either of us—especially you. I really miss you, Dad. It's weird, these past two weeks I've felt closer to you than ever just because I saw how much you were going to miss me. I miss waking up and reading the newspaper with you the most. I *loved* having you all to myself, early in the morning, sitting on the counter and reading and discussing the paper with you. I *really* liked the way you handed me the "Life" and "Dear Abby" sections before I asked for them!

Thanks for all your encouragement, Dad. Whenever I feel discouraged I think of all the times you wanted to quit but didn't. I'm very proud of you and all you've accomplished.

Dad, I love you so much, you're the best dad in the world!
Thank you for giving me an education.
Never forget how much you mean to me.
I love you!

I happen to know that the father who received this note got a tear or two in his eye when he read it, and who could blame him? It's the kind of note any parent would love to get after spending eighteen or more years raising a child from that day she comes home from the hospital and begins the incredible process of growing up. A note like this says that this father did a few things right—that he brought his daughter up without tearing her down.

This book is dedicated to, and designed for, all parents who would like to get a note like this someday when their children leave the nest. You may be wondering how this dad (and his more-than-capable wife) pulled it off—what their secrets of successful parenting might be. Come with me through the following pages and we'll find out, but along with that we'll be looking at something more important: how to raise each of your children to have a good self-image and a sense of positive, healthy self-worth that will take him or her through any crisis or challenge life presents.

BRINGING UP KIDS WITHOUT TEARING THEM DOWN

PART I

Self-Image? Why All the Fuss About Self-Image?

. . . Where and how to buy image insurance for each of your children

■

. . . How your parenting style was determined long ago, and what you can do to improve it

■

. . . Why "dysfunctionalism" can be a cop-out and how to have your family function as effectively as possible

■

. . . Some sobering reasons why parenting is not a part-time job

Chapter One

WHY YOUR KIDS NEED ALL THE IMAGE INSURANCE THEY CAN GET

■

The Priceless A-B-C's of Self-Worth

As I caught a "friendly skies" flight to a seminar recently, I passed one of those familiar flight insurance booths on the way to my gate. It occurred to me that, as a psychologist, I, too, deal in a very special kind of life insurance. I don't exactly sell it, but I help people find out where to get it.

My kind of insurance isn't sold in airports or on the thirty-second floor of some bank building. And it isn't available through your friendly good-hands people or any other major or minor carrier. The insurance I handle is symbolized in a conversation I've had with many mothers, which might typically open with Mom struggling into my office with her two-year-old in tow. Mom is dragging her leg as if she is wearing a ball and chain, and a quick look at her midsection tells me that the little fellow clutching that leg will soon be joined by baby brother or sister. After we exchange pleasantries, Mom gets right to the point.

"Dr. Leman, I'm not sure I'm ready to be a parent. My two-year-old is driving me crazy and another child is due soon, as you can see. I'm having all kinds of second thoughts, but most of all I keep wondering if I'm a good mother. I've got shelves of parenting books, but the experts seem to disagree and I wind up confused. Can you help me? How can I know what to do in any situation? How can I know what's *right*?"

"I'm not sure I can help you know exactly what to do in every situation," I reply. "That would take a perfect parent and there aren't any. All parents make mistakes. I've made plenty of my own with our four kids, and you'll make mistakes with yours. But instead of worrying about what's right, I'd like to have you think about taking out 'image insurance' on each of your children just as soon as possible."

"Image insurance? What's that?"

"It isn't any official policy that you can buy anywhere," I try to explain. "It's simply your unswerving commitment to developing a healthy self-image in each of your children."

"A healthy what?" Mom asks.

"A healthy self-image, which means your kids are responsible and capable, confident but not cocky, sensitive to the needs of other people but not doormats, always trying to do their best but never getting hung up on perfectionism."

"That's a tall order, Doctor. I'd just settle for having little Tyler here say 'yes' just once instead of 'no! No! NO!' "

"Believe it or not," I say with a chuckle, "Tyler is only doing what many a self-respecting two-year-old always does. He's testing his limits—pushing out those boundaries a little bit to assert his newly discovered independence. It's no reflection on you as a parent, and it's part of how he builds his self-image."

"I'm not sure I completely understand what is involved in building his self-image, but what you said a moment ago makes it sound like the most important thing in a child's life."

"In a way it is. Our self-image is how we see or picture ourselves. If we see a loser, we'll be losers. If we see someone who counts only when he's in control, we'll turn out to be pushy, overly aggressive, dominating, and insensitive. If we see someone who is loved and accepted, we'll be much more apt to love and accept other people as well. You see, however we act from even our earliest years is tied to our self-image. That's why I urge all parents to take out image insurance on their kids—to do all they can to help them grow up feeling good about themselves because that means they'll feel good about everyone else and get along better with people in the bargain."

The reason I work hard to sell new parents on the importance of plenty of image insurance for their children is because I've seen too many tragic results of what happens when kids grow up with a poor self-image. Parents really can't spend too much time learning how to build their child's self-image and sense of self-worth.

As Dr. Don Dinkmeyer, a colleague from whom I have learned much about parenting children, says: "A child who sees himself as worthwhile and useful has no need to develop destructive patterns. He does not turn to drugs and rebellion. He possesses a cooperative spirit, a sense of responsibility, and positive attitudes towards his family. His relationship with his parents is one of mutual trust and respect."[1]

SELF-IMAGE IS AS COMPLEX AS A-B-C

Whenever I talk to parents about taking out image insurance on their children, I begin with the A-B-C's of self-worth. While they may sound simple, building them into your child takes time—a lifetime, to be exact.

"A" is for acceptance and affirmation. Children who feel accepted and affirmed tell themselves, "Hey, I'm lovable. Mom and Dad really care about me." Along with my colleague, Randy Carlson, I am part of a daily radio program called "Parent Talk" that reaches over 130 stations in just about every state of the union. Recently we devoted an entire broadcast to the subject of self-image and building a good sense of self-worth, and during the program one woman called in to say this:

This is one area that I'm glad my mom and dad did a great job in. . . . I am not a very quiet person. I was not petite. I was not blonde. I was not a cheerleader. You know, I wasn't any of those neat things, but, boy, I had music and I could do plays at school and they encouraged me every day to do my best in those things. And they came and they were there. And I think that has been the secret with my own children. Not only did my husband and I tell them to go out and do it, but I think you need to be there for them.

This mother is describing what showing acceptance and affirmation is all about. To *be there*, to encourage, to hug, to pat, to support is to accept and affirm your child. All this should start early—the earlier the better, as I'll explain later.

In her memoirs, comedienne Carol Burnett remembers being bathed in the kitchen sink of the old house in which her family lived when she was just two years old. She is quite sure she was not much more than two because she could fit in the sink! Her mother kept the door of an old woodstove open, and she could actually see the heat waves in the air when she was sitting in the sink having her bath. Best of all, though, she remembered her mother drying her, holding her, kissing her, and putting her to bed. She sums it all by saying "It felt good."[2]

"B" stands for belonging, which is the other side of the acceptance coin. A feeling of belonging is one of the earliest building blocks in anyone's self-image. When a child feels he belongs, he tells himself, "I am worth something. I'm important. I fit in."

Children don't get very far in life before they run smack into situations where they're "on the outside looking in." They aren't welcome in the "in group." Maybe they find themselves without any friends or anyone to talk to. It's bound to happen sometimes to just about every kid.

One of the most moving stories I've ever heard is an old tale about a little boy who didn't fit in at school. His classmates ignored him. He was never chosen to play in any games. He had to stand and watch on the sidelines. He had to walk to and from school alone. Valentine's Day approached and he became very excited as he told his mother how he planned to give every child in his class a valentine. His mother smiled, but to herself she wondered and worried, "And how many will give him a valentine in return?"

The big day came, and the mother stood out in front of her home, waiting for her son to return from school. A group of his classmates came up the street, chattering excitedly and comparing all the valentines they had received from each other. And then her son came, walking alone as usual. She could see his hands were empty, but as he came up to her he was still able to say, "Mom, I gave everyone a valentine. I didn't miss a *single one.*"

Somehow, that little boy was able to survive an overwhelmingly cruel rejection. He was still able to believe he was important and worth something. In fact, he was more concerned with giving than receiving. I'd like to think that his mother and father had a great deal to do with that. When a child feels he belongs at home, he can stand a great deal of rejection out in the world.

"C" is for competence. Children with a good self-image are capable and they tell themselves, "I can do it!"

Along with my mother and my wife, my big sister, Sally, has always been one of the key persons in my life. She is an author in her own right[3] and a true genius in teaching small children. My family spends every summer in western New York State in a cottage on the shores of Chautauqua Lake, near the town where Sally and her family live. Last summer our little four-year-old daughter, Hannah, went to a different kind of vacation Bible school directed by my sister. The theme of the school was "Camp Can Do" and from the songs, to the memory work, to the handcrafts, the whole purpose was to show even the youngest children how unique each of them is and what they all can achieve if they just try.

Hannah came home excited every day, eager to show me what she could do or had done. As part of learning that they are special, every child at Camp Can Do had made her own T-shirt with her name and handprints on it. The symbolism was profound. Fingerprints say you are different, unique, not like anybody else. And along with that the children learned every day that they had ability, that they could do things, achieve things, make things.

I was pleased because it was obvious Sally and her staff were accomplishing a lot more than providing "good child care." As far as I'm concerned, their main objective was helping build my daughter's self-image in a positive and healthy way.

Feeling that you belong is important, but there is nothing like being able to do something, however simple or small. Actually doing something makes you feel worthwhile and capable. One of my early memories is of playing softball at the age of five with my uncles and other members of our family. I clearly recall hitting the ball and running around the bases *twice*. In retrospect, it's obvious that my uncles and the other older players deliberately missed the ball or made wild throws, and then they smiled as they watched a little five-year-old dash determinedly around the bases. I didn't realize what they were up to, of course, but I can tell you that it felt like a million dollars.

A GOOD SELF-IMAGE IS PRICELESS

The A-B-C's of self-worth add up to a healthy self-image. As Dorothy Briggs points out, "Children have two basic needs. Their self-respect is based on two convictions: I am lovable and I am worthwhile."[4]

When a healthy self-image gives you high feelings of self-worth, it is what Nathaniel Branden calls "the integrated sum of self-confidence and self-respect. It is the conviction that one is competent to live and worthy of living."[5]

A good self-image is a priceless possession, but the concept still worries and even frightens some parents. When I speak at seminars and workshops and mention self-image and helping our kids feel like "somebody," some respond with reservations they've been taught by *their* parents.

Won't all this talk about self-image and self-worth make a child self-indulgent, self-serving, and just plain selfish? Won't building up a child's self-image backfire and turn out a conceited, arrogant little brat who grows up to be a conceited, arrogant adult?

This kind of nonsense is worthy of the category I like to call "Bull crumble!" Conceited, arrogant little brats grow into conceited, arrogant adults because of having a *poor* self-image, not a *good* one. A healthy self-image doesn't *breed* selfishness or arrogance. It *prevents* it.

A POOR SELF-IMAGE CAN
LEAD TO REAL TROUBLE

Youngsters who grow up feeling they are "nothing" or "worthless" become troubled kids who struggle in school and have difficulty making friends. Or they make the wrong kind of friends who have similar problems. Often they grow up living fearful, insecure, defeated lives. It is not unusual for this kind of child to wind up in reform school or in jail. Numerous studies show that our reformatories and prisons are full of youngsters, as well as men and women, with terrible self-image problems. They grew up feeling they were nothing and nobody, so to become somebody they turned to crime and the result was arrest, trial, and imprisonment—all of which only added to their downward spiral of feelings of even greater worthlessness.

Our special guest on "Parent Talk" the day we focused on building a healthy self-image in children was Karen Johnson, director of the Explorer Program, conducted by New Life Treatment Centers in southern California. Karen and her staff work with twelve-, thirteen-, and fourteen-year-old children who have gotten into drugs or other related problems. When we asked her if the kids who come to the New Life Treatment Centers are there because of self-image problems, she said, "Probably the majority of the kids under care in our hospital, as well as the ones enrolled in our Wilderness program, are there because of self-image problems."

"Do you have *any* kids who have a great self-image?" I asked.

Karen's reply: "I would say no."

The New Life Centers Wilderness program zeros in on helping take youngsters' self-image from zero or below to a respectable level where they no longer feel that they are worthless and "can't do anything." The program includes a three-week campout in the wilderness. At the beginning, when they face such challenges as rock climbing and rappelling down the face of a cliff, the youngsters say, "I can't . . . I can't . . . I can't."

"What's so fascinating about our program," Karen related, "is that we can move them from a place of saying 'I can't' to saying 'I can.' We focus on helping them achieve success, and they walk away with experiences that no one can ever take away from them."

Karen works with children who have slipped over that crucial line and have already gotten into trouble because of poor self-image. You may be thinking that your child is in no danger, but please think again. I believe that few would argue with the fact that *every* child in America is in danger of being tempted and possibly succumbing to the use of drugs.

One of the key reasons children do get hooked is because they feel they aren't accepted, that they don't belong, that they can't do much of anything. All this adds up to feeling worthless. They are offered drugs by people—sometimes by children little older than themselves—who promise them good times, friends, and plenty of kicks. It's no wonder that kids try drugs. Why not? Here is their ticket to being *accepted*, to feeling that they *belong*.

When a parent sits in my office and tells me, "You make self-image sound like the most important thing in a child's life," she has no idea of how right she is. For every child, a positive self-image isn't a nice ideal—something we want to work on after being sure he or she learns phonics. Simply put:

A Positive Self-Image Is a Must

When a child grows up with less than a good self-image, he or she will be handicapped and possibly emotionally crippled for life. I've had adults sit in my office and tell me, "I'm fat," when in truth they were quite slender. Others have said, "I'm ugly," when, in fact, they were very attractive. But the most tragic ones are the teenagers who tell me, "I'm stupid . . . no good . . . defective . . . a retard . . . a failure." And then very often they add the crushing clincher, "My dad (or mom) says so."

Of course, it's true enough that a lot of us have grown up with a poor self-image and now, as adults, we're "getting by." Some of us may have learned to conquer feelings of low self-worth and we're functioning fairly well. But how much better it would have been to have grown up feeling affirmed and accepted, feeling as if we belonged somewhere and were worthwhile and feeling capable, competent, and able to do whatever we set our mind to. What about our own kids? What can we do to build a good self-image in each one of our children, especially if we don't have a very good one ourselves?

IMAGE INSURANCE TAKES MORE THAN MONEY

I wish I could just send parents out to buy an image insurance policy that would take care of everything, but that's not the way it works. Concepts such as "self-image" and "self-worth" are relatively easy to describe, but raising children to have strong feelings of self-worth is difficult and demanding. Parents who come to me for help often admit that they don't know how to "do it right." And why should they? They have had no training for what just might be the most challenging task in all of life—parenting.

It's ironic that in our society you need a license for just about anything—even keeping a dog—but there are no "parent licenses" being issued that I know of. Parents are expected to "wing it," and they muddle along, hoping that if they just "love little Buford enough," everything will come out okay.

Well, everything isn't coming out okay. Millions of kids are growing up with a poor self-image, lacking good feelings about themselves. And that's no surprise, because they are being raised by parents who don't have good self-images either. It's not unusual for parents to say, "Well, I'd like to help my child have a good self-image, but I don't have a great one myself. My own parents (or teachers, coaches, etc.) made me feel worthless a lot of the time."

"Great," I tell them cheerfully. "You have the problem half solved already because you're willing to admit your own weaknesses. Now at least you can be aware of how your insecurities can affect your relationship to your kids."

At this point I usually get a puzzled look. "What does *that* mean," Mom or Dad might ask, "especially when my kids are being brats and driving me crazy? Obviously I have weaknesses, but when my kids misbehave so badly, it makes me feel even more worthless as a parent and a person."

FIVE IMAGE INSURANCE PRINCIPLES YOU CAN USE DAILY

There is no need to feel defeated when your children misbehave and/or you have a bad day. To begin with, when your children make mistakes, misbehave, or act as if they are planning on making historians forget Attila the Hun, remember Image Insurance Principle #1:

Don't Take Misbehavior Personally

At crunch times—especially the "piranha hour" just before dinner—it helps to remember two things: (1) *All kids* misbehave and disobey at least occasionally; and (2) *all parents* struggle at times with feeling inadequate and even worthless. There are no perfect parents and, when your children act less than perfectly (which is practically all the time), I repeat, *don't take it personally.* Simply realize that they are growing up and they're being kids while they're at it.

I know this doesn't make their disobedience, laziness, forgetfulness, what have you, any less annoying or irritating, but it does help you understand what's happening. Why does Billy refuse to do his homework? Why does Janie have such a messy room? Why is it seemingly impossible to get Billy and Janie to bed on time each evening? Instead of wringing their hands over problems their children cause, parents need to stay calm and remember Image Insurance Principle #2:

All Behavior Has a Purpose

Alfred Adler, the father of individual psychology, took as a basic premise that all human behavior has a goal of some kind. He said: "No human being could think, feel, will, dream without all these activities being determined, continued, modified and directed toward an ever-present objective."[6] My Adlerian colleague Don Dinkmeyer puts it this way: "Behavior is best understood when it is recognized that the child always makes decisions to serve a purpose for him."[7] In other words, children will choose certain behaviors because they will get certain results that they want.

For example, I remember Buster, age six, who was afraid to go to bed by himself. "Too dark," Buster would plead. "Stay with me!" And so Mom or Dad (sometimes Mom *and* Dad) would stay with Buster until he fell asleep. Usually he was out in a few minutes, but occasionally he kept them tied up for a half hour or more. If Mom or Dad tried to leave while Buster was still awake, he would turn on the "water power" to make them stay.

As I worked with Buster's parents, I tried to explain what was happening. By being afraid of the dark, that fear served a purpose in Buster's life. In short, Buster was in control.

Buster was a powerful little guy, but he didn't hold a candle to another child I learned of who controlled his mother so completely that at nap time he would force her to lie down with him on the rug and then wrap his fingers in her hair before he went to sleep. When Mom would try to get away after he dropped off, he would feel the tug of her hair and scream bloody murder to make her stay!

As a parent, be aware that your child, sweet little ankle-biter that she or he may be, is always thinking, measuring, evaluating and deciding how to act—and often, how to act up.

When kids act up, a lot of it may seem like mindless or aimless fooling around, but don't you believe it. When little Buford tries to drive little Hilda crazy with his pestering, you can be sure there is method in his madness. When Hilda doesn't come for the fifteenth time after being called for dinner, you can be sure she has her reasons.

Whatever little Buford or Hilda do or don't do, they are working out how they see life and how they see themselves fitting into life around them—particularly their family. To put it another way, everything little Buford and little Hilda do is a reflection of their self-image—how they picture themselves in their own little world.

All children soon develop their own idea of how to succeed and stand out. In effect, they decide how they are going to "make their reputation in the world." Don Dinkmeyer believes that whatever children choose to be, they will want to be the best: ". . . the greatest athlete, the most helpful girl in the class or the cruelest boy in the block. Because we live in a culture that emphasizes the values of being superior in contrast to being equal, the child develops a reputation that gives him status, and then he behaves in ways that establish and fortify this image."[8]

If your child is misbehaving, one of the first things to look for is what is motivating him or her to act in that manner. Crucial to understanding your child is to learn *how a child thinks.* I always like to say that we must "Get behind a child's eyes." The more you can learn how your children see life and how they are trying to meet their needs, the more you can do to change their behavior by directing their search for status and significance toward goals that are more productive, beneficent, and acceptable.

Learning the basic lesson that all behavior has a purpose will send you well on your way toward mastering Image Insurance Principle #3, a concept that is the foundation of building a healthy self-image in any child:

Love Them No Matter What

In other words, love your kids *unconditionally.*

All the "experts" (including me) talk a lot about unconditional love, which is much different from "hoping you can love them enough and everything will somehow come out okay." Unconditional love is real, tough, and resilient. Unconditional love can cover a "multitude of sins," but it isn't done by simply "hoping" it will happen. It will happen only if you make it happen.

Nobody—and I mean nobody—has cornered the market on achieving or even explaining unconditional love. Loving a child "unconditionally" is a beautiful ideal and a vital target for every parent to shoot at every day. Will you hit that target every time? Of course not, but the better you understand your children and why they act the way they do, the more frequently you will at least hit the outer ring of the target. Occasionally you will even hit the bull's-eye!

Because unconditional love is so important, much of this book is geared to helping parents learn more about how it works and how to do it better. (See, for example, pages 70–73 in Chapter 3 for some practical tips.) The more often you hit the target of unconditional love, the better self-image your children will develop, because they feel loved and secure, even during the difficult times when you would like to wring their precious little necks!

Another key to taking out image insurance on your children is to value them as they are, not as you would like them to be all the time. Never forget Image Insurance Principle #4:

Parents Don't Own Their Kids

Instead, parents should remember that their kids are gifts from God, who are on loan for the few years in which we have the privilege and opportunity of bringing them up to become healthy, functioning adults. Of course, we all talk about "our kids." Mothers especially will tell me, "My kids are doing this or that." In one sense our children are ours to raise, protect, train, and nurture. But in another much more important sense, they arer't ours at all. *Each child is his or her own, unique person, and he or she should be valued as such.*

One of the best ways to value your children is to discover their assets and strengths and spend time encouraging and emphasizing them. I often say that if children don't have something that they are really good at by the time they get to high school, their self-image is in for some heavy weather. It's absolutely imperative that you bring your children up positively, always finding and affirming the little things they do in life. Then, when the children walk into that turbulent world called adolescence, they can be saying, "Hey, I'm a somebody."

For some kids, being "somebody" may mean blowing the tuba in the band at the Friday night football game. For others, it may mean being the point-after-touchdown specialist at that same game. Many kids, of course, aren't that visible. Many are "just average" but they can all develop an interest, skill, or ability, from stamp collecting to building models, from earning their own spending money to developing their own neighborhood business before they are seventeen.

The point is, everybody has to fit in, and the question is, what are you, the parent, doing today to make your children fit in? Remember the woman who called in during a "Parent Talk" show to say she wasn't the prettiest, the smartest, a cheerleader or anything "outstanding"? In her case, she had music and she got interested in drama, and that made her somebody—a somebody who grew up, got married, became a parent, and developed somebodies of her own. It can be done!

If you value your children, you will affirm them constantly. If an apple a day keeps the doctor away, at least one positive statement every day to your child will certainly help keep a bad self-image at bay. In other words, bring your kids up by building them up. Don't tear them down with a critical, negative attitude.

Yes, you will have to correct them and point out where they have made mistakes and where they have been just plain disobedient, irresponsible, and so on, but there are so many things you can say that are positive, so many words you can use that build children up rather than tearing them down. And when the time for discipline comes, keep Image Insurance Principle #5 in mind:

The Tail Does Not Wag the Dog

In his book *Bradshaw On: The Family*, John Bradshaw, whose television series of the same name was seen nationally on PBS, points out that the family is a system and that each person in the family plays an important part in that particular system. Bradshaw writes:

> Like all social systems, a family has basic needs: a sense of worth, a sense of physical security or productivity, a sense of intimacy and relatedness, a sense of unified structure, a sense of responsibility, a need for challenge and stimulation, a sense

of joy and affirmation, a spiritual grounding. A family also needs a mother and father who are committed in a basically healthy relationship and who are secure enough to parent their children without contamination.[9]

Bradshaw has much to say about how families can get contaminated, particularly by bad parenting. In Chapter Two we'll be looking at two particular styles of parenting that always contaminate the family: authoritarianism and permissiveness.

To avoid contamination and to keep the family on an even keel, it must be understood that no one member of the family is greater than the family as a whole. To put it another way: The whole is always greater than the parts. Although in authority, neither Dad nor Mom can put personal desires ahead of the good of the entire family. And when it comes to the children, the tail never wags the dog When a child runs the show, he or she quickly becomes spoiled, which affects the whole family.

When children are raised permissively, they become particularly adept at disrupting schedules and routines to suit themselves. Mom may make scrambled eggs for breakfast, as she does every Tuesday, but little Harlan decides he wants buckwheat cakes. And so, wanting to please her little darling, Mom makes a special meal just for him.

Schedule and order are key tools in making sure the tail does not wag the dog. Remember, the whole is always greater than any of the parts—even darling little Harlan.

As I've already pointed out in Principle #2, a favorite battleground for children is bedtime or nap time. This is a battle well worth fighting, not only because the children need their sleep, but because it keeps children from thinking their agenda is more important than that of the rest of the family.

When I run into parents who complain, "My child won't take a nap," I chuckle, because I know that isn't exactly true. Yes, there are children who seem tireless and who refuse to take an afternoon nap, for example, but they usually fall asleep a little later on the floor as they watch TV. Why? Because they're tired. The point is, kids *do* get tired. They do need a nap, perhaps not every day, but on most days they can use the rest.

All the Leman kids have followed schedules, some of them more willingly than others. Holly, our tightly wired firstborn, was the hardest to convince that "It's time for a nap now." She fought every inch of the way, and even when she finally did take a nap, she would wake up grumpier than before she went to sleep. Holly was a child who "woke up hard"—not at all in a good mood. Sometimes she would even wake up swinging.

No matter, we kept Holly on a schedule and it paid off. Today, as a college student, she still admits waking up isn't her favorite sport, but she is one of the most self-disciplined, well-scheduled—and unspoiled—people I know.

REALITY DISCIPLINE TEACHES
RESPONSIBILITY AND TEAMWORK

Obviously, the parenting style that most easily spoils a child is permissiveness, but the answer is not swinging the pendulum to the other extreme—authoritarianism. The answer is in helping children learn to become responsible and accountable for their own actions through an approach to parenting I call Reality Discipline: "a consistent, decisive, and respectful way for parents to love and discipline their children."[10]

Reality Discipline is a simple system that can work in any kind of family setting, where cooperation and teamwork are necessary for success. In the film *Hoosiers*, basketball coach Norman Dale (Gene Hackman) returns to tiny Hickory High School where he himself once played, to coach a team of mostly average players whose collective self-image is shaky and defeatist. Coach Dale is encouraged when he finds one boy, Jimmy, who is a deadly shot. The coach hopes to build a winning team around

Jimmy, but he has difficulty getting everyone to follow his instructions to play as a team.

As Hickory plays an early season game, Coach Dale finds it necessary to bench one of his starting players, a boy called "Rade," because he continues to ignore the order to make at least four passes before taking a shot. The coach puts in his sixth man, a boy who isn't very good but tries hard to be a team player.

In a few minutes, however, another starting player for Hickory fouls out. Automatically assuming that he is going back into the game, Rade jumps off the bench, but his coach quickly tells him to "Sit down!"

Just then a referee comes up and says, "Hey, Coach, you'd better put someone in. You have only four men on the floor."

Coach Dale gives Rade a hard look, then turns back to the referee and says, "My team is on the floor!"

Hickory loses the game, but Coach Dale doesn't mind. He had a point to make and, it's hoped, a lesson to be learned by all his players. That lesson was "The whole is always greater than the parts. No one player is more important than his entire team."

Coach Dale's strategy pays off. As the film progresses, his players realize what it means to build a team that pulls together. Their confidence increases with every game, and they go on to win the high school state championship of Indiana, a miraculous feat for as tiny a school as Hickory.

You may or not be a basketball fan, but I think you can see how this story applies to the family. The players are the "children," and the coach is the parent. When one player starts making the entire team revolve around him or her, teamwork, cooperation, and unity are hindered. If the situation continues, the team can be severely hurt, even destroyed.

Players on any team must know and believe that the whole is more important than the parts. This idea doesn't depreciate any of the parts: In fact, the whole exists to allow every part to develop its fullest potential toward personal fulfillment. In other words, when each part contributes to the success of the whole each part enjoys greater feelings of healthy self-image and self-worth. To put it in terms of the A-B-C's of self-image, when each family member becomes responsible and supportive to the whole family, then each family member enjoys feelings of acceptance, belonging, and competence.

TO RESPOND IS BETTER THAN TO REACT

One other thing is so important it's almost another principle in itself: When parenting, it's always better to *respond* to your child than to *react*. A response means that you are in control, that you are making choices, and that you aren't simply controlled by the same old knee-jerk reaction when children misbehave or just drive you a little crazy while they are acting like the children they are.

The five principles just outlined form a foundation for how to go about bringing your kids up without tearing them down. As you use these five principles, you will develop what Don Dinkmeyer calls a "response repertoire" for dealing with your children, lovingly, consistently, and effectively. The better you understand your children's behavior, the more effectively you can parent them in the endless variety of situations that occur through the day. As Dinkmeyer puts it, "Parents must learn how to expand their response repertoire with children and how to select responses that are effective."

You can build your child's self-image without completely losing yours, but image insurance does have a price. It will demand the very best you have to offer in commitment, dedication, and persistence. Many times you will think you are at war with your children. There is some truth to that. I often facetiously tell seminar crowds, "Children are the enemy." But, ironically, the real enemies are not our children. Pogo said it long ago: "We have met the enemy and he is us." We have to understand ourselves—

where we came from, how our parents parented us, and who we have turned out to be. We'll look at all that in Chapter Two.

Words to Remember . . .

- Image insurance is your unswerving commitment to developing a healthy self-image in each of your children.

- Children with healthy self-images are responsible and capable, confident but not cocky, sensitive to the needs of others but no doormat, always trying to do their best but never getting hung up on perfectionism.

- When children see themselves as worthwhile and useful, they have no need to develop negative attitudes and destructive behavior.

- The A-B-C's of self-worth are: feeling that you are accepted, feeling that you belong, feeling that you are capable—that you can do it.

- A healthy self-image doesn't breed selfishness or arrogance, it prevents it.

- Five image insurance principles to remember and use constantly:

  Don't take misbehavior personally.

  All behavior has a purpose.

  Love them no matter what.

  Parents don't own their kids.

  The tail does not wag the dog.

Actions to Try . . .

- Talk with your spouse about the concept of image insurance. How is each of you taking out image insurance on your children? Specifically, how do you make them feel accepted and affirmed, that they belong, that they are capable, and that they can do it?

- Try applying the five image insurance principles to your parenting this week and make a few notes on what happens. Ask yourself questions such as this:

    When my children misbehaved today, did I take it personally?

    When my children drove me a little crazy before dinner last night, did I remember that all behavior has a purpose?

    How well did I practice unconditional love? Am I intimidated by this term, or am I willing to try to "love my kids no matter what"? When I fail to do so, am I willing to admit my errors, put it behind me, and try again?

    What specific ways did I try to treat each child as a unique person? How am I helping each of my children learn to be good at something, no matter how simple or ordinary that something might be?

    Did the tail wag the dog today? Specifically, what did I do today to teach my children teamwork, cooperation—that the whole is always greater than the parts?

Chapter Two

"OH, NO! I TOLD MYSELF I'D NEVER DO THAT TO MY KIDS!"

■

How You Were Parented Is How You Will Parent

Her name was Cindy. She was in her mid-thirties, a bit too thin, with that "slightly worn around the edges" look that you see on so many mothers of young children. I had just finished an opening session of a weekend parenting seminar, and she stopped me afterward, introduced herself, and said: "I liked what you said tonight about taking out image insurance on our kids, but I have a problem. As hard as I try to build up my children, I keep slipping back into doing things I vowed I'd *never do*, because that's what my parents did to me while I was growing up."

"Give me a 'for instance,' " I said, and then waited for what I suspected would be a familiar story.

"Well, my parents always yelled at me. I could never please them, no matter how hard I tried. Even if I brought home seven A's, my dad would say, 'What about this B?' They were always raising the standards and it drove me crazy."

"And now you do the same with your kids?" I asked.

"I can't believe I have to say this, but yes, I do. My nine-year-old daughter gets straight A's, but I'm always after her to do better, just the way my parents were with me."

"Is that your major concern?" I wondered.

"No, it's my four-year-old son I'm really worried about. He's been a problem since he could crawl—before that, for that matter. He's into everything, very strong-willed. Can throw a temper tantrum like you won't believe. I'm spanking him more and more—and sometimes too hard. . . ."

"And were you spanked as a child?"

"A lot," she admitted. "And I hated it. I said I'd never do it to my kids, but here I am doing it anyway—it's almost like I have no choice. It's like a big magnet is drawing me into doing what I don't want to do."

"Well, Cindy, these are the kinds of questions I deal with in my office where I can go into them in depth. But I would say this. Don't give up on yourself. Your magnet analogy is right on. There is a perfectly good explanation for what is happening. If you can make it, be sure to attend the session on life-style tomorrow morning. Along with a lot of other things, you were taught a certain style of parenting by your own parents, and, no matter how much you may want to do things differently, you're going back to what you learned through their example."

As I watched Cindy walk away, I was sure that I had been talking to another parent who had grown up under authoritarian parents herself and who was now struggling not to revert back to the same kind of destructive style of parenting that had been used on her.

Every parenting style really boils down to one question:

HOW DO YOU USE YOUR PARENTAL AUTHORITY?

Yes, parents *do* have authority over their kids. Authority is clearly implied in being a parent. The word parent means "source, progenitor, guardian, and protector." The question is not, Do you have any authority? The real question is, Do you use your authority in a nurturing way? Is your style of parenting constructive or destructive?

AUTHORITARIANISM HAS BEEN
AROUND A LONG TIME

The authoritarian approach to parenting (also called autocratic or dictatorial) has been around ever since the first caveman waved his club at his kids and said, "As long as you live in *this* cave, you'll do things my way or I'll throw you to the saber-tooth tigers."

Today, of course, authoritarian parents have become a bit more sophisticated, but the basic attitude is the same. Children raised by authoritarian parents get distinct messages:

"Obey, or else. Don't talk back. Children should be seen but not heard. As long as you live under my roof, you'll do it because I say so, and that's that!"

Authoritarian parents love the motto "Spare the rod and spoil the child," which they mistakenly believe comes from the Old Testament. The Old Testament does talk about the rod, but the actual text of the verse says: "He who spares the rod hates his son, but he who loves him is careful to discipline him."[1] It's my conviction that when King Solomon used the word "rod," he meant it as a tool of correction and guidance rather than as a weapon to strike and injure.

In the Twenty-third Psalm, written by Solomon's father, King David, there is a verse that says: "Even though I walk through the valley of the shadow of death, I will fear no evil, for You are with me; Your rod and Your staff they comfort me."[2] Obviously, there is no thought here of punishing and hurting. And there is no fear that the rod will be laid across our backs or backsides if we happen to make a wrong turn in the path.

Authoritarian parents who believe the spare-the-rod philosophy are people who desperately need to control their children. Authoritarian parents demand obedience—as instantly as possible. Questioning, asking "Why?" and, heaven forbid, disobeying the rules are grounds for swift and often severe punishment. If children try to explain what happened, they are considered "mouthy and disrespectful."

Authoritarian parents don't believe in wasting time with dialogue. It is a bit of an understatement to say that, in the authoritarian home, verbal give-and-take is not encouraged. Not only is verbal give-and-take discouraged, it is not even considered an option!

All authoritarian parents share one basic characteristic—*they always are in complete control of those under their authority.* Being in control means making all the decisions. Authoritarian parents are absolutely sure they know best. They are strong on control but weak or sometimes nonexistent on live and compassion.

A controlling environment is a common denominator in all child abuse cases. Every few months, it seems, we learn of a child who is found chained, locked in a closet, or has been punished or beaten so severely that permanent injury, or even death, results. One of the most bizarre cases I have ever come across involved a five-year-old girl who was made to stand at attention for hours in the backyard under a blazing sun without and food and water. She was not allowed to go to the bathroom and, when she finally lost control of her bladder, she was beaten with a leather belt and forced to eat a bar of soap while standing naked in a corner.[3]

This kind of sadism is an extreme example of authoritarianism, but it graphically illustrates the *need to be in absolute control* that is always present when parents act in an authoritarian way. The most common scenario that I see is the young teenage girl who winds up in my office after being "kept under wraps" by parents, usually a father, who fear she will "get into trouble." Later, at age eighteen or nineteen, this girl may marry prematurely, simply to get away from her parents. The marriage seldom lasts, and later, when she is in her late twenties or early thirties, this woman winds up having the adolescence she never had a chance to have in her teens.

But there are even more subtle ways of using "absolute control" on children. One day a woman called while our "Parent

Talk" show was in progress to tell us rather proudly that she had her little eight-year-old son's summer "all mapped out." She had him busy from dawn to dark with summer school, practicing his trumpet, and any number of other activities that gave him not a moment's rest. I suggested to this mom that possibly she was overdoing it "just a little." Why not give the boy a chance to be a little boy and enjoy at least part of his summer by kicking back and doing whatever he liked?

Mom didn't care too much for my suggestion. She had *her* plans made, and, of course, her son was all penciled in to those plans. As far as she was concerned, she was doing him a favor by providing all these wonderful activities for him to enjoy.

One reason authoritarianism appeals to some parents is that it seems to work—for a while. In fact, it may seem to work through most of a child's growling-up years. But make no mistake: Children raised by authoritarian parents are keeping score and biding their time. Some day, in one way or another, they will have their shot and let their parents know that, underneath the facade of obedience, they are angry, hurt human beings who are "mad and [aren't] going to take it anymore."

I have counseled more than one pregnant teenage girl who was simply paying her parents back for the years of spankings, beatings, groundings, and dominating control of her life. When I served as an assistant dean at the University of Arizona, I dealt with a number of youngsters from authoritarian homes who came to college and, for the first time, found themselves free to make choices. Many of them chose to raise the roof and go slightly crazy.

We had the most trouble with freshmen who couldn't believe that they were really out from under Mom and Dad's authoritarian thumbs. We used to say that if we could get through the first semester, things might calm down a little and we'd make it through the year.

PERMISSIVENESS: LOVE GONE TO SEED

Authoritarianism used to be considered the old-fashioned, Victorian approach to raising children. In recent years, however, it has enjoyed a resurgence among many parents who have become sick and tired of the other extreme in parenting style: permissiveness.

While the authoritarian parents are absolutely sure they know best, permissive parents are absolutely sure that the only correct concept of parenting is to love, love, love. They are devoted to meeting every need of their little ankle-biters at every stage of life. Permissiveness is unconditional love gone to seed. Not surprisingly, the permissive parent is strong on giving loving support but very weak on control.

Bywords in the permissive home are such statements as: "Whatever you want to do, honey. . . . Well, I guess you can stay up and watch the movie—just this once. . . . Well, I guess you do need the car more than I do—I'll catch the bus. . . . Yes, I know it's hard to get up—I'll take you to school, I'm going right by there on the way to work."

Obvious in these statements are many attempts on the part of the parent to "feel noble" or to assuage his or her own guilt. After all, if you want to stay up and enjoy the movie yourself, why deny your child the same privilege, particularly if the film is a wholesome one? And isn't letting your teenager use your car while you take the bus a splendid way to meet the child's every need, which, of course, is your mission in life? And, of course, it's a noble mom or dad who can understand why it's hard to get up and who is always able to "be there" to bail the child out.

While at the University of Arizona, I also dealt with a goodly number of freshmen from permissive homes, who couldn't behave any better than the kids who had authoritarian parents. While children from the ultra-authoritarian home get into trouble

29

because they finally have a chance to rebel, children from ultra-permissive homes get into trouble because they just keep doing what they've been doing all their life—acting irresponsibly and with no concern for anyone but themselves.

I had many parents who would call me, ready and eager to fly out to help solve the difficulties that their teenage sons or daughters had gotten into due to irresponsible behavior. My reply was always the same: "Thank you very much, but please just stay there and we'll deal with it. If we really need you, we'll give you a call."

Permissive parents are always eager to snowplow the roads of life for their children. As attractive as permissiveness can look with its seeming nobility and sacrificial aspects, it starts backfiring very early, usually by the time a child is two or three years old. There is no sadder sight than permissive parents trying to "reason" with spoiled brats who know they are in control and that their parents are really at their mercy.

I have seen it again and again while counseling parents and their children:

Permissiveness Leads Straight to Rebellion

Parents come to me wondering "How can little Henry treat us this way? We've given him everything."

Exactly. And because Henry has had everything, he wants still more. There may be some child-rearing specialists who believe that children are basically good, but I am not among them. Yes, children are cute, sweet, and lovable, but they are also basically selfish, greedy, and self-centered until they are nurtured, trained, and lovingly disciplined. To bring up children and not meet their needs for nurture and training is to create a little Frankenstein who controls the entire family. In a home with permissive parents, children have the authority and the parents are the servants. For example:

The entire family is headed out for pizza, but little four-and-a-half-year-old Hilda the Hostage Taker wants to go to McDonald's. When she finds out that "we're going for pizza," she throws herself on the floor and screams and carries on until everyone gives in and decides that perhaps visiting Ronald McDonald is a good idea after all. Maybe *he* can handle Hilda—they can't

Another classic product of permissive parenting is the little fellow we might call Baxter the Barbarian. He is a total menace, particularly in someone else's living room (curse the luck, *your* living room!). While Mommy implores Baxter to put down that vase or to stop kicking the stereo, you sit there gnashing your teeth and desperately trying to think of a diplomatic way to tell Mom her parenting style isn't working.

One other example of the fruits of permissiveness is a little guy I observed just the other day in a supermarket. I wasn't officially introduced, but let's just call him Freddy the Fussy Shopper. While trying to find the cereal aisle (we were plumb out of Cheerios), I came upon Mom and four-year-old Freddy who was perched regally in a shopping cart, poised like Ben Hur for a chariot race.

"Oh, do you want this one, honey?" Mom inquired. The child was pointing to a box of crackers that had a surprise in it. Since Freddy couldn't read, I guess he could tell which crackers were which by the special emblem on the box announcing the big surprise inside. "Yes, that's right," said Mom, as she pointed to another kind of cracker, "those don't have a surprise and these do."

I stalled around, acting as if I were looking for crackers myself, and just listened as Mom and her four-year-old master made their way down the aisle to the peanut butter section. Again, Mom asked Freddy what kind of peanut butter to buy, and he was quick to give his opinions. I stuck with them until the next aisle over, and as I left to find Cheerios, the mom was asking Freddy what kind of spaghetti in a can she should get this week.

Now perhaps this mother thought Freddy was cute by asserting himself so loudly, but in reality Freddy was doing the shopping. He was making the decisions and Mom was carrying out his bidding. I'm not saying that a child can't ask for a certain product now and then, but in this particular instance Mom was the servant and her four-year-old, issuing orders from his shopping cart chariot, was the master.

And that's always the telltale sign of permissiveness. *The child is in control.* And because the child is in control, the parent often resorts to bribery to keep the peace.

"Just sit there and let the barber cut your hair and then I'll give you some candy," Mom begs her three-year-old. Or we find Mom with her same three-year-old who hasn't eaten any dinner and who is now fussing for a bedtime snack.

"Potato chips," chirps the child eagerly.

"No," Mom says firmly.

"But I'm hungry," her three-year-old shrieks.

"Oh, all right," Mom says wearily, and the snack is provided.

The routine is always the same. The parent says no, the child cries, and the parent gives in. I know of one case where a twelve-year-old girl who loved horses whined and complained so much about not being able to have her own horse that her parents moved seventeen miles farther from the father's employment to buy a home with property zoned for horses. That twelve-year-old got her way. Today she is thirty-four years old, single, unusually fond of horses, but so emotionally distant from people that she needs therapy.

Between the poles of authoritarianism and permissiveness are many gradations of the same kinds of errors. Some authoritarians, for example, can be syrupy sweet, loving dictators, so to speak, who still dominate and control their children. They still use an iron fist, but they cover it with a velvet glove. And some permissive parents seem to be in control but their kids know different. The kids go along most of the time and even seem to be obedient. But when push comes to shove, they know exactly what buttons to press to get their own way.

HOVERING PARENTS MAKE A BIG MISTAKE

A special breed of permissive parenting is the mom I call a "hover-mother." Fathers can show this same kind of behavior, but I see it much more often in moms who worry constantly that their child is going to be hurt and must be helped, assisted, and comforted at every turn.

For example, little Billy, age thirteen months, teeters on shaky legs as he hangs on the edge of the coffee table. Suddenly he decides to take off and gets all of three steps before winding up on his bottom. His mother has a great opportunity to let Billy learn what it's like to fail and then get right back up again. But, instead, she rushes to the rescue, asking Billy if he's hurt and giving him other hugs and reassurances. But this is not the time for a rescue; this is the time to smile and encourage Billy to try again.

Take this scene with Billy and multiply it by hundreds, if not thousands, of instances where the child is protected, helped, and comforted in the face of the slightest adversity, and you have the hover-mother syndrome.

I know of one hover-mother who won't let her children play with the neighbor kids, because she's afraid they might catch cold. She has two daughters and a little boy, but none of them ever plays with anyone. This isn't a seasonal policy; it lasts all year! Hover-mother is "protecting her children from germs" but she's not doing much for their social lives—or their self-image.

This kind of overprotection doesn't help children; it actually harms them, particularly later in life when they have to deal with the real world. In a letter to our local paper, a woman wrote about another mother who wouldn't let her nine-year-old daughter attend a party because the entertainment included ice skating and none of the girls attending had ever gone ice skating before. The woman's letter continued:

> Being a sheltered child myself, I know what it's like to reach adulthood unprepared for reality. It's like being all warm and cozy and then being suddenly dumped into a vat of ice water. It's taken me twenty years to get over that shock and to realize that my parents just love me too much and couldn't bear to see me get hurt.
>
> I still have an unreasonable fear of people. But getting hurt is what it's all about. How can we ever grow and learn if we aren't hurt sometimes? Mom is not always going to be there to kiss our wounds.[4]

Native to Indonesia is the upas tree, which is poisonous and grows so full and thick it kills any vegetation that might spring up beneath its branches. The upas tree shelters and shades, but it also destroys. Hovering parents should beware of becoming upas trees. They may not actually kill their children, but they do cripple them and, in some cases, the children remain babies all their lives.[5] My advice to Hover-Parent is:

Love Them but Let Them Go

Remember Image Insurance Principle Number 4: *You don't own your children.* Let them become individuals with thoughts and feelings of their own. Stop looking on them as extensions of yourself.

BOTH EXTREMES DESTROY THE SELF-IMAGE

The reason I have described authoritarianism and permissiveness at some length is because different versions of these two parenting styles often pop up in the families I counsel. Both styles destroy children's self-image and sense of self-worth. Authoritarianism leaves children without the A-B-C's of self-image —unaccepted and unaffirmed, not belonging and not feeling capable.

Authoritarian parents may have children who are extremely submissive due to the parents' demands and setting of severe limits. The problem is, demands that are too severe and limits that are too constricting stifle children's curiosity. Children of authoritarian parents often find learning to be an unpleasant task. I'm always a little concerned when parents tell me, "Little James is very obedient." When children are "very obedient," they may have had all of their curiosity squeezed out of them. Little James may easily fall into that sad category of children who don't express themselves much and who can't carry out a task unless it is clearly stated and minutely outlined.

Children parented by authoritarians often grow up to be very passive, lacking drive, creativity, and initiative. Their self-image is so battered and bruised they are content to be followers, trying to obey the wishes of others.[6]

At the other end of the spectrum, permissive hover-parents also destroy the A-B-C's of self-image because they rob the child of the experience of learning from his or her mistakes and failures. When hovering parents deny their children opportunities to conquer obstacles or achieve the difficult, these children soon begin to doubt themselves. This kind of child begins to feel, "My mother thinks I'm a baby."

Instead of feeling affirmed, accepted, and valued as a person, children feel, "I'm not good enough. They do it so much better than I do, so why should I even try?"

When you teach your children that others will do for them, they back off from life rather than meeting its challenges head-on. Permissively parented children also lack feelings of really belonging. Because no demands are placed on them, their wishes are always granted, and they can get plenty of help, they have few if any opportunities to contribute and enjoy the feeling of "Hey, I helped, I'm part of this!"

What makes a parent become authoritarian or permissive? Does it just happen after the children arrive? Do parents try parenting for a while and then decide on a certain style they'll use the rest of the way? Of course not. Everyone comes to marriage and parenthood with a predetermined set of views and values gained a long time ago, starting from the cradle. It's a simple and seemingly obvious truth:

How You Were Parented
Is How You Will Parent

You may disagree and tell me you are doing a lot of things different from how your parents did, and I'm sure you are. Nonetheless, I'm certain powerful forces have molded your personality, and when push comes to shove, you will revert back to —or be strongly tempted to revert back to—what you learned while growing up. If you doubt this, all you have to do is look back at your own family atmosphere, your birth order (place in the family), and your early childhood memories. All of these are integrated into a portrait of who you are today and the parenting style that you tend to use with your children.

WHAT WAS YOUR FAMILY ATMOSPHERE LIKE?

I often ask clients or people in a seminar session: "What was your home like when you grew up? Was it warm, friendly, supportive? Or was it cold, indifferent, hostile, or chaotic?" Whatever your family atmosphere was and whatever the style of parenting your mom and dad used, you absorbed all of this like a sponge.

Let's return to Cindy, the mom I met at a local weekend seminar who decided to call and make an appointment the following Monday. Apparently she had attended the life-style session I had recommended, and it had convinced her that she was making the same mistakes in parenting her children that her parents had made on her. Also motivating Cindy was the fear that her mistakes could develop into something very serious—possibly even child abuse.

After Cindy filled out the standard information form we use with all our clients, I greeted her warmly and said, "Well, I guess I know why you're here. You want to talk about what you mentioned to me the other day at the seminar."

"That's right," she said. "Why can't I shake these bad habits that my own parents taught me about parenting? It's getting scary, particularly the anger I feel toward little Billy. Just this morning before I left the house he made me so angry I shook him till his teeth rattled."

"This all goes back to the family atmosphere you grew up in. As soon as you were aware of your little world, you began making decisions about how to get along and how to solve your problems. As a little tyke, you developed your own 'plan for life,' so to speak, and from that plan came a certain style of thinking and acting that you did in definite patterns."

"What do you mean by definite patterns?" Cindy asked.

"It's sort of like the theme in a piece of music—there is actually a rhythm to how you deal with life, and you learned the tune a long time ago when you were a toddler. By the time you were four or six, at the latest, the grain of your wood was set, so to speak, and that's what makes you be you."

"And you're saying I learned all this from **my** parents?" Cindy wondered.

"I believe your information sheet says you were firstborn in your family?"

"Yes, that's right. I have a brother, Roy, who is five years younger than I am, and a sister, Meryl, who is the baby of the family. She's eight years younger."

"As a firstborn in the family, a great deal of your basic life-style came from interaction with your parents and possibly other adults. Your younger brother and sister learned from their parents, but they also developed much of their life-style from interacting with older siblings. But to go back to your original question, your parents are the ones who influenced you for the most part, and, by the way, they taught you an awful lot about parenting, even when you were very young."

"I don't see how I could have learned all that when I was that young," Cindy challenged me. "Can you explain how it works?"

"The way I usually try to explain this is to do what I call a 'mini-life-style sketch' on a person. Let's begin by asking you to pick one of your parents and give me a brief description of that parent. What was he or she like?"

"Well," Cindy said slowly. "Dad was very strict, but he did love us. He was a hard worker and a good provider. He wasn't around much—because he worked a lot as an engineer—but when he was home you knew it. We didn't dare sass him. He could make me dissolve into tears with just a look."

"Anything else on Dad?" I inquired.

"He wasn't much for discussing things. What he said went. And he could have a temper. You might say he was the boss."

"I believe when you talked to me at the seminar, you said you had been spanked a lot as a child."

"Yes, that's true. I guess I started out kind of strong-willed but my dad took that out of me. He spanked me until I was almost twelve years old."

THE PATTERN WAS BEGINNING TO EMERGE

As we talked I had been making several notes: (1) Cindy picked her father to describe first, which told me that he was the more significant parent in her life. (2) She used the word "very" several times. That gave me a clue about her own personality, which I had already pretty well figured out.

"Okay, that's good. Now tell me about your mother."

"Well, Mom was a very sweet lady," Cindy recalled. "She still is, for that matter. She is what you call a good mom—always there for you. Very supportive of Dad and all of us children. She always does a lot to please."

After making a few notes on Mom, I continued, "Okay, now I'd like you to give me a description of you between the ages of five and twelve years old. What was the little girl Cindy like?"

"I remember that I was a reader—still am, for that matter. And I loved crossword puzzles. I only had only one really good friend—her name was Jane. I was a very good student and never any trouble in school—one year I even got selected for a gifted class. I guess if you had to put a label on me, I was a Miss Goody Two-Shoes."

All the while Cindy talked, I continued making brief notes and the pattern was becoming very clear. Her father was:

STRICT, BUT LOVING, WORKED A LOT, NOT HOME
MUCH. HAD A TEMPER, THE "BOSS"—A
CONTROLLER

As for Cindy's mother, my brief notes included:

SWEET, GOOD MOM, ALWAYS THERE, SUPPORTIVE,
LOVING—A PLEASER

My notes on Cindy pointed to a quiet, studious girl, indeed, a Miss Goody Two-Shoes:

A READER, ONLY ONE GOOD FRIEND, GOOD
STUDENT, GIFTED, PROBABLY A PERFECTIONIST

"All this is very helpful," I told Cindy. "Now the only other thing I need on your family is brief descriptions of your younger brother and younger sister."

It turned out that Cindy's younger brother, Roy, was a typical middle child but with one interesting twist because he was also the firstborn male in the family. Because middle children often feel squeezed by the child above and below them, they usually become good negotiators and much more capable of getting along with others. It turned out that Roy had been very popular in school, but as the firstborn male he also had a strong competitive drive, which pleased his father a great deal. According to Cindy, "Roy was obviously the apple of Dad's eye."

"As a kid, Roy loved to figure out how things worked," Cindy recalled. "He always watched *Mr. Wizard* on TV—today he's a high school chemistry teacher, very popular with the kids."

"How does Roy get along with women?" I asked.

"Well, I guess he gets along fine—he always got along well with Mom and now he's engaged to someone who also teaches at his school—he met her a little over a year ago, and they're planning to get married soon."

"And what about your little sister, Meryl?"

"Well, I was a lot older and we weren't very close as sisters. I was like another mom to Meryl. She was the little clown of the family and she got away with murder, by the way. My parents let her do a lot of things that Roy and I never got to do. They bought her a car at sixteen and I barely ever got to use my dad's car unless he happened to be in a good mood, which wasn't very often."

"Did you resent having to care for Meryl so much when she was little?"

Cindy paused and then admitted, "To tell you the truth, I guess I did. I had to cancel a lot of things I wanted to do with my own friends because I always had to take care of Meryl. It made me angry."

BEING FIRSTBORN HAD BEEN
TOUGH ON CINDY

As I tallied up my birth-order notations on Cindy, Roy, and Meryl, I came up with the classic three-child family. As the first-born, Cindy had always been under pressure, having to care for her baby sister, plus trying to toe the mark and meet her father's austere expectations. Roy, the middle child, had turned out to be easygoing and popular. As a firstborn (and only) male in the family, he had basked in his father's approval and, in some ways, had dethroned Cindy as the real firstborn of the family.

As for Meryl, she was the classic baby—a comedienne who got away with murder. As a baby of my own family who did the same thing, I could relate to that quite easily. But the most interesting thing about Meryl was that she had been a source of irritation to Cindy. In a sense, she had symbolized what parenting was like. When Cindy had married and her own children came along, she was having trouble accepting them, especially when they did things that reminded her of her own childhood.

The key figure in Cindy's entire life-style sketch was her father. Because Cindy was the firstborn in the family, her mother and father had been her main models, and, of the two, her extremely authoritarian father had been more significant. When Cindy talked, it became evident she was a black-and-white thinker, someone who believed "It's either right or it's wrong." She had gotten this from her dad, and the fact that she had used the word "very" to describe her father in several instances pointed to her perfectionistic nature, which she had also learned from him.

The perfectionism she had learned from her father was a big part of why she was finding it so hard to be patient with her own children. The hard spankings from her father had stuck with her, and, as much as she had hated them, they had become a model for her own parenting. Fortunately, she had realized that her spanking of Billy was becoming too severe—that she was slipping over the line.

FINALLY, A TRIP TO THE MEMORY BANK

I would explain all of this to her soon enough. But first I wanted a few of her childhood memories. Another important part of Adlerian therapy is the memories we have as very young children—the younger, the better. A person's childhood and the words and emotions used to describe them hold the keys to understanding who that person is as an adult.

Childhood memories are one of the most more reliable explanations of "why you are the way you are." These memories are like tapes playing in your head, and they combine with the basic life-style you learned as a child to determine how you will respond to what happens to you every day. In Cindy's case, they were involved in her response to her own children when they misbehaved, made mistakes, or did other things to irritate her or make her angry.

"Cindy, you've given me some valuable information about your dad, your mom, and yourself, and there's one more thing I'd like to have. Can you share with me two or three of your earliest childhood memories?"

Cindy sat in silence for almost a minute before responding. Then she said, "I remember being in this spelling bee in fourth grade. Everyone had been eliminated but me and Herman Miller, the smartest kid in the class. The teacher asked me to spell 'anthem,' and I missed it. Herman spelled it right, and I lost. I was mortified."

"Any other memories, something possibly when you were even younger?"

"I remember being in dance class—I think I was only five and it was my first recital. I got out there to do my little tap-dance number and midway through I forgot the next step. I just froze and then I ran off the stage in tears."

Cindy's childhood memories confirmed my suspicions of her perfectionism. Although she had been an outstanding student and successful in many other ways, the first memories that came to her mind were failures that had devastated her.

What a difference between Cindy and Karen Johnson, director of the Explorer Program. The day we interviewed Karen on "Parent Talk" (see Chapter One), I could sense from her manner that key people in her life had affirmed her when she was very young. She was a successful, confident young woman, and it was my guess that she had had very affirming parents, particularly her father. Sure enough, when I asked Karen about her childhood, she said:

"What I knew growing up is that my parents always told me I could do whatever I put my mind to. As long as I went out there and did my very best, I could achieve whatever I wanted to in life. There never was anything like 'No, you can't do that.'"

I asked Karen to reach back into her memory bank and pull up a couple of early childhood memories, and here's what she told us:

"The first thing that comes to mind was playing in our swimming pool with my dad. He really liked to throw me around and I loved it. The second thing I remember is a Christmas morning when we got these life-size stuffed animals bigger than I am today. Somehow getting my own giant stuffed animal made me feel so appreciated and loved—it was great."

In contrast to Cindy, Karen Johnson had positive childhood memories—in the pool having fun with her dad . . . Christmas morning, receiving a giant stuffed animal and feeling good about that. It was no wonder that Karen had enjoyed three different careers before the age of thirty—in television news, in her own business, and as director of the Explorer Program for New Life Treatment Centers. Childhood memories seldom fail to confirm that "the little boy or girl you once were, you still are."

CINDY'S HUSBAND WASN'T
HARD TO DESCRIBE

To complete our first session, I decided to cover one more important area with Cindy. "Would you like to have me describe your
husband?" I asked.

"How could you possibly know about Hank? You've never
met him."

'Oh, yes, I have," I assured her. "Not in person, of course,
but I've gotten a fairly good picture of the man you would be
likely to marry. I do these life-style sketches a lot, and while I
miss now and then, I'm usually very close. If you don't mind, I'd
like to tell you what I've been hearing about what your husband
is like. It will help you understand your own parenting style and
what we can do to change it."

"Okay, go ahead," Cindy said, settling back as if she almost
dared me to describe her husband very accurately.

"Hank is a very strong person, a controller in many ways,
but it is my guess you get along fairly well. . . . How am I
doing so far?"

"You're close," she admitted. "I'm not completely sure I
know what 'controller' means, though."

"It's my guess Hank is a flaw-picker," I continued. "Controlling people are often perfectionists who find fault. Is Hank critical of you and the kids?"

"In a way, I guess he is," Cindy said. "He's quiet and soft-
spoken, but he does let me know when something isn't cooked
right or when his shirts aren't quite right—stuff like that."

"How does he treat the kids? Does he have the same problems with them as you have?"

"Well, he bawls them out for bad table manners and not
keeping their rooms neat, but he doesn't get as angry as I do. I do
all the disciplining because I spend a lot more time with them
than he does. He's gone all day at work and I'm home all day

with Billy, who is slowly driving me crazy. When Jennifer gets home from school, I guess I take some of it out on her."

"If at all possible, I'd like to have Hank come in with you at your next appointment. I'd like to talk with him about how the two of you can become a stronger team in parenting your children. Does he know about your problems with the kids—especially being too hard on Billy—and what you're afraid is going to happen?"

"I don't think so. I don't share with him much about that. I guess I've been too ashamed."

"I can understand that. Cindy, you're what I call a pleaser who, down deep, is a perfectionist. Your dad made a great impression on your life, but you could never please him enough as you were growing up. He was always critical and not there for you a lot. Nonetheless, he taught you your perfectionism and you also learned your authoritarian approach to parenting from him."

"If I learned so much of this authoritarian perfectionism from my dad, why am I a pleaser?" Cindy wanted to know. "That really doesn't seem to follow."

"Oh, yes, it follows quite easily for two reasons. First, you were always trying to please your dad, but you didn't succeed. Second, you watched your mother model what a wife is supposed to be like—someone who probably walked on eggs while trying to please her husband and be supportive of the whole family. All this combined to make you someone who tells herself, 'I count in life only when I please other people. I count only when I'm right, when I'm perfect, and when I can achieve something to prove my worth.' "

"And this is why I married Hank," Cindy mused, trying to put the pieces together.

"Exactly. When you got married, you looked for a man who was strong and controlling. You appear to have married a guy who has a critical nature, but fortunately he also seems to be fairly supportive and loving. What he needs to hear is that he should be helping you more with the parenting instead of leaving so much of it on your shoulders."

"Then you think I can change?" Cindy wanted to know.

"Oh, yes, there are many things you can do and, now that you have a little better picture of why you are the way you are, I think we can get started. But the key is to never forget that the little boy or girl you once were, you still are. You'll always be tempted to go back to that life-style you learned from the cradle on. But you can change your behavior, and it's obvious that you want to because you know what a burden all this is to have to carry through life. That's the main reason why we're talking today."

"But just what am I supposed to do about all this?" Cindy wondered.

"For starters, I believe you can do a great deal to curb the hard spankings and shakings of Billy if you'll just learn to take smaller bites of life. Make a real effort simply to slow down and quit trying to please everyone all the time. That way you'll be more relaxed, less tired and irritable, and more able to be patient with Billy."

THE GOOD NEWS CAN OUTWEIGH THE BAD

As I worked with Cindy over several more months, it turned out that slowing down and taking smaller bites of life was a key to improving her parenting style. Eventually she learned to take it easier on her firstborn, and her hard spankings of little Billy stopped. Cindy learned other ways to discipline him that were far more effective. Many of these techniques are shared in other parts of this book.

While my life-style sketch of Cindy may not fit you, it does demonstrate how we get a view of life and a way of operating in life at a very early age. This way of operating—this style of interacting with the world—never leaves us. It follows us right up through grade school, high school, and into adulthood.

When we become parents ourselves, we find ourselves doing certain things and then wondering why. It's no wonder, then, that Cindy would say, "Oh, no, I told myself I'd never treat my kids that way." And, of course, "that way" was the way her parents had treated her. I see it over and over. Ironically, with all the good intentions in the world, *parents are doing exactly opposite of what they should be doing to get good results.*

In Cindy's case, her perfectionism had blended with an authoritarian approach that was slipping toward child abuse. With you, the problem may be permissiveness, or, as it is with so many people, you may swing back and forth between authoritarianism and permissiveness on a pendulum of inconsistency. And, as I've said in another book, *Making Children Mind Without Losing Yours,* to be inconsistent in your parenting style—to go from one approach to another—is a great way to raise a yo-yo.[7]

But suppose a parent wants to change? Can it be done? Or is a parent doomed to say, "Oh, no, I said I'd never parent my children that way and here I am trapped in patterns I learned from my own parents."

Well, there is bad news and good news. The bad news is that the grain of your wood is set. Your basic life-style was determined a long time ago. Your birth order had much to do with your choice of certain roles you wanted to play in life. And your childhood memories confirm the life-style you chose and your perceptions of your world, even your world today as an adult.

The good news is that you can change your behavior. You can "know yourself" well enough to be able to recognize what you are doing to your children and stop it before you start. You don't have to blow to and fro between the winds of authoritarianism and permissiveness. You can learn to be firm but fair, in loving authority over your child, in control but not a controller, with flexible rules, not rigid ones. In short, you can have a functioning family. We'll look at what that means in the next chapter.

Words to Remember . . .

- Parenting style always boils down to how you use your authority over your children.

- Authoritarians use the rod and warp the child. They always have to be in complete control.

- Permissiveness is love gone to seed, and the "crop" always gets spoiled. Sow permissiveness and you will reap rebellion.

- Hover-parents can kill a child's self-image with too much kindness (or too much control).

- Both authoritarianism and permissiveness destroy the child's self-image.

- Your family atmosphere, birth order, and childhood memories can tell you the kind of parent you will be. In most cases, how you were parented is how you will parent.

- While the grain of your wood is set, you can change your behavior. You can break the cycle of poor parenting that gets passed from one generation to the next.

Actions to Try . . .

- Talk with your spouse about your individual parenting styles. Which of you is authoritarian? permissive? What can both of you do to bring your styles closer together so you can be a united front as parents?

- If one or both of you is in the "hover-parent" category, what specific steps could you take to give your child more opportunities to take reasonable risks and have more opportunities to learn from his or her own mistakes?

- Try doing a "mini-life-style" sketch on yourself by using the following questions:

What is your birth order: Only child; firstborn; middle child; baby of the family?

As you were growing up, what was the atmosphere in your family like: cold and/or hostile; warm, friendly, supportive; neutral, neither warm nor cold?

Pick the parent who has the most influence in your life and put down some words or phrases to describe that parent.

Now pick the other parent and put down words or phrases to describe him or her.

Next, put down words or phrases that would describe you between the ages of five and twelve years old.

Put down two or three of your earliest childhood memories (preferably below the age of five or six). Be sure to note the emotions present in the memory (were you happy, sad, etc.?) as well as whether it is negative or positive.

Go back over your answers to see if you can find any telltale words or phrases that give you clues about how you parent your own children today. Pay particular attention to how you have described your parents.

■ To get more out of reading the rest of this book, sign the commitment statement below:

While I realize the "grain of my wood is set" and that the life-style that I learned as a child does much to influence me even today, I am willing to change my behavior in order to become a more effective parent.

Signed _____

Chapter Three

WHAT DOES A FUNCTIONAL FAMILY LOOK LIKE?

■

How to Escape the Trap of Dysfunctionalism

One of the bywords of the late 1980s and early 1990s has been "dysfunctional." Bookstores are full of discussions on codependency, shame and guilt, compulsive addiction, and the "wounded child within." As John Bradshaw, whose nationally acclaimed television series (*Bradshaw On: The Family*) has been seen by millions, observes: "Addiction has become our national lifestyle."[1]

My clients often reveal their knowledge of the new buzz words during my first life-style interview to gain clues about the family atmosphere in which they grew up (see Chapter Two). For example, a client might say, "Dr. Leman, I think you should know I came from a dysfunctional family. I'm attending ACOA [Adult Children of Alcoholics] meetings on a regular basis."

"So you are an ACOA," I respond. "I'm a Republican myself."

At this point my client may look shocked, but I have my reasons for sounding a bit facetious. I go on to explain that it's always helpful to get background on a patient. The fact that a person's mother or father was and still may be an alcoholic is an important part of the family atmosphere background. In this sense, terms such as "dysfunctional" and "codependent" are certainly legitimate, but I try to steer people away from using these labels. In my experience, it's too easy for a person to tell himself, consciously or unconsciously, "I'm codependent. My family was dysfunctional. I can't do much to change the way I am."

This kind of talk is self-defeating and will hinder any changes clients might be able to make. It's too easy to label yourself "dysfunctional" and then say you can't really change, that you're a victim of bad luck—or bad genes. My reply is always the same: "Okay, I hear what you're saying. Life has kicked you squarely in the teeth, but what are you going to do about it? Are you going to continue sitting there, pointing at your parents, saying it's all their fault? Or are you going to pick yourself up and move forward and work on some things?"

One of the real dangers in the recovery movement that has swept the country in recent years is making parents the scapegoats who are the cause of everyone's problems. Unquestionably, parents—even well-intentioned ones—can make mistakes and cause varying amounts of damage to their children, which may not surface until years later. But parents are not the only cause of a child's problems. One of the truly sorry sights today is that so many people are calling themselves adult children of one problem or another. According to an article in *USA Today*, "There is a growing backlash among both professionals and just plain folks against the best-selling premise that somehow we are all 'adult children,' damaged goods who need to repair what well-intentioned parents did to us."[2]

As one adult daughter of an alcoholic put it, "All of us have a story. . . . But talking about what your parents did to you has become as much of a disease [as the parents' original problem]."[3]

My whole approach to counseling is based on the belief that a person *can change*. As we saw in Chapter Two, it's true that by the time a person reaches adulthood, his or her basic life-style has been determined. The grain of the wood doesn't change, *but behavior can be changed*. People can learn how to counter knee-jerk reactions that come out of the life-style they learned as children. But people can't change if they continue to tell themselves that they are dysfunctional and, therefore, they're stuck.

Because I assume my clients are seeing me to get help and to make some changes, I want to downplay the dysfunctional and focus on how to become more functional. I want clients to be thinking about such questions as: "What do I really want to change? What do I need to do to become a more functional spouse and parent and help my family become more functional? How far do I want to go? Am I really ready to change or at least modify the way of looking at life that I learned back in childhood?"

Notice I keep using the phrase "more functional." Every person or family is functional to some degree. A dysfunctional family, however, is operating without certain things that are necessary to everyone's sense of well-being and feelings of self-worth. Any psychologist or counselor would probably define "dysfunctional" a bit differently, but I believe that in the dysfunctional family certain basic psychological needs are not being met. These include people's needs to:

Be loved and accepted.

Be secure and relatively free of threat.

Belong, to feel a part of a group.

Be approved and recognized for the way
in which one functions.

Move toward independence, responsibility,
and decision making.

According to Don Dinkmeyer, when children's needs are met, they attain "an inner psychological stability. Failure to feel and perceive self as accepted, loved, secure, approved and responsible are forces that stimulate misbehavior."[4]

It shouldn't be hard to see that all of the basic psychological needs just listed relate directly to the A-B-C's of self-image that I talked about in Chapter One. If these needs aren't met, a child's self-image and self-worth erode rapidly. And, as we've already seen, misbehavior, and eventual breaking of the law, are directly related to a poor self-image.

When a family is functioning well, it will be meeting basic psychological needs by obeying certain rules for living together successfully. At the Leman house, we call our basic rules for a functional family the "Magnificent Six":

1. Be firm but fair.

2. Ask—and give—respect.

3. Learn from mistakes.

4. What you see is what you get.

5. Real love includes limits.

6. Walk, don't just talk, your values.

These are the same rules I advocate for any parent who comes to see me with child-rearing problems. The rest of this chapter provides a brief description of these rules and some case studies to show you how they work. The rest of this book illustrates and develops these rules in more detail.

RULE #1: BE FIRM BUT FAIR

This is the cardinal rule on which all the other rules are based. I spent a great deal of Chapter Two describing the two major errors that bring parents and their children to my office for counseling: authoritarianism and permissiveness. Authoritarians tell the child: "My way or the highway." Permissive parents say: "Have it your way, honey, and can I drive you anywhere?"

Both these approaches fail to meet the basic psychological needs listed earlier in this chapter. Both approaches leave children feeling unloved, insecure, not belonging anywhere, unapproved of, unrecognized, and operating in a dependent, irresponsible way. Both these approaches destroy or erode children's self-image or sense of self-worth. When used to extremes, both approaches lead straight to a seriously dysfunctional family.

Within the firm-but-fair approach, however, is a great deal of flexibility—and freedom to fail. Children have freedom to think, ask questions, and disagree with parents. Children have freedom to feel—angry, frustrated, sad, afraid, and so on. They have freedom to express their feelings in an appropriate way.

Anger, for example, is always a problem, but it does no good to treat children's anger with authoritarian methods: "You will *not* be angry! That's an order!" Nor does it help to be permissive: "Mommy is sorry she made you mad, but please don't hit the baby with your truck—it isn't his fault."

The firm-but-fair approach acknowledges children's anger— "I can see you are upset"—and then works out a way for them to express that anger in a nondestructive or nonabusive way: "If you want to scream, you'll just have to do it in your room. When you calm down, you can rejoin the rest of us and we can talk about it."

To be firm but fair is to be flexible, avoiding the extremes of being too rigid or a wimp. Instead, you are willing to listen, understand, and, on occasion, bend a little. For example:

Eleven-year-old Roger has neglected his regularly assigned chores—cleaning his room and the dog pen—again. He is supposed to have these tasks done by Friday night each week, but it is now eight-thirty Saturday morning and his soccer game starts in half an hour. His mother has discovered his chores aren't done, and she is already running late for an appointment of her own. She tells her husband what happened. Dad calls Roger in and says, "Your room isn't clean and the dog pen is still filthy. Our agreement is that these chores are always to be done by Friday night."

"But, Dad, there was such a good program on TV and I just forgot."

"Well, I think you'd better get your room cleaned up and the dog pen too—right now."

"But, Dad, I'm going to be late for my soccer game. The team needs me. I'm the only goalie we've got!"

"Roger, ol' buddy, I know you're going to be late, but you're just going to be later if all you do is argue."

Roger rolls his eyes and goes off muttering to clean his room and the dog. Twenty-eight minutes later he is ready to leave for the soccer game. By the time his dad drives him across town to the field, he is a good thirty-five minutes late and the game is under way. Roger's coach is not too happy and decides to leave him out until the second half. Roger's team loses by one goal—a goal scored in the first half, when he didn't play.

Let's look back at this situation to see why I call it "firm but fair." If Roger's father had wanted to, he could have been strictly firm and said, "No game for you this morning. The rule is 'No chores, no soccer.' " Instead, however, he bent a little bit and let Roger do his chores, then drove him to the game. Being late was consequence enough for Roger in this situation, but if he continues failing to get his chores done by Friday night, then his dad will probably have to simply say "No game at all."

Being firm but fair leaves the parent in charge but provides a flexible atmosphere in which children can learn from their mistakes without feeling crushed or stifled by authoritarian insensitivity. Being firm but fair applies the Golden Rule of parenting:

Treat Your Kids As You Would
Want to Be Treated

In the firm-but-fair family, everything is designed to function to build a sound self-image and sense of self-worth, in *all* the members, including the parents.

RULE #2: ASK—AND GIVE—RESPECT

Parents often tell me that they want their children to learn to be respectful. Some mothers have sat crying in my office, sniffling the same complaint made famous by Rodney Dangerfield: "Dr. Leman, I don't get any respect from my children. They act like little savages."

I realize that turning sweet little savages into respectful, responsible citizens is no easy task, but it can be done. The key is not to demand respect from your children. In order to gain the respect of your children, you have to treat them with respect as well. In other words,

Respect Is a Two-Way Street.
Model Respect by Being Respectful Toward Your Kids.

Authoritarian or autocratic parents often make their children "toe the mark" by demanding respect, and woe unto the kid who doesn't give it to them. What these parents don't realize is that they are not getting respect, they are only receiving their children's begrudging obedience, which comes out of fear. The children are biding their time, and there will come a day for payback. I deal frequently with families where the "respectful" child has decided to pay back the parents in dramatic and even devastating ways.

On the other hand, being respectful of your kids doesn't mean you put them in charge. After all, you are the adult and you are in healthy authority over your kids. Never forget that. You can still be firm in stating your expectations, but at the same time remember that all the expectations in the world will not do you much good if you act disrespectfully toward your children and treat them like second-class citizens, or worse.

I often suggest to parents that they check themselves on how they are talking to their children as they try to do everyday correcting and teaching—of table manners, for example. What does your child hear? In the authoritarian home, he's used to hearing harsh judgmental comments, such as:

"Get those hands washed before you come to dinner. They're filthy!"

"Sit up straight—keep your elbows off the table!"

"You'd better eat all your vegetables or there will be no dessert for you!"

I'm not saying that washing before dinner, sitting up straight, and eating vegetables aren't important. But I am saying there is a gentle, respectful way to help children learn table manners and there is a harsh, disrespectful way.

Linda Albert, who directs the Family Education Center of Florida, uses a phrase I like very much: "the language of respect." If you want to use the language of respect with your child, it means that you

> will have to recognize and get rid of the disrespectful words most of us have in our everyday vocabulary. Throw away the words that you would find insulting, humiliating and sarcastic if someone were to use them in speaking to you. Children will also be hurt by them. Throw away the commands, the demands, the direct orders. Children rebel when they hear them. Throw away the shouts, the yells and screams. Children become parent deaf after hearing them for a while.[5]

Admittedly, maintaining a balance between being too harsh and being too soft is not always easy—even for psychologists who write books about it. Not long ago my teenage daughter was kidding around with me, but she crossed a line when she called me a "moron" in front of several of her friends. I promptly dressed her down right in front of her friends and let her know "that kind of language isn't necessary, young lady."

After her friends left, Krissy was sitting glumly in her room. By then I had cooled off. She had not shown me respect, but at the same time I had not been respectful of her. I had simply retaliated and used my parental authority to chastise her disrespect for me.

I knocked on her door and went in and told her, "I'm sorry, I shouldn't have yelled at you in front of your friends. Honey, you know I like to kid around, but you went too far."

"Okay, Dad. I'm sorry—it won't happen again."

As I turned to leave, Krissy added, "Uh . . . Dad. . . ."

"What is it?"

"Thanks for apologizing. I won't forget."

RULE #3: WE LEARN FROM OUR MISTAKES

The firm-but-fair family functions by holding children accountable and responsible for their actions. This isn't done punitively with a we're-watching-you—don't-foul-it-up! attitude. Instead, parents are always available to help children learn from their mistakes while carefully balancing the need to be responsible with forgiveness and love. Firm-but-fair parents point out what is wrong and invoke logical consequences when necessary, but always within a context of loving forgiveness.

For example, sixteen-year-old Betsy has had her driver's license for just three weeks. Over the Thanksgiving weekend as she is hurrying to pick up a friend to do some Christmas shopping, she backs into Grandma's car parked at the far side of the driveway. She barely dents Grandma's fender but, nonetheless, the damage will run at least $150 to $200 minimum, possibly more.

Betsy is mortified. She comes in the house crying, trying to explain what happened. Her parents remain calm. There is no screaming, no threats to take away her license or her keys. As Betsy continues to sob and vow that she'll "never drive again," Dad comes over, puts his arm around her, and says, "Honey, accidents happen. It's just metal. It can be fixed as good as new. Everything's going to be okay."

And then Dad works out a deal with his daughter. He goes ahead and gets Grandma's car fixed and, because he has $500 deductible, that means paying for the repairs out of his own pocket. But then he arranges with Betsy to pay him back over the next few months.

To be firm but fair always allows for failure. When children feel they can never fail, they are hampered and become afraid to try, risk, create, grow, and learn. When parents are understanding, they can turn a failure into a good learning situation.

RULE #4: WHAT YOU SEE IS WHAT YOU GET

As a baby of the family, I have never been much on perfectionism. I find real joy in doing all I can to help firstborns (who make up a major portion of my practice) loosen up and quit trying to live flawless lives. And I hope everyone reading this book—particularly firstborn parents—will loosen up too, because there simply are no flawless parents. We all make mistakes and some of them can be dillies.

I'm still living down the time I cut Holly off at the ankles over something we've both long forgotten. But I'll never forget the fire in her twelve-year-old eyes and what she said: "You ought to read some of your own books!"

I've had more than one tense encounter with Holly, some of which were her responsibility and some of which were mine. But this time, to be honest, her remark took the wind out of my sails —and almost collapsed my mast. A few minutes later, as she was leaving for school, I stopped her, looked her in the eye, and said,

"You know, you're right. I *should* read my own books. I was way off base and I'm sorry. I apologize."

As kids are prone to do, Holly tried to act nonchalant as if nothing really had happened. "Oh, that's okay, Dad, see ya," and off she ran for the car. She may have wanted me to believe it was no big deal, but we both knew different.

The thing that has saved the day for me more than once with Holly, as well as my other children (and not to mention my wife!), is to be transparent and to admit I'm not perfect. A lot of parents try to do the right thing, say the right thing, and act in the right way. Ironically enough:

PRACTICE MAKES IMPERFECT

By that I mean it's too easy to slip back into who you are. Your life-style will get you every time. That's where transparency becomes your powerful ally and tool. Instead of covering over mistakes, own up to them. Then you don't have to cover them up because they're taken care of and the way is cleared for forgiveness.

Being transparent is only one part of the all-important area called "communication." Unfortunately, the "C" word has been used so much that it has become a worn-out cliché. Nonetheless, to have a functional family, clear and open interaction between parent and child is an absolute necessity. We will look at this a lot more thoroughly in a later chapter.

RULE #5: REAL LOVE INCLUDES LIMITS

In Chapter One I discussed the vital need for parents to unconditionally love their children, but admitted this isn't always easy. While none of us can love unconditionally on a continual basis, we all can demonstrate real love by balancing love with limits. Real love means that we are kindly and compassionate, but we are also firm and fair. In fact, we can't have real love for our children without reasonable, healthy limits to guide and to nurture them.

Sometimes a parent may ask, "Aren't limits 'conditions'? How can you set limits if you are trying to unconditionally love someone?" Limits don't put conditions on your love; limits help channel your love and give it the substance that makes it real and lasting, not artificial and temporary.

The trick is to invoke the limits without making your children feel "Mom doesn't love me." According to Ross Campbell, author of *How to Really Love Your Child*, some studies show that 93 percent of all teenage children feel that nobody loves or cares for them. Campbell observes that surely more than 7 percent of all parents love and care for their children, but the catch is that their children don't *feel* loved and cared for.

Campbell says, "The love we have in our hearts for our children isn't automatically transferred to them through osmosis. Children don't know we love them simply because we feel love for them. We must communicate our love for our children in order for them to feel secure in it."[6]

To "communicate" suggests words—talking, writing, and so on. I believe, however, that parents, especially parents of young children, actually can communicate love more effectively without words. Every child needs plenty of hugs, holding, cuddling, kissing—what the textbooks call "tactile stimulation." Then follow up with plenty of talk—kindly words, loving words, appreciation and encouragement. But go easy on the praise because, strange as it may seem, praise usually doesn't help and can even hurt. I'll talk a lot more about that in Chapter Seven.

Another way to love your children is to simply enjoy them. Enjoy their earliest smiles and laughter—even their drools and spills and accidents. Watching young children explore, particularly from eighteen months to three years—can actually be fun, even though that includes the infamous period called "the terrible twos." Yes, the twos can test any parent, but they don't have to be terrible. More on that in Chapter Nine.

Perhaps I can't emphasize enough that your children need to be touched, particularly the boys. Research shows that as badly as children need physical contact, few of them get enough of it. Supposedly preschool girls get the most touching and cuddling. Some studies say they get five times more than preschool boys. Could there possibly be a connection between this and the fact that little boys have six times as many psychiatric problems as little girls?[7]

The connection is obvious. Our society has always taught its males to be nontouchers or nonhuggers. As a rule, parents think it's more important to touch and hug little girls than boys. After all, little boys are supposed to grow up to be "big strong men" who don't need all this hugging and touching. Not surprisingly, there is a price to be paid for this lack of tactile stimulation, and boys pay it.

One of the basics in teaching children that they are accepted and belong is the power of touch. Because boys are touched less, they are much more apt to grow up having difficulty getting close to people or in learning to develop intimacy with others—their wives, for example. Many of the psychiatric problems men develop are often connected to feeling alienated—literally "not in touch" with others.

Never underestimate the awesome power of the simple hug. One doctor studied forty-nine different cultures throughout the world to determine what effect physical affection and body touch has on children and adults. He learned that the more violent societies were the ones where there wasn't much fondling or caressing in the family.[8]

I realize that with all of the "horror stories" coming out today about incest and child abuse, some parents shy away from cuddling and hugging. My only comment is that parents who are predisposed to doing the wrong kind of touching will do it anyway. Healthy parents will do the right kind of touching, and all their kids need plenty of it.

Along with touching, you can show your love for your children by looking and listening. How often through the day or even through the week do you tune in and focus on your child, looking the child in the eye and talking lovingly and kindly? And how often do you stop to listen for feelings instead of hurriedly urging the child to give you the facts so you can go on with your busy schedule?

Parents often complain that they can't get their children to tell them what's happening at school or to talk about much of anything. Perhaps a major reason is that, when the children were very small, they were brushed off so frequently they decided that Mom and Dad just weren't that interested. In the functional family, Mom and Dad are always interested, and they let their children know it.

RULE #6: WALK, DON'T JUST TALK, YOUR VALUES

One of the biggest mistakes a parent can make is to think "All my kids need are good care and lots of love. When they're older they can pick their own philosophy of life and decide for themselves about the way they want to live."

That may sound good on the surface, but only because it's surface thinking. To raise children without sound values, beliefs, and morals is to raise children who don't know what they believe or who they are—both of which are vital parts of a good self-image. When I deal with thirty-five-year-old adults who claim they have some kind of identity crisis, I can often trace it back to a childhood home where teaching sound values was neglected or ignored. Either the parents had few or no values that they wished to convey, or they preached certain values and didn't practice them. There is no more powerful way to teach than by modeling or, more simply, by example.

Parents fail to realize that how they live each day speaks volumes about what they really value. The choices they make, the words they use, the TV programs they watch, the way they treat others, the way they obey or disobey the law—all are sure-fire communicators of what they think is really important. In one sense, everyone has "values"; it is a question of what kind.

Zig Ziglar, a master salesman and motivational teacher, has written several best-selling books, including *See You at the Top*, which is the basis for an "I CAN" course taught in over five thousand schools with over 3 million participants. As he conducts seminars around the world, he often polls the audience to identify the qualities of the most successful people they know. According to Ziglar, it doesn't matter where he is, the age of the audience, or the occupations and professions represented. The answers he gets most often are:

HONESTY . . . POSITIVE MENTAL ATTITUDE . . . FAITH . . . LOVING . . . DEPENDABLE . . . COMMITMENT . . . SENSE OF HUMOR . . . PERSISTENT

While Ziglar calls these traits and characteristics "qualities of successful people," they could easily pass for traditional values, and many of them do at the Leman house. They are probably values in your home as well. Other values that Ziglar often hears named by the crowds he polls include character, integrity, hard work, enthusiasm, compassion, loyalty, responsibility, caring, and friendliness.

Frankly, I think values such as character, integrity, hard work, and compassion are more important than some of the "big eight" Ziglar claims are the most popular around the world. And, at our house, we would add such values as courage, trying to achieve excellence (but not perfectionism), being fair, forgiveness, humility, being respectful, being a good sport, being understanding, and stopping to think.

Granted, that's quite a list. You could make your own list. It might include many of the characteristics I've just named as well as others that are of particular importance in your home. The point is, we all know of values that have "stood the test of time." We know they are things worth believing and practicing even though we may not always practice them as well as we would like. Something about "eternal values" makes them difficult to practice consistently. Human nature doesn't always want to cooperate.

ETERNAL VALUES ARE WORTH IT

Some educators and counselors believe that values are where you find them—that is, whatever you feel is a value is a value for you. This point of view advocates a system of thought called "values clarification." According to this system, people use basic questions to determine what their real values are.

A leading exponent of values clarification is Sydney Simon of the University of Massachusetts. Simon believes that the "traditional approach has become increasingly less effective because direct transference of values only works when there is complete consistency about what constitutes desirable values."[9] For Simon, values clarification is a process that helps people arrive at finding their *real* values. People aren't concerned with any ultimate set of values. Instead, they decide what values work for them.

I agree with Simon that people don't always practice the values they claim to hold, but I disagree when he claims that: "The 'eternal verities' seem to be less than eternal; familiar 'shalt not's so often don't relate to the complexities of our daily lives."[10]

After eighteen years of counseling families, I am convinced that there still are eternal values that *do* relate to our daily lives.

Further, parents should and can try to transmit these values to help their children develop a solid self-image and a good sense of self-worth. For example, being honest has never hurt anyone's self-image; cheating, lying, stealing, shading the truth, and the like often destroy self-image and self-worth.

One of the most cherished values in our family is faith. From what I have seen behind counseling doors, there is no better builder of self-image and a sense of self-worth than to know that you are the handiwork of an all-powerful Creator—that you are *somebody*, not an "it" or an accident.

In this highly mobile age in which we live, people move away from their roots. I often counsel with patients who "used to go to church back East, but now that they've wound up in Tucson, they've sort of drifted away." Without apology and also without pressure or a judgmental approach, I urge them to get back to a church or synagogue of their choice, because I know that this is where they can rediscover a sense of who they really are and their personal worth.

Another advantage to practicing your faith is that it can help your children grow up with positive moral values. Having a solid faith in God can be a tremendous advantage for children who must grow up in a culture where having it all, going for the gusto, and enjoying pleasures now and not worrying about "later" are all rules that so many people live by.

The AIDS crisis alone is reason enough to never give up on teaching your kids eternal values such as being thoughtful, tender, gentle, kind, committed, and moral, all of which are part of responsible sex. The tragedy of Earvin (Magic) Johnson, whose NBA basketball career was cut short when he contracted AIDS after years of practicing "free love" and promiscuous sex, stunned the nation. Magic immediately told the world what had happened to him and he retired from professional sports, vowing to preach the message of "safe sex" (using condoms) wherever he could. A few days later, Johnson added that the best way to avoid AIDS is to abstain from sex until married. Although Magic

Johnson is hardly a good role model of practicing abstinence until marriage, at least he tried to let young people know that practicing traditional values is the only way to be truly safe when it comes to sex. (For more on "safe sex," condoms, and the like, see Chapter Eleven.)

Senate Chaplain Richard Halverson describes the moral state of our country today well when he says, "We demand freedom without restraint, rights without responsibility, choice without consequences, pleasure without pain. In our narcissistic, hedonistic, masochistic, valueless preoccupation, we are becoming a people dominated by lust, avarice and greed."[11]

If parents are not willing to take a stand and teach their children such eternal values as morality, where will their children learn them? Will they somehow "clarify" the values they get taught by friends at school who haven't been taught any values either?

IT HELPS WHEN MOM AND DAD AGREE

Before leaving the subject of values, I want to stress that it's critical for a husband and wife to try to mesh their values as closely as possible. A woman called in on our "Parent Talk" hotline recently to complain that she and her husband "saw discipline issues a bit differently." Her husband had just purchased their three-year-old son a Batman costume and the little fellow had become a Batman fan. Her husband thought it was cute because he had grown up with Batman and had looked upon the comic book hero as one of his personal heroes.

But Mom didn't see Batman in the same light. She felt that the comic book, as well as the television show and the movie, were too violent for three-year-olds. And her reservations were being proven right. Her little boy, who had been a fairly easygoing child, had developed a belligerent attitude and had begun striking other children and even other adults, often without any provocation.

As we dealt with this mother over the phone, we pointed out that she didn't have a disagreement over discipline with her husband. Her real problem was the conflicting values held by her and her husband. I also pointed out that she has a three-year-old who is now exhibiting powerful behavior. And that thirst for power will probably continue to grow as long as the little fellow is encouraged with violent heroes such as Batman.

On top of all this, her mother-in-law was planning to give the child all kinds of Batman gadgets and paraphernalia for his fourth birthday, which would be coming up in about a month. We advised this mom to try to sit down with her husband and talk seriously, but calmly, about their values disagreement, which centered around a seemingly "innocent" character like Batman.

"Do everything you can to explain to your husband that you feel Batman is just too violent a character for a three-year-old to imitate," I told her. "Just because your husband 'grew up with Batman,' it doesn't make him suitable fare for a three-year-old mind. There is no way to know for sure that watching Batman going 'POW! BIFF! BANG! SOCK!' is making him belligerent, but it is safe to say it isn't helping him learn to be kinder and gentler. Keep in mind, too, that wherever there is a powerful child, there is usually a powerful parent who is setting an example that is teaching that child powerful behavior. You and your husband need to analyze what your child is seeing as he watches the two of you interact with each other and rest of the family."

Our conversation with this mother illustrates the awesome power of modeling or "setting an example"—good or bad. Parents often think that children are "deaf" and aren't really listening to them when they talk. Children may act deaf at times, particularly when you're trying to lecture them, call them for dinner, and so on, but they are not. They do hear you—far more often and more clearly than you realize. As you speak and as you exhibit certain behaviors, they are deciding on what is right and wrong, what is good and evil—the way they want to live.

ARE THERE ANY REAL ABSOLUTES? ABSOLUTELY!

If parents live before their children without any absolute values, the children will grow up believing there are no absolutes—that there are no beliefs worth holding dear and following as best they can.

Recent generations have proved that this is exactly what has happened. In *The Closing of the American Mind*, which made bestseller lists, Alan Bloom wrote: "There is one thing a professor can be absolutely certain of: almost every student entering the university believes, or says he believes, that truth is relative."[12]

In other words, there are no absolutes. We have friends who have taken great pains to teach all their children moral absolutes, such as waiting until marriage to have sex. Heather, their oldest child, has just entered college. She is suffering a kind of "culture shock" as she runs into girls in her dorm who think nothing of sleeping around with any number of different partners. Heather is discovering firsthand what it's like to road test her self-image in the "real world." Her mother and father aren't there and people are constantly knocking on her door, wondering if she wants to go out to "find some guys and do some serious drinking."

One of the girls who's been doing a lot of sleeping around has come to Heather to confide in her and ask her why she is so different from all the rest. It's hard for Heather to handle all this, but she is learning.

For the functional family, there *are* absolutes, and it's time parents said so. If you have been trying to teach absolute values and your kids have been giving you strange looks, don't be intimidated. If a value isn't an "absolute," it can't be valued very much. Make no mistake, what you believe about right and wrong is crucial. How you live those beliefs is even more crucial.

Just because transmitting absolute values is difficult doesn't mean parents should give up and just let children decide which values are best for them. For my money, this comes very close to "following your feelings," and one reason my office continues to have visitors is because people have done just that. The fact is, hurting others is wrong; telling lies is wrong; telling the truth is right; loving others is right; being dependable and committed is a good idea. On and on I could go.

Not only are traditional values good and right, they help children meet their basic psychological needs, which were cited earlier. When children hold sound values, the children are more apt to feel loved and accepted, to feel secure, that they belong, that they are approved of because they can make responsible choices. The point is, to be loved you must value love; to feel secure you must value security and making others feel secure. To feel responsible you need to value responsibility and being responsible to others. *Values are not a one-way street.* What you believe and how you live will come back to you many times, and it will either build your self-image or tear it down.

Functional families aren't perfect. But they do function well enough to try to obey certain rules that make them function better. You may have been noticing that it takes *time* to practice these rules and make them work. In Chapter Four I focus on this indispensable ingredient for having a functional family. It really isn't part of the Magnificent Six, because it's not just a rule, it's practically a philosophy. It towers above all the rules, for without it the rules won't work very well, if at all.

Words to Remember . . .

- Words such as "dysfunctional" and "codependent" are legitimate terms, but beware of using them as cop-outs because you aren't willing to really change your behavior or your habits.

■ No matter what kind of childhood you had, remember that your parents are not the only cause of your problems. Only you can decide what you want to change.

■ When a family is dysfunctional, basic psychological needs are not being met, including the need to:

Be loved and accepted.

Be secure and relatively free of threat.

Belong, to feel a part of a group.

Be approved and recognized for the way in which one functions.

Move toward independence, responsibility, and decision making.

Six magnificent rules for having a functional family are:

1. Be firm but fair.
2. Ask—and give—respect.
3. Learn from mistakes.
4. What you see is what you get.
5. Real love includes limits.
6. Walk, don't just talk, your values.

The firm-but-fair approach to parenting is flexible enough to give a child freedom to fail.

■ The Golden Rule of Parenting is: *Treat your kids as you would want to be treated.*

■ Respect is a two-way street. Model respect by being respectful toward your children.

- It takes an understanding parent to turn a child's failure into a good learning situation.

- To be a transparent parent, always be willing to admit to your children that you are not perfect.

- Remember that your children don't automatically know you love them. They must *feel* it.

- To raise children without sound traditional values means raising children who don't know what they believe or who they are, both of which are vital parts of building a good self-image.

- Always be careful of the example you set. Children hear and watch you far more often than you realize.

Actions to Try . . .

- Sit down with your spouse and discuss how well the basic psychological needs are being met in your family. What is each of you doing to make your children feel loved and accepted . . . secure and free of threat . . . that they belong and are really part of the family . . that you both approve and recognize them for their abilities and accomplishments . . . that you are helping them become more independent, responsible, and able to make decisions?

- This week take specific pains to practice the Golden Rule of Parenting with your children. In other words, treat them as you would want to be treated. Make a deliberate effort to show respect to your children, just as you expect them to show you respect. Try something as simple as saying "Please" when you ask them to do something, or "Thank you" when they do something for you. Also try giving them choices and options instead of just telling them what to do.

- During the coming week, try being more transparent in front of your children. That is, admit "Mommy was wrong," or "Daddy goofed." Your children will love you for it.

- Make a concerted effort this week to enjoy your children—not only when they make you smile but when they fail.

- Make a list of the traditional and eternal values, such as honesty, forgiveness, humility, and being a good sport, that you hold and that you want to communicate to your children. Then look for ways to model these values.

Chapter Four

DO YOU HAVE TIME TO BE
A FUNCTIONAL FAMILY?

■

Imprinting Your Child Is All-Important

If someone were to ask you, "Is parenting a sacrifice or an investment?" how would you answer? Maybe both words would seem to apply. If I have to be honest, however, the word "sacrifice" comes more easily in mind. It takes time and energy to raise kids—and money—*lots* of money.

I've read all kinds of numbers on how much it costs to raise a child to age eighteen—and $100,000 is getting to be a low figure. If you throw in the college years, the numbers can climb in a hurry. I heard somewhere that providing for the needs of a family of four—Mom, Dad, and two kids—is well over a million-dollar operation by the time you're finished with putting the kids through school. I don't doubt that a bit, especially after getting the bills to keep two daughters in college.

In addition, Kevin II is now in high school and our little Hannah is now only five years old. Although we are tickled to death with little Hannah, every now and then it does get a bit overwhelming to realize that we'll still be raising kids in our sixties. The other day I groaned to Sande, my wife, "Can you believe it? If you count putting Hannah through college, we won't be through parenting until almost the year 2010!"

"Two thousand and ten?" Sande said absently as she sorted another huge stack of laundry. "Wasn't that a movie about a computer that took over a spaceship?"

"No, I think that was '2001' . . ." Then I stopped and just shrugged. I could see Sande wasn't interested in talking about sacrifice. She was in her usual happy state, content to be a mom of a five-year-old even though she's in her early forties. She doesn't seem to mind spending the money or the energy, and it takes a lot of energy—which I notice has grown much scarcer since Kevin was small. But if having Hannah has emphasized anything, it's how much *time* it takes to be a parent. And if you want to be a good one, it takes a great deal of time, indeed.

WHY TAKING TIME IS SO CRUCIAL

In Chapter Three I listed six laws for a functional family, but towering above them all is this:

You Have Only One Swing, So Make It a Good One

To explain what I mean, I want to use an analogy from America's favorite pastime: baseball. In high school I played third base well enough to earn a letter, but not quite well enough to get a college scholarship. No matter, I still loved the "grand old game," and after getting married and hanging out my counselor's shingle, I found myself managing a local city league softball team, where I played third and occasionally filled in as a pitcher.

One particular game will always stand out in my memory. We were playing for the league championship, and the game had come down to the final inning and our final turn at bat. We managed to rally and score a few times, but when the dust cleared we were still one run down with men on second and third and two outs. Striding to the plate was Murph, our second baseman, who hadn't had a base hit in his last five games—in fact, he hadn't even gotten the ball out of the infield.

"C'mon, Murph," we all shouted, but, to be truthful, there wasn't a lot of enthusiasm. The probability of Murph getting a hit was about equal to winning the lottery with an out-of-date ticket. Our feeble cheers soon turned to groans as the opposing pitcher put two quick strikes past Murph, who stood there, bat on shoulder, as if frozen by fear.

Suddenly I got an idea. I won't dare to call it a brilliant idea—in fact, I guess it would be better described as a desperate one. Calling time out, I strode out to the field and called Murph up the third-base line where we could talk quietly, unheard by the other team. Looking deep into Murph's eyes, which seemed a bit glazed over, I said, "Murph, you've got one pitch."

"What do you mean, one pitch?" he asked, looking nervously around.

"Hit the next pitch or I'm pulling you out of the game and sending in a pinch hitter," I told him.

Despite his incredible hitting slump, Murph was an excellent fielder and one of the outstanding players on our team. The idea of being pulled out of the game was almost more than he could stand. I could see the anger flash in his eyes. Silent, he stalked off back to the plate. I went back to the bench to watch and pray that my off-the-wall strategy would work.

Smiling with anticipation, the pitcher whirled his arm in the familiar windmill delivery used by so many softball hurlers. The ball blurred toward the plate and Murph swung viciously, connecting squarely and sending the ball on a line to deep left center field. Two runs scored and our team won. Murph was a hero and I was a managerial genius.

Later Murph stopped me as I headed for my car and asked, "Why did you tell me to swing at that next pitch or I would get pulled out of the game? How did you know I'd hit it?"

"I didn't," I told him. "But I had to do something to wake

you up. I'd rather you went down swinging than stand there with the bat on your shoulder and lose the game for sure."

I believe this story contains a parable for all parents—a parable that has to do with how they spend their time. Raising children is a lot like being at the plate with two outs and everything riding on the next pitch. You can stand there with the bat on your shoulder, hoping to draw a walk. You even can ask to be pulled for pinch hitter, but the truth is, you get only one swing at being a parent, and you might as well make it a good one.

THE FIRST FIVE TO SEVEN YEARS ARE CRUCIAL

If you're expecting your first child or have young children under age seven, the next section is especially for you because:

There Is No More Important Time
in Your Child's Life Than Now

Most parents know, or at least can recall hearing it somewhere, that the first five to seven years of a child's life are the most important in developing the child's personality, character, and emotional makeup. In Chapter Two we looked at how children develop their own personal life-style, their way of seeing the world and responding to it. The question is, how much of a part do you want to play in helping your children develop their life-style during those first seven years or so? Is that your main priority, or does your career or some other interest take precedence?

As I tried to say in my softball illustration, you get only one swing at molding your child's self-image at the most crucial time in his or her life. I admit my softball analogy breaks down a little bit because parenting lasts a lot longer than a seven-inning softball game or a nine-inning hardball contest. And, in truth, parents come to the plate a great many times while their children are

77

in their care. Rome wasn't built in a day, and neither is a child's positive sense of self-worth. It takes years to build a good self-image in a child, and those years have to be broken down into concentrated periods—weeks, days, hours, and minutes that you spend guiding, teaching, loving, hugging, touching, and just plain enjoying your kids.

But the one-swing analogy makes a lot of sense when you realize that there are critical moments in your child's life when you get only one opportunity to leave a positive mark on your child. Any basic textbook in psychology usually contains an account of the work of Konrad Lorenz, who is credited with coining the term "imprinting" because of his studies of baby ducks and how they learn to follow their mother. What Lorenz and other psychologists who worked before and after him learned is that the period for a baby duck to learn to follow Mom lasts only about twenty-four hours. According to Lorenz, the imprinting of the baby duck reaches its maximum point at seventeen hours; at twenty to twenty-three hours, the imprinting effect is just about complete.[1]

Another study of songbirds done by a psychologist named Konishi in the 1960s demonstrated that "song learning in birds is also restricted to a very short period of time and is irreversible. It cannot be repeated later, nor caught up with if that period is missed. Nor can it be changed."[2]

Lorenz and many other psychologists believe that there are very real implications in the imprinting concept as far as human beings are concerned. He admits that it is a very big leap from ducks and songbirds to human infants, but the correlation is there.[3]

I believe Lorenz is right. Obviously, human babies have longer periods for imprinting than ducks. Imprinting, especially by the mother as she bonds with her baby, goes on throughout infancy, particularly during the first year or so. If Mom isn't there to do that imprinting, somebody else will. That somebody else is usually a caregiver of some kind.

Research shows that imprinting starts immediately at birth. For example, one study determined that if a mother is with her newborn the first hour following birth and at least five hours in each of the next three days, she will have a much greater opportunity to be an effective parent. In fact, this kind of study has shown that, when a mother has increased contact with her baby in the first few days and weeks after birth, the baby cries less and grows more rapidly. The mother also has increased affection for her baby and more self-confidence and is much less likely to engage in any child abuse in the immediate years to follow.[4]

THE PROS AND CONS OF WORKING MOMS

On the other hand, if a mother has her baby and goes back to work in the next few days, weeks, or even months, she has less opportunity to bond with her child. Other caregivers will do much of the imprinting, and the mother can only hope that she has chosen people who are stable, loving, and capable.

Throughout the 1980s, in particular, and on into the 1990s, the debate has continued about the pros and cons of the "working mother." The largest survey ever done on child care in the United States revealed that there are more kids than ever in our day care programs, but that these programs are declining in quality. According to a report in *USA Today*, in 1990, 46 percent of all mothers were in the work force compared with 26 percent in 1970, and some 8 million children under thirteen are currently in day care programs of some kind.

In the survey, conducted by the National Association for the Education of Young Children (NAEYC) and other agencies, 2,089 day care center directors were questioned, along with 583 family care providers. The average recommended ratio of children to adult staff members is one adult for every three to eight children, depending on the age involved. But in most day care facilities, child/staff ratios are nearly double that.

According to the report, the average caregiver's salary has fallen off at least 25 percent in adjusted dollars since 1976, with hourly rates ranging from $5.43 to $7.40 per hour. In addition, nearly 50 percent of the programs reported a turnover averaging *half* of their staff every year. One spokesperson for the NAEYC said: "When salaries are low and turnover high, you get poorer quality programs, worse social development and academic scores."[5]

Despite these glum figures on day care, author Faye Crosby has come out with a book that was praised as a "fresh perspective for the two-job couple of the 1990s." In *Juggling: The Unexpected Advantages of Balancing Career and Home for Women and Their Families,* Crosby's thesis is that women with husbands, children, *and* jobs have the happiest lives.

According to Crosby, the research she has studied shows little evidence that women who "juggle" career with being wives and mothers don't show any more stress than other women. Not only that, but women who juggle different life roles seem less depressed than other women. "Jugglers," as Crosby calls them, rate higher on average in self-esteem and happiness. She believes that when a woman confines herself to one life role, no matter how pleasant it may seem, she may become starved emotionally and psychologically.[6]

It seems that you can find research that backs one view or the other, but what really counts is what is happening in the typical home. I have counseled many women who felt guilty about working. Sometimes they had to work due to economic pressures; in other cases it simply was a personal choice because staying home to raise children left them frustrated and unfulfilled.

I SYMPATHIZE WITH WORKING MOMS, BUT . . .

I've always had sympathy for working moms because I was raised by one. I clearly remember the day—I was about twelve—when I flattened one of my friends as we stood talking together after riding our bikes. He made some crack to the effect that "Your mother must not love you very much or she wouldn't work." The next thing he knew he was lying in a tangled heap with his bike and I was nursing some sore knuckles. Why did I hit him? Obviously, his remark made me angry. I knew my mother loved me. But perhaps I also hit him out of frustration because I wished she had been around more often as I was growing up.

So, as much as I sympathize with moms who have to work—especially single moms who seldom have any other choice—I still come down on the side of having parents do everything they can to keep at least one parent home as the key caregiver for children through grade school and preferably well into high school. And, if at all possible, this person should be the mother.

I am well aware of how many fathers have stepped forward to pick up the parenting slack in two-career families. Instead of asking his wife to go on the "mommy track" at work, a husband will take the "daddy track" and put aside his own career for a few years while he becomes the major caregiver in the home. I applaud these fathers, but I doubt that their rather small tribe will increase a great deal.

I realize there are some who believe men and women have the same abilities to nurture and care for children, but I've seen little proof of this in my own counseling. I have worked with thousands of couples over the years, and I just haven't found the evidence for sameness. On the contrary, I observe men and women as very different in their needs and natural abilities. I believe men and women think differently, act differently, and communicate differently.

GOOD MOTHERING IS
EVERY CHILD'S BIRTHRIGHT

While it may be true some men are staying home and doing a creditable job of nurturing their children, I believe they are adapting to a role that is far better suited to the woman, particularly when children are very young, in the first few months and years of life. Dr. Brenda Hunter, a psychologist who specializes in infant attachment and the effects of infant day care on children, makes the basic difference between men and women one of her key premises in her book, *Home by Choice.* This book is one of the best discussions I have seen to date on how a child is affected by the mother working full or even part time.

Hunter recalls what it was like to be raised by her own mother, who worked full time.[7] Not surprisingly, she became a working mother during the growing-up years of her own two daughters, so she has personally experienced the empty places that can be left when mothers aren't there to do their irreplaceable work in a child's life.

In her forties, Hunter earned a degree in psychology and became aware of the fascinating and highly complex nature of infants and the attachments they form with their parents. She realized the mistakes she had made as a mother as well as her own mother's mistakes by being out of the home too much. Hunter became convinced that "good mothering is every child's birthright."[8]

In her book, Hunter frequently mentions the work of British psychiatrist John Bowlby, who wrote about the centrality of a baby's emotional bond or attachment to his mother. Bowlby calls this bond the "foundation stone of personality," and he goes on to say, "The young child's hunger for his mother's love and presence is as great as his hunger for food. When mother isn't there, the child inevitably generates a powerful sense of loss and anger."[9]

One psychologist, Evelyn Thoman, uses the metaphor of "the

dance" to describe the dialogue that goes on between a baby and its mother. This dance "is a timeless form of communication, infinitely more complex, subtle and meaningful than a polite ballroom waltz. The baby's dance—which is actually communication at its most basic—comprises rhythmic arm movements, eye shifts, head tilts, coos, cries, fusses, gazes, and dozens of other behaviors."[10]

Brenda Hunter makes the key point that the baby "moves rhythmically in response to Mom's voice and facial expressions. As Mom communicates her emotional state to baby, he dances synchronously in response to the messages he receives."[11] She goes on to say something I believe every mother should think about:

A Woman's Baby Is Programmed to Fall in Love with Her

"During that first year," writes Hunter,

a mother isn't just feeding, diapering and playing with her baby. She is teaching him lessons about love and intimacy he needs to know his whole life long. If a mother is absent, he will fall in love, or try to, with whomever she has left in charge. A mother who elects to re-enter the work place needs to grapple with this and decide if she can live with the consequences.[12]

I see it in my own counseling chambers; I read and hear it in the media; and I get it firsthand when talking with parents as I crisscross the country: More women are deciding that the price of working is just too high. During one TV talk show out of Chicago, the question was asked a studio audience of some two hundred people: Given that money is no concern, should a mom stay home with her kids? Eighty-two percent of the studio audience, mostly women, said yes.

A June 1989 *New York Times* poll of nearly 1,500 adults revealed that 83 percent of the working mothers and 72 percent of the working fathers said they were torn by the demands of their jobs versus a desire to spend more time with their families. A 1987 survey of 800 women had 88 percent agreeing with the statement: "If I could afford it, I'd rather be at home with my children."[13]

According to an article in the *Washington Post*, figures released by the U.S. Labor Department early in 1991 revealed that for the first time since 1948, there was a slight downturn in the number of women entering the work force. According to the president of the Families and Work Institute, which does a lot of highly regarded research on women and work, this organization is seeing more and more women saying it's not worth trying to be mothers and hold down full-time jobs.[14]

I'm seeing the same trend. One of my clients, a female attorney who told me "I *love* law," admitted that she wanted a career. Before having a child, she vowed, "I'll always work. No staying home for me." Then she had her first child—a son—and went on a three-month maternity leave. But at the end of that time, she discovered that she didn't want to go back to her beloved law practice after all.

"I fell in love with my son," she told me. "The thought of having someone else around for all the special moments—standing for the first time, the first steps, the first words—was more than I could handle. I talked to my husband and told him, 'I think I want to stay home with our baby.' He agreed and that's just what I did."

True, this attorney had to go on what is derisively called in the corporate and business world "the mommy track." In her law firm, her decision labeled her as someone who preferred being a parent over climbing the corporate ladder. But she was glad to do so and it all went back to one basic fact: "I fell in love with my son."

And, meanwhile, of course, her son was falling in love with his mother. There is simply no substitute for Mom.

GUILT TRIPS AREN'T THE REAL ISSUE

I suppose everything I'm saying here could be called "laying a guilt trip on working mothers." I repeat: I have great sympathy for working moms, and the last thing I want to do is make them feel guilty. It's my guess that if they do feel guilty, they felt that way long before coming across this book or any other comments about the problems that arise when both parents work. But what I'm hoping is that if you still have an opportunity to make a choice, you'll think more than twice about how your little ones will grow up. Will you be there to imprint them with your indelible, irreplaceable stamp or not?

I don't have space here to go into a thorough discussion of working mothers. Many good books do that. I will say, however, that despite all of our modern technology and libraries full of material on how to raise children, babies need today exactly what they needed fifty years ago. A baby's basic needs haven't changed one bit. Therefore, I give the following recommendations:

If at all possible, only one parent should work during a child's growing-up years—and that means at least through junior high. Ideally, Dad should be the one out on the job and Mom—for many reasons already stated—should be the one who stays home. If this means that Mom must put her career on hold—the mommy track—so be it. This can be a very hard decision, and I do not minimize it at all. But facts are plain: By choosing to be a parent, you are taking a step that has to preclude other things. If you're a parent, your first priority is your children. Contrary to the popular saying, you *can't* have it all.

If both parents have to work, then try to keep one parent's (preferably Mom's) hours to a minimum, at most half-time. In *Home by Choice,* Brenda Hunter claims that if a mother works even twenty hours a week, her child is at risk, but sometimes a mother has no choice and must make the best of it.

Make the best of it by getting the best child care you can possibly find. Don't bail out by simply running to the nearest kiddie kennel and depositing your children there early in the morning and then picking them up about twelve hours later, assuming that they have had good care all day long. When seeking child care, put child care agencies somewhere down your list. Start first with the children's grandparents. If they are willing, able, and very loving, they can make the best child care substitutes for Mom available.

If grandparents aren't in the picture, try finding a grandmotherly woman who will care for your children in your home while you are working. Be sure she has very complete and very good references, but don't be above popping home by surprise, if you can, just to see what's going on.

If you must use a preschool or other kind of child care agency, check it out in minute detail. Talk to other parents who have been using the preschool and see what they think. (See "Checklist for Finding a Good Child Care/Preschool" on pages 99–101 for more pointers.)

Whatever you do, be sure you don't pick the kind of kiddie kennel that was featured recently in a national television report. In this particular preschool, small infants were brought to the preschool attendant in their car seats and then *left in those car seats all day long.* There was no hugging, cuddling, singing, kissing, or any kind of tactile stimulation. This kind of situation is the kiddie kennel at its worst. Dogs and other pets often get far better treatment.

IMPRINTING IS A LOT MORE THAN NOSTALGIA

Keep in mind, however, that no matter how good a preschool or any child care agency might be, it can't replace Mom's special imprint. Picture the scene. It's a small, midwestern town on a cold, blustery, January day. Mom had planned to do some shopping, but now she has decided to stay home, make a fire and sit, just rocking little Festus while singing to him. That's imprinting.

Two years later, we find Mom cuddled up on the couch in front of the fire on the same kind of January day, reading little Festus a storybook. That's imprinting.

Now it's several years later and little Festus arrives home after another day in first grade. He bangs through the door hollering, "Mom, Mom! See what I drew at school?!" The smell of freshly baked cookies is in the air, and there Mom is with a glass of milk as well. More priceless imprinting.

Jump ahead two more years and we see Dad getting off work early and meeting Mom at the school auditorium just in time to see little Festus perform in a leading role in his class play. That also is imprinting.

These aren't just cozy, little nostalgic scenarios. They are the kind of positive imprinting that should be reality for every child. As young children grow, they are drawing conclusions about who they are, what kind of world surrounds them, and how they want to be treated and how they want to treat others. If their world is supportive, loving, kind, and warm, they'll grow up with a positive self-image. They'll believe they have real worth, and they'll treat other people accordingly.

IS THERE A POSITIVE SIDE TO WORKING?

I realize I've made a strong case for moms to stay home in order to imprint their children at every opportunity, but don't get the idea that a working mom can't imprint her kids at all. She can do a great deal—it will just take more planning, effort, and sacrifice. The child care agency or caregiver will do some imprinting, but the working mom can do several things to make the situation as positive as possible. If you are in this situation, consider the following options, which I call "the positive side of working."

First, consider working at home. The advantages are obvious:

You're close to your kids, you avoid the commuter hassle, your hours can be flexible, and if you are in business for yourself, your overhead should be very low. Perhaps best of all, you avoid those inevitable moments when you get the guilties after dropping off your ill or unhappy child at a day care center.

In *Home by Choice*, Hunter devotes an entire chapter to describing mothers who figured out how to translate their skills and education to marketable at-home careers. Hunter herself recalls moving to Seattle from London and needing money to supplement her income. She tried to find the perfect "half-day job," but nothing turned up.

Just as she was thinking she would probably have to go to work full time outside her home, a friend called. She learned that his organization wanted to publish a quarterly newsletter and needed somebody with editorial skills to produce it. Hunter, who had spent several years teaching English and writing at the college level, believed she had the writing skills but would have to learn how to work with printers.

Within a few days, her editorial consulting firm was born. She was able to produce the newsletter on a half-time basis, spending enough time with her daughters and also getting out for essential adult contact and stimulation that she needed.[15]

You may be thinking, "That's great—for Brenda Hunter. But I don't have any editorial skills . . . what can I do at home?"

Have you thought about starting an accounting service, running an aerobics class, or providing an answering service at home? Some other ideas could be running a bed-and-breakfast inn, cake decorating, catering, or a cleaning service. Also, think about doing pet sitting, possibly for unusual animals; music instruction; setting up a shopping service; being a toy maker, a tutor, a wardrobe consultant; or offering word processing and secretarial services. There are many other ideas.[16]

Before launching a work-at-home career, you need to ask some questions: What do you really enjoy doing? Do other people see you with any particular skills and talents? Do you have any talents that are hidden or that you haven't tried before? And possibly, most important: Do you have the makeup to work at home? Do you have a self-starter type of personality? Can you organize yourself? Do you meet deadlines and do you enjoy working alone?[17]

Working at home isn't for everyone. Some women have tried it and decided it was better to go back to the office. But if it works for you, you could turn it into something nice for you and your child.

If working at home just isn't feasible, think about taking your child to work. I know of moms who bundle their babies up in the morning and take them down to the office, or the store, complete with portable crib or playpen. There they tend to their jobs and their children throughout the day. I've seen this done in a flower shop and in a fabric store. Again, this isn't for everyone. You would need the kind of job where you could be interrupted—sometimes frequently—by your child and be able to tend to his or her needs. But the point is, some people are doing it. Perhaps you could too.

Sounds nice, you say, but kids aren't allowed at your place of business. What do you do then?

I recently acquired new empathy for this kind of question when I spoke at a parents' seminar. During part of my talk I strongly emphasized the need for mothers to imprint their children and the need to stay home from work, if at all possible. Afterward, a woman approached me at the front of the auditorium and, with tears in her eyes, she said: "Dr. Leman, I heard what you said about spending time with your children. I have two little girls and I'd love to do just that, but I'm a single mother and I have to work two eight-hour shifts to keep the bills paid. There just isn't much—if any—time left."

Then she started to sob, very softly, as if she didn't want to bother anyone. I put my arm around her and said, "You know, the Kevin Lemans of this world need to remember there are a lot of moms just like you." I talked with this mother briefly and tried to reassure her about what she could do, even though she was in what some people would call an impossible situation.

One obvious point I made was: *No matter how much you have to work, always let your children know how much you love them—every day.* Help them understand why you have to go to work. It's not what you really want to do. Your children are your first choice, but you have no other choice for now. Also, even a mother who works two eight-hour shifts gets *some* time off. A working mom needs to budget her time carefully. Let some of the housework go, if necessary, to focus on your children. No matter how impossible a situation might be, the important thing is that your children feel loved.

I've spent a lot of space in this chapter talking about how important mothers are in a child's life. Does this mean that Dad is off the parenting hook, free to concentrate on his career and curing his slice? Not on your pacifier! Dad plays an equally important but different role in the task of parenting, which ideally is a team operation. Everything I say in this book is based on that idea of teamwork. The best upbringing a child can have is by *both parents* who are dedicated to each other and to their task.

I often tell seminar audiences that, as badly as children need the love of their parents, children have an even greater need to see their parents loving each other. Research shows that when asked what they fear the most, children don't list nuclear war or stranger-danger. Their major fear is that "Mommy and Daddy might get a divorce."

It doesn't matter if you have a two-career family, a one-and-a-half career family, or a one-career family. None of these work well unless Mom and Dad remember where their real priorities must lie—in loving each other and then loving their children with everything they've got.

PORTRAIT OF THE FUNCTIONAL PARENT

If you were asked to do a working sketch of a functional parent —one who is doing the job reasonably well—what would it look like? I'm sure your portrait would include words like:

LOVING . . . FIRM   BUT   FAIR . . . CONSISTENT . . .
AFFECTIONATE . . . FORGIVING . . . SACRIFICIAL . . .
ENCOURAGING . . . WISE . . . HUMBLE . . .
STRONG . . .

Many more words could be added, but I have two that might not necessarily make the average list:

Date Book

Open the "month-at-a-glance" calendar (or its equivalent) of a functional parent and you will see certain dates blocked out. Depending on the time of year, it will say "Johnny's Little League game, 2:00 P.M.," "Janie's soccer game, 4:00 P.M.," "Trent's basketball game, 10:00 A.M." Whatever little Johnny or Janie or Trent is playing, Mom and Dad will have it down and they'll be planning to be there. Also penciled into the date book will be the children's and award ceremonies, not to mention birthdays and graduations. In the functional family, the priorities are clear:

PEOPLE ARE ALWAYS MORE IMPORTANT THAN THINGS

People—particularly family people—are more important than meetings, sales reports, golf games, working late, luncheons, or shopping expeditions. Functional parents value their family and they live out that value every day.

"Dad, Be There by Three-fifty"

Being there for your kids doesn't get easier as the children grow older. In fact, it can become even more demanding. You can't tell yourself that you're going to concentrate on your children the first few months of their lives or even the first few years and *then* you can ease off. Your availability must continue throughout children's lives if you want to imprint them in a way that builds self-image and a sense of self-worth. In fact, the older children get, the more dates that get filled in on your calendar. Children need love all their lives. As they grow older, it takes more, not less, love to fill their emotional tank.

I remember very vividly when Krissy, a senior in high school at the time, reminded me that Senior Recognition Day was coming up soon. She would be playing in a volleyball game, along with some other activities, and she wanted to be sure I would meet Sande and be there for everything.

"Dad, you and Mom need to be there by three-fifty," she told me. Before the volleyball game is a program at which all seniors get flowers and parents are introduced.

I was grateful for the reminder. I knew the volleyball game started at five-thirty. It might have been easy enough to get there late for the rest of it.

These days Krissy makes it a special point to tell me what time to arrive for just about every one of her games or events. Not only does she want me there for the game, she wants me there for the *warm-ups*. Times have really changed. When Krissy was a younger teenager, she was "cool." When I'd go to her basketball or volleyball games, she wouldn't acknowledge my arrival openly. Like most parents of teenagers, I had to learn to live with being sort of anonymous.

In another book I describe how I drove out into the Arizona desert for what seemed like hundreds of miles to watch Krissy's basketball team play some tiny school in a drafty cracker-box gym. I walked in just as warm-ups were being finished, and

Krissy never looked my way once. But as the game got going and she got fouled, she wound up on the free-throw line, directly opposite of my seat. Again, she never looked over at me, but I could see her one hand go behind her back and her pinky finger do a funny little wave, as if to say "Hi, Dad—glad you're here."

I had to settle for pinky-finger waves when Krissy was a sophomore, and even a junior, but when she became a senior she'd start giving me a smile and a direct wave of her hand when I walked in. It was a great feeling. So, if you're a parent whose teenagers seem to prefer to ignore you in public right now, hang in there. Some day things can and will change.

QUALITY COMES OUT OF QUANTITY

One of the scourges of our current times is a term that was introduced several years ago: "quality time." I'm not sure who coined those words, but it's my guess they didn't want to take enough time with their children, so they dreamed up a mythical concept that sounded good. Quality time is based on the presupposition that you don't have much time to spend with your children, and, therefore, you want to "put everything you've got" into the few minutes you may have available. This may be true for some people—that mother I talked to who works two eight-hour shifts a day, for example—but, for a lot of people, quality time is not only a myth, it's a cop-out.

From what I've seen, you just don't get together with a child, press some imaginary button, and turn on quality time. The quality moments with your child don't happen on cue: They happen of their own accord while you're spending time together. I for one am a firm believer in spending as much quantities of time as I can in the hope that the quality moments will happen.

One of the best examples of how quality time occurs is the story told by Zig Ziglar in his book, *Raising Positive Kids in a Negative World.* It was a Sunday evening, well past nine o'clock, when Zig, his son, Tom, and one of Tom's friends, Sam, decided to go out running together. They finished their run, Sam peeled off to go home, and then Zig's son said, "Dad, let's walk."

The two of them walked on, "cooling down" for another ten minutes. According to Ziglar, those ten minutes were among the most meaningful he had ever spent with his son. He doesn't even remember what they talked about, but he vividly remembers that he never felt closer to his son than during those precious moments. It was, indeed, "quality time." But how had it come about? Ziglar points out that earlier in the day the two of them had gone to church together. Then they'd been at lunch together, as well as spending the entire afternoon together. They'd also had dinner together and then they had gone out running. Ziglar said, "We were totally relaxed, at ease, and were communicating together—that's what made those ten minutes so great."[18]

Tim Hansel, author of *What Kids Need Most in a Dad*,[19] has shared a concept on spending time with children that really hit home with me when I read it. It seems that he found an article with a headline that said "If you're 35, you have only 500 days left to live." The writer of the article pointed out that if a person subtracts the time spent working, engaging in personal hygiene, cleaning house, and doing all the odd jobs of life, that person has 500 days left to live as he chooses.

Stunned by this revelation, Hansel decided to develop some statistics for the amount of parenting time he had. Figuring that a parent has children from birth to age eighteen and giving a parent one to two hours a day (which he felt was generous), he came out with 273 days that parents have to spend with each child.[20]

I don't know about you, but when I realize that I have (in some cases had) only 273 days each to parent my children, the distinctions between quality time and quantity time get pretty blurred. Holly and Krissy are in college, so my 273 days with each of them are just about gone. Kevin is in high school, so well over half of my allotted time with him has ticked by. Hannah, however, is turning six, and I have quite a few of those precious days left to spend on her. The point is, with each child, I want to spend all the time I can, and that's why that date book becomes so important.

A MESSAGE FOR ALL MOMS (AND DADS)

Not long ago, one of Ann Landers' readers sent in an essay that she believed needed to be read by every mother, everywhere. It was written by a mom to her little four-year-old daughter in the form of an apology for missing a great deal of her babyhood by "wishing she would grow up faster." The essay, of course, really isn't for four-year-old eyes. This mom planned to save it and give it to her daughter when she was fully grown, married, and having children herself. Landers ran the entire essay and, as you read it, you will see why. It's a message every mom (and dad) should heed:

Dear Daughter: Although you are only 4 years old and will not understand what I am saying, I feel the need to write this letter and put it away for you to read many years from now.

When you were an infant and the newness of being a mother wore off, I couldn't wait until you grew up. At first I found myself wishing, "If only she would start walking!" And then, "If only she could start talking!" One day I suddenly realized that you were out of diapers. You were indeed walking and talking, and pretty soon you would be going off to school.

I remember the morning your father and I brought your baby sister home from the hospital. You and I had been apart six days. When the door opened I saw you standing there with your angel smile. You seemed so big compared to the baby I was holding in my arms. It was hard to imagine you were once that small.

I suddenly realized how much of your babyhood I had wished away. Being a mother is demanding. It robs you of so many freedoms, and I resented the fact that I had so many added responsibilities. And then I looked down at your soft curls and your trusting eyes. Suddenly I felt so ashamed. My heart almost broke.

I cannot relive those first four years, but I have been trying to make them up to you—and to myself. I hope and pray that when your first child is born you will be wiser and more mature than I was. I hope you will enjoy every phase of your child's growing up and not wish they would hurry and pass so you could be free of the "burdens" of motherhood.

You and I will have our share of heated words and angry battles in the years to come. There will be days when we will find it impossible to please each other. I will secretly wish that you would hurry and graduate from high school so I could send you off to college and be rid of you.

Life rushes by all too rapidly, my darling daughter, especially the lovely days and the beautiful times. Be smarter than your mother was. Don't let a single moment slip away unsavored or unappreciated. These days are priceless and afford you the greatest opportunities for fulfillment. Never again will your heart be so full.

All my love,
Mother[21]

The mom who wrote this essay never heard of image insurance, but she's not only talking about insuring her child's self-image, she's insuring her own as well. The first, and biggest, down payment on image insurance is a parent's time. I don't know the ages of your children. They may all be quite young and you have a lot of imprinting to do. Perhaps they are teenagers heading out of the nest and your imprinting opportunities are just about over. But one thing I do know: *The ducks are on the pond.* If imprinting doesn't happen now, it doesn't happen later. There is no remedial duck school, and the saddest words a parent could ever utter are "If only I had spent more time with my kids when I had the chance."

Whatever the age of your children, there is still time to imprint their minds and hearts with your love and guidance. You are at the plate and the game is on the line. The pitcher is winding up. You only have one swing, so make it a good one.

Words to Remember . . .

- The ultimate law for having a functional family says: "You only have one swing (so much time), so make it a good one (spend it on those you love)."

- While it takes years to build a good self-image in each of your children, the first five to seven years are the most important.

- There are critical moments when you get only one opportunity to leave a positive mark on your child. If you aren't there, those opportunities are gone forever.

- Imprinting, especially by the mother as she bonds with her baby, is critical during the first months and years of life.

- A baby's emotional bond or attachment to his mother is what one psychiatrist calls "the foundation stone of personality."

- You can find all kinds of pros and cons on working mothers. The bottom line is: Children pay a price when Mom isn't there.

- As the 1980s turned into the 1990s, survey after survey showed that working women would much prefer to be home with their children. More and more couples are cutting their standard of living in order to let Mom be home with the kids.

- If at all possible, only one person should work during a child's growing-up years, which extend at least through junior high.

- If both parents must work, they should make every effort to get the best child care they can possibly find.

- If you have no choice and both of you must work, go out of your way to let your children know how much you love them—every day—and prioritize what time you do have so you can focus on your children as much as possible.

- Functional parents are loving, firm but fair, consistent, affectionate, forgiving, sacrificial, encouraging, wise, humble, and strong. They also have date books or month-at-a-glance calendars with plenty of dates with their children already scheduled.

- Quality moments with your children come out of spending as much time with them as you can

Actions to Try . . .

- Sit down with your own date book or calendar and take a good look at how many dates with your children you have actually planned. If getting to their Little League games, dance recitals, and class plays are only on a I'll-try-to-make-it basis, you are losing the battle to be the most important part of imprinting their lives.

- Sit down with your spouse and talk about your family's schedule. Keep coming back to the question: "In our family, are people more important than things?"

___

Checklist for Finding a Good Child Care/Preschool

While the lines between child care agencies and preschools are becoming more blurred, the essential difference is that parents send children to *preschool,* usually no more than twenty hours a week, to give them a head start with learning as well as opportunities to socialize with other children. A *child care agency* provides proper care and supervision for whatever time is needed, usually while both parents work. Child care agencies often provide learning activities, but that is not their chief goal.

Several basic criteria should fit either child care agencies or preschools:

1. The facility should have flexible visitation rules that allow parents to come in and observe at any time. In addition, the facility should have a good security plan that includes a sign-in/sign-out system so that not just anyone can walk in off the street, posing as a friend or some distant relative.

2. Reputable facilities check out their employees. This can include an FBI check of fingerprints or at least a check with the local police department. The obvious reason for this kind of check is to be sure the facility isn't hiring a known pedophile or person with some other kind of criminal record.

3. The facility should have a clear-cut policy for dismissing the children. Who picks up the children each day? In these days of rampant divorce and separation, all child care/preschool facilities need to be extremely careful. Some facilities even require lists of people who are *not* allowed to pick up the child under any circumstances.

4. The physical condition and the appearance of the facilities are extremely important. Are they neat and clean? Is equipment clean and up-to-date? Are there colorful decorations? Are there plenty of toys that are in good repair—blocks, dolls, trucks, cars, balls, and the like? Also, what about hands-on stuff such as clay, sand, watercolors—anything that allows children to be creative. Ask yourself, "If I were four years old, would I want to play here?"

5. What are the facility's emergency procedures in case of accident or sudden illness? And what are the policies concerning children who

are ill or who are "coming down with something"? Stay away from facilities that are too permissive about taking half-sick kids. Some schools or agencies may have areas where they can isolate children who aren't feeling well, but the best place for a sick child is home in bed.

6. What are the credentials of staff members? This is especially important regarding preschools, but it doesn't hurt to ask for credentials, or at least experience records, on day care workers. The point is, do the people who are going to be taking care of your child know what they are doing? Also, keep in mind that turnover is usually much greater in child care facilities than it is in preschools. Occasionally you will find some preschool workers who have been with a facility for many years.

7. What are the facility's policies regarding discipline of children? Does the director of the facility allow any staff member to yell, scream, or use heavy-handed punitive measures with the children? This is extremely difficult to ascertain in one interview or one phone call. If at all possible, try to spend some time at the facility, observing what goes on before enrolling your child there on a permanent basis. Ideally, you should try to spend the entire day and see what happens with children of all ages. Of course, staff workers will be on their best behavior while you are there, but you can still learn quite a bit about how patient they are and how they react to various situations. Note especially if the smaller children, including infants, are held and talked to.

   Beware of any facility that is hesitant to allow you to come and observe. If you feel you are not that welcome, try somewhere else.

8. What is the ratio of adult staff members to children? As a rule, with two- and three-year-old children, for example, there should be no more than eight children in the care of each adult staff member.

In regard to preschools, I recommend:

1. Enroll your three- or four-year-old (*never* younger) for a maximum of three hours a day, four days a week. Four hours a day, five days a week is too much for a lot of little kids.

2. Pick a preschool that does not overemphasize academics. Some parents go to incredible lengths to get their children enrolled in

prestigious kiddie kolleges and urchin universities, but there is little long-term proof that this does much for children except cause them stress and pressure. I believe creative activities and stressing social skills are much more important than trying to prepare three- or four-year-olds to score high on their SAT tests in high school.

3. Along with too much stress in academics, beware of preschools that offer a lot of busy work—ditto papers loaded with things for the kids to color, dot-to-dot pages, and the like. A little of this is okay, but be sure the school also offers opportunities to be creative.

    Good creative activities include painting at easels, using uncooked spaghetti and glue to make pictures, doing finger-painting with pudding, using different-colored Jell-O cubes to make designs, and so on.

4. Discourage perfectionism with your preschooler. Some preschool teachers will "touch up" a child's art projects so they look "more perfect." This kind of teacher doesn't want anything going home unless it "really looks correct." Let any preschool you choose know that you want to be sure that what comes home is your child's work, not the teacher's.

5. Steer away from situations where the teacher does a lot of direct instruction and the kids passively absorb knowledge. Look for schools that encourage children to talk and share their ideas and opinions.

6. Preschools should provide "walking field trips" rather than sending them off on elaborate field trips by minibus or van. A stroll in a nearby park, around the neighborhood, or even in the preschool yard, with everyone holding hands and looking at all the wonders around them, can be a fabulous experience for little kids.

7. Finally, whether you're looking for child care or a preschool, don't make "a convenient location" your most important consideration. A better facility that is a little farther away is well worth the extra time it will take to drive there and back. Remember, you are trying to benefit your children and provide them with the best situation possible, rather than just making things convenient for yourself.

PART II

They May Not Be Perfect, But You Can Help Them Be Awesome!

. . . Why all kids are "the enemy"—the conspiracy to
get your attention

■

. . . How to raise children to be responsible,
cooperative, conscientious—and several other
parent fantasies

■

. . . Why the one-minute manager is only
partly right

■

. . . How to stop praising your children and start
doing something beneficial for a change

■

. . . Why active listening really works—and how
to do it

Chapter Five

"IF THEY'RE SUCH 'GOOD KIDS,' WHY ARE THEY DRIVING US UP THE WALL?"

■

Four Key Causes of Misbehavior

Flamboyant tennis star André Agassi is well-known for several things, including a commercial he did for a large camera maker that ends with André, sunglasses pulled low on nose, delivering his famous punch line: "Image is everything!"

I've never appreciated the egotistical overtones of this ad. However, as I watch it, I'm struck by how true the words are in regard to every person's *internal* image. As I said in Chapter One, parents need to take out all the image insurance they can on each of their children, because the self-image children develop will, in a real sense, determine their destiny. Their self-image will affect their thoughts and feelings, their ability to cope in a world that is demanding and even dangerous. Their self-image will mold their attitudes and have a great deal to do with their behavior—or misbehavior, as the case may be.

Every case of child misbehavior that comes to my attention can be traced right back to how the child sees him- or herself stacking up against the world. Remember Image Insurance Principle #2? All Behavior Has a Purpose.

In this chapter, I want to talk especially about why all "misbehavior" has a purpose. Often misbehavior is simply an effort to gain attention that has gotten a little off course—or perhaps it's more accurate to say, an effort that has gone too far.

Rudolf Dreikurs, a child psychiatrist who understood kids about as well as anyone who ever lived, believed that when children misbehave, they may have any one of several goals in mind. Another way to classify these goals is to see them as levels of misbehavior, escalating from mildly annoying, to severely irritating, to downright dangerous and deadly. The four goals (causes) of misbehavior are to:

1. Gain attention.

2. Use power to control.

3. Avoid pressure and expectations.

4. Seek revenge.

As we look at each of these motivations to misbehave, we will clearly see that the children's self-image always plays a key role in what they do to annoy, control, or even hurt their parents.

ATTENTION-SEEKING CAN BE POSITIVE OR NEGATIVE

All of us are born with the basic need for attention. As I have said in another book, all children start out with this basic skill, which they hone to a sharp edge as they go about the business of growing up.[1]

Because every child starts out in life with a natural desire to please you—the parent—you have a golden opportunity. Since children are going to seek your attention ("Hey, Daddy, watch me!"), you might as well do all you can to teach them how to be a positive attention-getter rather than a negative one. How you interact with your children as they seek your attention is the critical issue.

For one thing, go easy on the word no. I'm not saying to never use "no," but I am suggesting that you use it sparingly. You'd be surprised at how often you can change your natural inclination to say no by rephrasing your message to say: "That's good, but why not try it this way?" or "It would be better if we did this."

By controlling the use of the word no, you put an automatic curb on possibly slipping into being punitive and judgmental. As you interact more positively with your children, you will find yourself taking time (there's that word again) to love them, hold them close, play with them, and be involved with their lives. As a rule, the word no says "I don't want to spend time . . . I'm too busy for you . . . I can't be bothered." But when you use phrases such as "Why can't we try it this way?" you're saying "I have time for you . . . I love you . . . you're important to me."

Two of the best strategies to encourage positive attention-getting in your children are these:

1. Don't overreact to what your child says or does.

2. Do show interest without putting on pressure.

For example, seven-year-old Tommy comes to Dad and says, "My friend, Kenny, is going to play T-ball. He wants me to play too. Dad . . . what's T-ball?"

"It's baseball, honey, you know. You play catch and bat the ball with Daddy sometimes."

"Oh, I like baseball."

"Well, maybe you'd like T-ball. I don't know. I guess you could try it. Do you know what a 'T' is?"

"No."

"Well, this afternoon we'll go down to the store and Daddy will show you—anyway, they set the baseball on the 'T,' you hit it, and then you run around the bases. It's just like baseball except there isn't any pitching. And you have uniforms."

"Uniforms?"

"I think for kids your age you get a shirt and a hat. And you have a manager and coaches, you practice and you play games. And the parents come to watch."

"Oh . . . you'd be there?"

"Sure. I'll come to your games."

"Dad . . . do I have to play T-ball?"

"No, you don't have to play. Some kids play and some kids don't—it's up to you."

This kind of conversation illustrates the laid-back approach to dealing with children. Some dads, upon being approached by a son about T-ball, might have eagerly started talking about how "You'll be the greatest. I can't wait to see you play and hit home runs." When children show interest in one activity or another, a typical reaction by parents is to be very enthusiastic, but this isn't necessarily the best approach.

Notice that Tommy wanted to know if he *had* to play T-ball. The whole thing was a bit scary to him—particularly thinking about coaches, managers, uniforms, games, and parents coming to watch. In this case the father was wise to be interested, patient, and kind, but not pushy or pressuring.

Let's take this T-ball illustration one step further. Suppose Tommy starts playing T-ball and decides that he likes it. He discovers that he can throw the ball, hit the ball off the T, and even catch it on occasion. He learns, "I do can do this, I'm pretty good at this. I like this!" Above all, Tommy learns that he gets attention by playing T-ball, and it's the positive kind that his parents feel good about. In Tommy's case, playing T-ball is a positive attention-getter and all is well.

Suppose, however, his little friend Kenny, who invited him to play in the first place, starts playing and decides he doesn't like it. He discovers that he can't hit the ball very well, that he can barely throw across the infield, and that when he tries to catch it, it hits him right in the face.

If Kenny is fortunate, he will have parents who will simply say, "Well, maybe you better let T-ball go for this year. You can try playing ball when you are a little older and see how you do." On the other hand, if he has pressuring parents, they might over-react and tell him, "Look, you wanted to play, we paid your fees, and you made a commitment. You're going to stick in there and finish out the year."

The result of this can be a very bad experience for Kenny. He may be getting attention, but not the kind that is positive to him or anyone else. And he may start to do negative things to get attention, such as whine, stall, get a stomachache, lose his uniform or his glove. And the upshot of it all could be that he will hate T-ball so much that he'll never want to play anything competitive again.

My concern is that parents be sensitive to what the pressures of competitive activities can do to children. I am not anti–T-ball (or any other activity, for that matter), but I am pro family. When Kevin was seven and played T-ball, I can remember helping coach at games and hearing some of his teammates come in off the field and ask, "Can I sit down? Can I sit out now?" It wasn't that they just wanted to rest while the team was at bat; they wanted to sit out a few innings, or possibly the rest of the game.

I'm not sure what motivated each child who asked to sit out, but I can make a few good guesses. Some were obviously feeling the pressure and didn't want to stay in the game because they were afraid they would make a mistake. In other cases, their fathers were at the game and had been shouting instructions (and sometimes criticisms) at them. Another possibility is that some of them were just plain tired, and at age seven, their tired-ness could have been mental as well as physical. Children that young might be ready to "compete" in T-ball, but the competi-tion should be kept at a very low key.

My advice is to limit your children's activities. Prioritize, and when they are very young—five, six, and seven—let them participate in only one activity. As they grow older, I would say two is the limit, as a general rule. Kids can burn out very quickly in activities, especially sports. And the myriad of activities in which kids can get involved can easily pull the family in too many directions and in some cases pull it apart.

HOW TO GET THE BEST BEHAVIOR FROM YOUR CHILD

To help your children see that positive attention-getting is the best way they can go, always try to do the following:

Recognize and encourage achievements.

Place a premium on cooperation.

Make sure that your family environment is creative and invites the children to experiment.

Always let children know that failure is not fatal.

Don't reward or encourage competition between siblings.

Expect the best of your kids in all situations. Encourage them to shoot for excellence but not perfectionism. (See "The Difference Between Excellence and Perfectionism," page 112.)

I deal with clients who are driven by the demons of perfectionism. This is especially true of super-moms who find themselves in my office, totally exhausted and wondering why. To get their attention, I tell them, "Perfectionism is slow suicide." And if I see them laying their perfectionistic hang-ups on their children, I could easily add, "Perfectionism can lead to first-degree murder of your child's self-image."

Pressure, expectations, or stress is the root cause of a lot of negative attention-getting. When your children start seeking attention in negative ways, look for where they are being pressured, where life is closing in on them to give them stress and bad feelings about themselves. When this happens, they are headed over that fine line between attention-getting and what I call power trips, using powerful behavior to control those around them, particularly parents.

A POWER TRIP IS YOUR CHILD'S REACTION TO YOU

There is an invisible but very real line between negative attention-getting and a power trip. Children cross that line when they decide they will *make* you pay attention to them on *their* terms.

It's important to remember, however, that children don't just "decide" to take a power trip. They are usually reacting to the way they're being treated by the parent. Children enjoy being led, but they don't like being driven. When parents use their authority without patience and understanding, children will often retaliate with powerful behavior. I recall being on a panel with psychiatrist Grace Ketterman, who has written many fine books on child rearing, and hearing her say something well-known to counselors but that should be taken to heart by all parents:

> "Whenever You See a Powerful Child,
> You Know There Is a Powerful Parent"

When parents use their authority without patience or understanding, they are taking their own kind of power trip; and often their children will retaliate with powerful behavior. They may talk sassy or have temper tantrums. But they also can take subtle power trips by turning "mother deaf" and just not hearing when being called to dinner or being reminded it's bedtime in five minutes.

Rudolf Dreikurs points out that children

> resist our attempts to overpower them and show us their power instead. A vicious round develops in which parents attempt to assert themselves and the children declare war. They absolutely will not be dominated or coerced. All attempts to subdue them are futile. Children are by far more clever in a power contest. . . . the home becomes a battlefield. There is no cooperation and no harmony. Instead, there is anger and fury.[2]

The Difference Between Excellence and Perfectionism

Always be aware that there is a vast difference between having standards of excellence and putting too much pressure on your children with perfectionism.

- Excellence shoots for high standards that are possible, but perfectionism tries to do the impossible.

- Excellence is known for "who I am," but perfectionism can find personal value only in "what I do."

- Excellence deals with disappointment, but perfectionism succumbs to depression.

- Excellence learns by failing, but perfectionism believes failure is disaster.

- Excellence learns from making mistakes, but perfectionism dwells on mistakes and can't shake their effects.

- Excellence is satisfied with doing its best, but perfectionism believes winning is everything; second place or below is nothing.

- Excellence has a good self-image no matter where it finishes, but perfectionism must win or its self-image suffers.

In many families I deal with, children go on power trips because parents are inconsistent, vacillating between permissive, then losing their temper and become very harsh and authoritarian. In other cases, parents may be using power and overcontrol while believing they are "doing it all out of love" for their children.

For example, I remember little Richey, who came out of a home where everything had been done for him by a hovermother who was constantly snowplowing the roads of life for her son. When I dealt with Richey, he was nine years old and one of the most powerful little buzzards I had ever met. Richey acted out in school. He got in fights and, in general, was in constant trouble.

His mother tried to have teachers arrange their classrooms by seating Richey in certain seats. If he didn't get a good grade on his first report card of the year, his mother would ask to have his seat moved away from a certain other boy who, in her opinion, was a "problem child."

The first day Richey came in to see me, I was reminded of Dennis the Menace, minus the slingshot. In Richey's case I almost expected a B-B gun, or maybe something of even a higher caliber. The smirk on his face told me, "Hey, Doc, you are not going to do a thing with me."

As I worked with Richey, I discovered his self-image was around minus one or two. His mother was divorced and he was cared for most of the time by his grandmother while his mother was working. In addition, he had two older sisters who either mothered him or treated him like a pest.

His father was totally out of the picture, and Richey had no male influence to identify with. Feeling guilty over the divorce, the mother decided to do all she could for little Richey out of love. Ironically, however, Mom's "loving attitude" only gained Richey's disrespect and misbehavior. As he misbehaved, Richey was the victim of a vicious cycle that continued to make him feel unaccepted and as if he didn't belong in his family. He admitted to me he didn't feel capable of doing anything for himself because his mother or sisters kept doing things for him. His powerful behavior was his way of saying "I'll show you!"

Because he lacked a father's love and involvement in his life, Richey felt hurt and resentful. His mother's overinvolvement and interference, caused in great part by her own guilt over the divorce, didn't help, and neither did the accommodating behavior of his two sisters. The end result was a little nine-year-old boy who resented his mother and sisters but who still had an unrealistic view of his importance in his family. His belligerent cocky arrogance was a cover-up for the pain he carried.

IS THERE A WAY TO AVOID POWER STRUGGLES?

There is a way to avoid power struggles with your children, but in order to do so you must be aware of what's happening and particularly aware of your own attitude. Let's look at a typical example of a child on a power trip as we watch little Suzie, age ten, who has been asked by Mom to clean up her messy room. She and Mom have been around and around about keeping her room clean and neat, but it has again reached the condition where it is difficult even to walk through the room without stumbling over something.

"Suzie, please get your room cleaned right now," Mom says impatiently.

"But I want to watch *Full House,* and then I want to call Mary and see if she got her new CD yet," Suzie whines.

"Forget the television program and forget calling Mary until that room is clean," Mom says firmly. "I've got some work to do in the kitchen, but I'm going to be back to check this out."

Twenty minutes later Mom returns and Suzie is sitting in the middle of her bed pouting, the room still totally untouched. When Mom sees the mess, she moves from irritable to downright angry. "Suzie, I thought I told you to get this room cleaned. Why haven't you done it?"

"I was reading my book; you're always telling me I should read more," Suzie said, stalling.

"You can read later! Now get this room cleaned right now!" With that Mom grabs Suzie by the arm, pulls her off the bed, and pushes her toward a pile of clothes and toys in the center of the room.

"Oh, okay," said Suzie. "I don't see why I have to always clean my room. It's my room and I like it this way."

This scene could go on indefinitely until Mom would probably resort to spanking Suzie or having Dad do it when he got home. An even more familiar scenario today would have Mom come home from work herself, find the room not cleaned again, and blow her cool because she's tired and hungry and fed up with having her orders ignored.

However you want to picture it, this is a classic example of a mother being drawn into a power struggle by her child. How can she avoid this? Simply letting Suzie go on with being messy is being totally permissive. But ordering, screaming, and finally spanking Suzie is authoritarian. The answer lies in Mom looking at her own attitude.

Note that the room had degenerated into an impossible mess, and Mom was already irritated and told Suzie so in an irritated tone of voice, which was a big tip-off about how she really felt. Suzie sensed that Mom was already angry with her, so her natural reaction was to resist.

Whenever we come to a child with a request that sounds like an order, the child is going to stiffen. Then, when we go to Stage II and become irritated and angry when the child doesn't immediately obey our orders, the child resists even more. As Rudolf Dreikurs says, "Firmness is usually expressed quietly, while power contests are generally accentuated by verbal battles and angry words."

The best way for Mom to avoid a power struggle with Suzie

over her room is to sit her down and simply say, "Suzie, your room is your territory and you can be messy—to a point. But when the room gets so messy that you're always late because you can't find anything, that's going beyond what is acceptable. It's your room, but the house rules say it must be shoveled out every Tuesday and Saturday. Until you get it cleaned, you watch no TV and you don't call or play with your friends. I'm not going to bug you, but there are limits and you have to work with me on that."

With this approach, Mom is using a little good-natured humor along with some key principles from Reality Discipline to set up a combination of love and limits. She is giving Suzie a certain amount of freedom, but she is letting her know that there are limits and when those limits are exceeded there will be consequences. As I said in Chapter One, Reality Discipline is a consistent, decisive, and respectful way for parents to love and discipline their children. It is not punishment, nor is it "smother-love." We will deal with Reality Discipline and the concept of love and limits in much more detail in the next chapter.

HOW TO KNOW IF YOU'RE IN A POWER STRUGGLE

Avoiding a power struggle does not mean simply giving up and permissively letting children do as they please. You are in authority. The key, however, is to not use your authority like a club or a leash. In general, everything depends on your *attitude*. When you start to feel yourself being drawn into a power struggle, ask yourself:

1. What is my general attitude right now? Am I trying to maintain order, or am I really trying to assert my authority?

2. Do I have a stake in this situation? Do I feel I "don't dare lose"? Is my prestige and my own self-image involved?

3. Am I calm, or do I really feel anger burning inside?

4. What is my tone of voice? One of the best measurements of my attitude and how I feel is my tone of voice. Am I insisting, demanding, and even threatening? Or do I just plain sound angry? If so, I'm definitely into a power struggle.

If your child's negative attention-getting or powerful behavior is really starting to get to you, what can you do? Several things, which I will describe at the end of this chapter. First we need to look at two other kinds of misbehavior and why it happens.

INADEQUACY: THE COMPLETELY DISCOURAGED CHILD

Children who display what has been called "complete inadequacy" are engaging in a subtle form of the power trip. They are acting out their discouragement in a very passive way. Instead of rebelling openly with angry retorts, bad language, getting in fights, flagrant disobedience, and the like, children who feel totally inadequate simply give up.

Totally inadequate children often have difficulty in school. They're behind in all subjects and flunking some of them. They play no sports and they refuse to help at home. Mom has tried to get little Irvin the Inadequate to help, but he is so clumsy or so slow or does whatever he's asked to do so badly that his parents have simply given up on him.

Little Irvin appears to have given up entirely. He is so out of it that he doesn't even want to try, because this would take initiative and effort. He's finding that the best way he can cope with his lack of self-image and self-worth is to become helpless.

Also, he exaggerates any weakness, particularly often complaining of not feeling good or being tired. He is skilled at holding "pity parties" at which he is the guest of honor.

Completely discouraged children often appear stupid, but they are anything but stupid. What they are really doing is playing a very subtle game. They are so afraid of failure that they'll do anything to stay away from having to try or make an effort. They think, "If I do anything or try anything, Mom will discover how worthless I am. I'd prefer that she just leave me alone."

When children give up to this degree, the parents usually wind up saying the same thing: "I give up!" They decide there just isn't any point in asking little Irvin to do anything because it will simply end in disaster and disappointment.

This, of course, is exactly what Irvin wants. If he can convince Mom and Dad he is worthless, they will get off his back and stop hassling him. But what a price to pay for relieving stress in your life. Irvin's self-image will remain puny unless he is encouraged and slowly brought out of his shell. Sometimes "getting tough" with some loving Reality Discipline can help, as it did in the case of a boy named Carl, who had his teacher believing he was so inadequate and unmotivated he could barely sit up straight at his desk.

CARL SEEMED TO HAVE A BROKEN SPIRIT

An elementary school teacher who regularly listens to "Parent Talk" called one day to tell us about Carl, who had everyone believing he was "simply not motivated." The teacher, and teachers before her, had tried everything they could to encourage him but nothing worked. In fact, this little guy appeared to be so inadequate he couldn't even hold his head up! Carl seemed to have a broken neck—and a broken spirit. He wouldn't respond to anything.

One day this teacher told her principal about her problem and then asked, "What should I do with this child?"

"Send him home," the principal said. "If he doesn't want to be here, he doesn't have to."

A bit shocked, the teacher could only think to herself, *What? Should I do something that drastic?* She did nothing for a couple of days and then, as she was listening to "Parent Talk" she heard us discussing a similar kind of child. I recommended the very same solution: "Send the child home from school."

That settled it for this teacher. Next morning she went up to the child, who was sprawled in his usual position in his seat, with his head lolling to the side as if his neck were broken.

"All right, Carl," she said. "Come on."

"Where are we goin'?" Carl wondered.

"You're going home," she said. "Get your coat and hat."

Carl was shocked. His apathy instantly turned into agitated desperation.

"Please, please, give me another chance," he begged, and then he started to cry.

The teacher took Carl to the principal's office and told him what she planned to do. "Have him call his parents," the principal said, "and ask them to come and get him."

Carl got his father on the phone. When Dad learned, "Teacher is sending me home!" he asked Carl to put the teacher on the line. When she told him that, yes, the school did indeed plan to send Carl home, the father responded, "Well, I'll bet he'll love that!"

"No, he won't love it," the teacher responded. "He's already been crying and begging for a second chance."

Carl's mother and father left work and came down to the school immediately, where they had a good talk with the teacher and the principal *with Carl present.* After explaining what was going on and why, the teacher gave Carl a list of homework projects. Then the principal said, "Carl, when you get this work done, you can come back to school if you want to."

Carl was back all right—at eight-thirty the next morning, saying, "I have everything done that you told me."

According to the teacher, being confronted with Reality Discipline caused Carl to become a totally new boy. He has taken a 180-degree change in direction. Now he walks into class with a smile on his face. No longer does he slouch in his seat; his head is up, his "broken neck" totally mended. He participates in class, raising his hand at every opportunity to answer questions or take part in discussion. He gets good grades—mostly A's and B's—and is a much happier boy. The teacher told him how pleased she was with his new attitude and then added, "I'll bet your mom and dad are happy too."

Carl nodded and smiled, and then the teacher said, "I'll bet you're happier too."

Carl smiled again. All he could say was "Yes," but that simple yes spoke volumes. Carl was a product of an educational system that had just pushed him along without challenging him or holding him accountable for what he did (or didn't do). He had everyone believing he was totally discouraged, unmotivated, and inadequate until two concerned educators—the teacher and her principal—decided to call his bluff. When they pulled the rug out from under Carl, notice that they didn't just send him home. They sent him home with homework assignments—with "something from every book on his desk," is the way the teacher put it.

This is a great example of Reality Discipline, because for once Carl was asked to assume responsibility and be accountable. The teacher and the principal were firm but still loving as they told Carl in so many words, "We still believe in you. It's up to you. It's your choice to make." Carl responded and became a different kid.

REVENGE: WHEN POWER TRIPS GET SERIOUS

Beyond power trips and inadequate behavior are the children who seek revenge. Children on an active or passive power trip are not pleasant to deal with, but children with the goal of revenge can be downright scary. When a power struggle intensifies and escalates, it can cause children to seek revenge. While their ultimate target is usually one parent or both parents, they may attack a sibling, or possibly a friend, in order to make their point.

For example, one boy of five went after his three-year-old brother while Mom and Dad were in other parts of the house. They came rushing when they heard the three-year-old's screams and found the older boy stabbing his little brother in the arm with a safety pin. The three-year-old got some punctures and the five-year-old got the attention he wanted—to be recognized as "really bad."

A child willing to stab his little brother in the arm with a safety pin again and again is in a very discouraged state of mind. Because he feels insignificant and unimportant, he is seeking revenge as a last resort. In all likelihood, little brother is outshining him and getting more attention from Mom and Dad than he is. He has finally become so discouraged that he resorts to something awful. He is convinced that nobody likes him, that he doesn't have any power, that he counts only if he can hurt other people as much as he feels they're hurting him.

What should Mom and Dad do with the five-year-old in this case? Punish him? If they do, his self-image will diminish even further, and his sense of self-worth will all but disappear. It has all but disappeared anyway. Also, the older boy will see punishment as revenge on him, and he will simply take more revenge in turn. The power struggle will become one of retaliation, answered by more retaliation.

What the parents must realize is that their five-year-old is unleashing his anger. He is literally resentful of his little brother's presence in his life. What can his parents do? Some helpful approaches would include the following:

Take stock of how they are treating their oldest son. Does he have to go to bed at the same time as his "baby brother," or does he get to stay up at least another half hour?

Does the older boy have any special privileges because he's older? Do the parents occasionally make a "big thing" about his being the oldest in the family?

Are the parents always saddling the older boy with "being in charge" of his baby brother—watching baby brother, doing things with baby brother when he'd rather be playing alone or with friends his own age? If so, the parents are creating a need in their oldest son to put distance between himself and "the Thing" that has bugged him ever since he came home from the hospital.

Parents who detect any kind of revengeful behavior in their children should take it *very* seriously. Most children who reach a full-fledged revenge level do not recover. Our prisons are full of adults who are proof of this terrible fact. When children act out physically in a revengeful way, they may well need evaluation by a competent professional.

Not all children in a revengeful state of mind are beyond help, however. The level of the revengeful child's discouragement is a key. Youngsters who get in serious trouble at home or with the law are almost always extremely discouraged. They tell themselves, "I've been hurt and therefore I have a right to hurt others."

ALL KRISTY NEEDED WAS TRUST—AND LOVE

Fourteen-year-old Kristy was brought to me after she'd been engaging in all kinds of revenge-seeking tactics. Her mother had been divorced when Kristy was six and had remarried a man who was trying to do the best he could in the difficult position of stepfather. Nonetheless, Kristy had been rebelling in all kinds of ways. She chose not to confront her parents openly with backtalk and screaming, but instead she had already run away twice, had been thrown out of a private school, and transferred to a public school.

Kristy admitted to me that she is stubborn, lazy, self-centered, tomboyish, and "hangs out with stoners but I'm not a stoner myself." Kristy had also been skipping school and had been caught drinking at school as well as in the homes of her friends. While Kristy never fought with her parents at home, she had been involved in several fights at school.

What was the cause of all this revenge-seeking behavior? After talking with Kristy and her parents, I determined that whatever was bothering her was buried deep beneath the surface. In a session alone with Kristy, I asked her if something was bothering her deep inside. She tried to just shrug her shoulders and act as if nothing were wrong. I didn't give up, however, and asked again, "Is there something way down deep, Kristy, something you'd like to tell me?"

Suddenly Kristy broke into tears and then her story poured out. She had been sexually abused by a fourteen-year-old babysitter when she was six—just about the time her parents had been divorced. She had never told anyone, but since reaching junior high she had been acting out the hurt and rejection she had felt. Kristy's self-image had plummeted due to the divorce, and the molestation had just about finished the job.

Fortunately, I was able to bring Kristy and her mom together to talk about all this, and eventually she was willing to talk with her stepdad as well. Because the stepfather really cared for

Kristy, he was willing to change some of the rather militarylike rules he had set up in the home. She was able to start trusting her mom and her stepfather. They responded by giving her more responsibility and more flexibility—on times to be home at night, for example.

Another thing they did was stop confronting her every day about her homework. Instead, they simply gave her the responsibility to get her homework in without being nagged or reminded. (At my suggestion, Mom did monitor Kristy by calling the school now and then and talking with her teachers about how things were going. The new arrangement worked beautifully. All Kristy wanted was some trust and to be helped to believe she was capable and could do things by herself.)

REMEMBER: ALL MISBEHAVIOR HAS A PURPOSE

To recap, when your children misbehave, it won't do any good to react with irritation, anger, or hurt feelings. Instead, you need a way to respond to your children so you can identify what is motivating their misbehavior. The two most common forms of misbehavior that most parents face are negative attention-getting and power trips. Children test their parents daily in these two major battlefields. Remember, how children behave or misbehave is a direct reflection of their self-image. If you want to improve or strengthen your children's self-image, you need a strategy for dealing with misbehavior. One of the best approaches I know of is a technique I call:

Stop, Look, Listen, and Learn

Suppose you find yourself saying, "Oh, no! I said I wouldn't let my child lure me into a power struggle, but here I am seeing red with my stomach churning. . . ." Instead of letting negative self-talk take over ("I'm a lousy parent"), take heart and encourage yourself for a change. You are catching yourself in mid-stride, so to speak, which is the first step toward changing your ingrained behavior by acting differently. A fancy psychological term for this is "cognitive self-discipline," but I call it the Stop, Look, Listen, and Learn Technique. Here's an example of how it works.

Suppose you've just cleaned the house. Several of your friends are due in forty-five minutes for a special luncheon you are hosting to honor someone in your women's group. You turn your back for a few minutes, and your seven-year-old gets out his Legos. When you return there is a trail of Legos from the front hall into the family room up and partway up the stairs.

On top of that, a mound of jelly and peanut butter has obviously oozed out of somebody's sandwich onto the living-room rug and lies in the middle of a small lake of Pepsi. Not only has your seven-year-old enjoyed Legos, he has enjoyed a prelunch snack as well.

Your normal knee-jerk reaction—and moms the world over will understand—is "I'll kill him!" After all, your friends are coming over for lunch, which is now less than forty minutes away. You start to scream: "JAMES ALLEN! COME IN HERE IMMEDIATELY!" But then you stop and catch yourself. "Oh, no! I'd said I'd never scream at my boy. . . ."

James Allen peeks his head around the corner. He has a horrified look on his face, sure that he is doomed. But instead of landing on James Allen with all your fury, you simply tell him, "Please sit here on this chair. I'll be back in a few minutes." Then you go out in the backyard, perhaps, or to another room in the house where you can walk up and down, or, if you prefer, sit quietly and take time to think. Your goal is to look at the situation calmly, to listen to the sound of your own self-talk telling you that screaming, spanking, and totally "losing it" won't help.

In less than five minutes you are back. James Allen is still perched on the chair, wondering what his fate will be. The peanut butter and jelly island is still in the middle of the Pepsi lake in the middle of the rug. Normally you would have run shrieking for a rag and some rug shampoo at the first sight of the mess. This time you have decided to stop, look, retreat to contemplate for a few minutes, and now it's time to listen to your child.

"Jimmy, I want to know why this house is such a mess. What has been happening here?"

"I'm sorry, Mom," Jimmy says tearfully.

"I know you're sorry, but why? Why all this when you know Mom is having people over for lunch in just a little while?"

"I wanted to play with my Legos," Jimmy explains rather logically—to him.

"Don't we have a rule that you talk to me before you bring out your Legos and we decide where you can set them up?" Mom reminds Jimmy. "And don't we have a rule not to eat sandwiches and drink pop in the family room on the rug?"

"Yes, but I was hungry."

"Well, there's also a rule about eating just before lunch. I would have been glad to fix you a peanut butter and jelly sandwich and a drink to eat in the kitchen for your lunch. Tell you what I'm going to do. I have some things to still prepare in the dining room. I'm going to leave you here with a pan of water, a rag, and some rug shampoo. I want you to clean up this mess on the rug, and then I want you to pick up every Lego and put the box away. Do you know how long ten minutes is?"

"I think so," says Jimmy.

"Then I want you to have all this done in ten minutes."

Mom goes off to finish setting her table for lunch and Jimmy is left to clean up the mess. Mom comes back in ten minutes, finds almost every Lego back in the box (he did miss a couple under a chair). As for the spot on the rug, Jimmy hasn't done a perfect job, but for a seven-year-old it looks quite good. Not wanting to "do it over" in front of her son, which would be a sure putdown to his self-image, Mom says, "You've worked hard. I appreciate all this help." Jimmy scoots happily off to play and then Mom touches up the spot, knowing that Jimmy will never notice the difference.

During all of this, Jimmy has learned that making messes has its consequences, and Mom has learned a little bit more about how to keep her cool and not just do the usual screaming, spanking, and punishing, and then spend most of her luncheon telling her guests all about it to boot.

WHAT ABOUT TEENAGERS?

The Stop, Look, Listen, and Learn Technique works well at almost any age, but perhaps it works even better with older children, who often feel nobody listens to them. For example, suppose your seventeen-year-old uses your car for the evening and comes in a good hour and twenty minutes past curfew time. Like most parents, you have been so worried about the kid you want to kill him when he finally does get home. But instead of screaming, putting the car off limits for at least two years, and other reprisals, you simply ask, "What happened?"

"Well," your teenager replies, "Bart couldn't get a ride, so I had to wind up taking him home. He lives way out of town, and on the way back I noticed I was almost out of gas, so then I had to drive around awhile to find a station that was still open. And I just don't know where the time went, but I got here as fast as I could."

"Let's sleep on it," you tell your teenager. (In this case, "sleeping on it" is equivalent to Mom perching Jimmy on a chair and retreating for a few minutes to gather her wits.)

The next morning you review the situation with your teenager and then you simply say, "Why didn't you call us when you knew you would be late?"

"Well, I'm not sure I had the change for a pay phone and stopping to call would have made me even later, so I guess I didn't bother."

"Hereafter," you say, "always carry change to make a phone call home if you're going to be late. And never be concerned about being a little later by taking time to make a call. We worried about you. We had no idea of where you were or what had happened, and you haven't been driving all that long."

You may want to go on from here to hold the teenager accountable for what happened the night before. Perhaps he can't have the car for next Friday night's game, but if that is your decision, be sure it is a logical consequence that you have set up before allowing him to drive at all. Or perhaps you want to give him another chance to act in a mature and responsible way. Don't issue any warnings, just remind him of your agreement and let him go back to work out the problem for himself. (For more on logical consequences, see Chapter Six.)

Whatever you decide to do, this kind of confrontation with your teenager has helped you stop, look, and listen instead of charging full speed into an unfortunate reaction that will only make your teenager more rebellious or at least far less interested in acting responsibly in the future.

Also, you have let your teenager know how parents think. He may think you were silly to worry. Like most teenagers, he believes that he is a good driver, that nothing could ever happen, that he is indestructible. So be it, but hang in there. With tongue in cheek, tell your teenager, "Look, I know you think your parents are rather ancient. We know our brain cells are dying fast, but the fact is we old folks do worry about stuff like this. You should know us by now, so humor us a little, okay?"

By good-naturedly letting your teenager know how you feel, you plant one more seed that may some day lead to more responsible, considerate behavior on his part. You have stopped, looked, and listened. And, in this case, perhaps your teenager is the one who has the opportunity to learn the most.

In the examples used in this chapter, you may have noticed that children of any age can be held accountable and made to face logical consequences for behavior without the parent having to punish, scream, hit, use abusive language, and so on. The principles that parents and teachers employed come from an approach to child rearing that I have already referred to in several places as Reality Discipline. I am convinced that it is the best approach to disciplining children and, over the long run, building their sense of self-worth.

With Reality Discipline you have a proven strategy for raising children to become adults who are mature, responsible, confident, and capable of functioning successfully in life. In the next chapter we will take a closer look at Reality Discipline to see just how and why it works.

Words to Remember . . .

- Children's self-images have a direct effect on their behavior, good or bad.

- All behavior has a purpose, and when children misbehave they have one of four goals in mind:

  1. Gaining attention.
  2. Using power to control.
  3. Avoiding pressure and expectations by appearing to be inadequate.
  4. Seeking revenge.

- All children are born attention-getters. How you respond to their attempts to get attention has a direct bearing on whether their attention-getting behavior will be negative or positive. Don't overreact to what your child says or does, and try to show interest without putting on pressure.

- To raise positive attention-getters, always try to do the following:

. . . Recognize and encourage your children's achievements, big or small.

. . . Place a premium on cooperation. Teach your children they are part of a team.

. . . Make sure that your family environment is creative and invites the children to experiment.

. . . Always let your children know that failure is not fatal. Failure is a stepping-stone to future success.

. . . Don't reward or encourage competition between siblings. (They're usually competitive enough!)

. . . Expect the best of your kids in all situations, but always be ready to forgive them if they aren't perfect.

- If you want to murder your children's self-image, teach them to be perfectionists.

- When children go on a power trip and seek to involve you in a power struggle, they may be reacting to your powerful behavior toward them. You can usually trace children's powerful behavior back to your own impatience or lack of understanding.

How to Tell What a Child Is Up To

Misbehavior always comes out of mistaken goals that the child is trying to reach. You can usually identify which goal the child is aiming at by your personal reaction—how you feel during and after the misbehavior. Here is one way to chart these four goals:

Goal 1: Attention-Getting
  The child's goal is to keep you busy.
  Your reaction is one of annoyance.

Goal 2: Power
  The child's goal is to show he or she is boss.
  Your reaction is anger.

Goal 3: Revenge
  The child's goal is to get even.
  Your reaction is to feel hurt.

Goal 4: Withdrawal
  The child's goal is to be left alone.
  Your reaction is to give up.[3]

― ― ―

Actions to Try . . .

- The next time you feel yourself being drawn into a power struggle, try to call time out and get away by yourself for a few moments to ask yourself these questions:

    . . . "What is my attitude at this moment? Am I trying to maintain order, or am I really trying to assert my authority?"

    . . . "Do I feel I don't dare lose the argument with my child? Are my prestige and own self-image involved?"

    . . . "Am I calm or is that anger burning inside?"

    . . . "What is my tone of voice? Am I insisting, demanding, or threatening? Or is my voice just plain loud and angry?"

- When you know you're in a power struggle with your children, operate with the principle that you must "Remove your sails from the children's wind." Children seeking a power struggle will huff and puff and try to get you involved in arguing and even screaming and shouting. Instead of hoisting your sails and going to battle, strike your sails instead. Don't engage in battle. Instead·

    . . . Decelerate the conflict by speaking quietly but firmly.

. . . Don't argue with your children. Simply state what is needed and then remove yourself from the scene (or remove the children by putting them in another room).

. . . If the children are old enough and in any kind of receptive mood, sit down and talk reasonably, pointing out what you expect and allowing the children some latitude in making choices.

. . . With younger children who display powerful behavior by refusing to obey, simply give them a choice:

"Do you want to go to bed under your own power or do you want me to take you?"

"Do you want to wear your sweater or your jacket?"

"Do you want to stop complaining (stop crying, stop playing ball in the house, stop bugging your brother) or do you want to have a time-out in your room?"

This way you give the child a choice, but no matter what the child chooses, the child is obeying your wishes.

- An old Spanish proverb says: "A wise bull knows when to charge." Pick your battles. Some things just aren't worth arguing about. For example, you're picking up your three-year-old at school or church. She has on a sweater, but you also want her to wear a jacket. It's not very cold out and she can easily walk to the car in her sweater without getting chilled. Instead of forcing her to put on the jacket, which will probably lead to screaming and lying stiff on the floor refusing to move, and the like, simply say, "You may carry your jacket to the car. If you get cold on the way, you can put it on."

- Use less talk and more action. Do not go on and on with lecturing, arguing, criticizing, or complaining about the burden you have to bear because you're a parent. Spell out what needs to be done and also spell out the consequences involved if the child refuses to cooperate or obey. And then be ready to back up what you have said with swift action. (For more on this, see Chapter Six, particularly Reality Discipline Principle #4.)

Chapter Six

HOW TO RAISE RESPONSIBLE CHILDREN

■

Combining the Power of Love and Limits

The letters and phone calls never stop flowing into our "Parent Talk" program:

. . . a thirteen-year-old has been lying to her mother,

. . . a three-year-old keeps wetting the bed,

. . . a seven-year-old won't clean his room,

. . . nine- and eight-year-old siblings are driving the family crazy with their fighting and bickering,

. . . a five-year-old has his mom believing he will starve to death because of his picky eating.

Problems seem endless, and always the solutions lie somewhere between the two extremes of parenting. Parents can go the permissive route and be all *love* and just live with the problems. Or they can choose the authoritarian path, crack down on their children with righteous wrath, and be all *limits*.

The worst destroyer of children's self-image is authoritarianism, followed closely by permissiveness. The most typical scenario, however, is the permissive/authoritarian seesaw. Here the parents' basic approach is permissive, or at least soft on enforcing the rules because they want to make sure children will like them. But finally, after being provoked beyond the limits of patience, the parents crack down with authoritarian fury. The word for this pendulumlike atmosphere is inconsistency. I also like to call it the yo-yo syndrome. The children are constantly jerked up and down, and back and forth, between one approach and the other.

As we have already seen, neither of these approaches builds children's self-images (not to mention the parents'). There must be a balance between love and limits. It isn't love unless there are limits, and it certainly isn't love if all parents do is limit the children, making all the decisions and attempting to control their every move.

There has to be a middle ground that is sane, healthy, and, above all, effective. I believe that this middle ground is Reality Discipline, which I define as a consistent, decisive, and respectful way for parents to love and discipline their children.

As you use Reality Discipline, you automatically will build the A-B-C's of self-image into your children's lives. Because your children are held accountable for their actions, they will learn that they are capable and able to please you and themselves. At the same time, your children will learn that they do belong, that they will feel worthy of being part of the family. They will know that they fit in. And, finally, your children will feel affirmed and accepted despite being disciplined.

The following note hangs framed on my office wall. It was written to me by my daughter, Holly, now a sophomore in college. At age seven, Holly wrote the following words in her own inimitable scrawl:

World's Gatist Father

My father is the gratist, for your the best, caring, loveing, THE BEST!!!!!! Even when you disaplin me, I love you the same.

Love, Holly

Besides those lines about my being the "gratist," the best part about Holly's note is that she uses the word "disaplin" instead of punish. Even at the tender age of seven she had already detected the huge difference between the two.

Reality Discipline, you see, is all about training and guiding your children. The world "discipline" comes from the word "disciple," which means "to teach," and that is what disciplining your children ultimately should be all about—teaching your children the better, more productive, more satisfying way to live in the family and the rest of the world as well.

In over twenty years of counseling, I have never dealt with a so-called problem child I couldn't turn around as long as the child's parents were willing to use Reality Discipline and let it do its work. That's quite a claim, and you may be thinking, *Okay, Leman, just how does Reality Discipline work?* To give you a quick overview, I would like to share six principles of Reality Discipline, which are developed in much greater detail in *Making Children Mind Without Losing Yours.* The foundation stone of Reality Discipline is the following simple but often misunderstood truth:

You Are in Healthy Authority over Your Kids

A lot of the books, articles, tapes, and videos that you can find today on raising children steer away from the word "authority" and substitute instead such words as "leadership" and "guidance." Parents are told that in this democratic day and age, they can no longer expect to be obeyed simply because they are parents. They must win the cooperation of their children if they hope to succeed. There is a certain amount of truth to this premise. I also think it's a good idea to win the cooperation of my children, but I also believe that a leader without authority is no leader at all, while a leader who misuses authority can become a dictator and a tyrant.

Healthy authority, however, doesn't beat children into submission in order to "teach them better." Rage and anger come out of fear and defensiveness. If you are in *healthy* authority, there is no need to get angry because there is no reason to be afraid.

Healthy authority rejects wrong behavior but always conveys love to the child. In a sense, when you use healthy discipline on children, you are giving them exactly what they want because children, despite what they may say and do, want discipline.

One of the major problems I see in so many families is that parents will discipline their children but fail to communicate love. It is as if they can't do a good job of disciplining unless they are angry, cold, aloof, and severe. Later, when they have cooled off, they find it possible to be friendly and loving toward the children again.

The trouble is, children are relentless. They never stop probing, testing—and, yes, even rebelling. Behind the basic goals of attention-getting, which can turn into power trips, acting inadequate, and even seeking revenge, is an even more basic goal than any of these: *finding out if you really do love them.* That's why balance is so important. As I wrote in *Making Children Mind Without Losing Yours:*

> *Balance is a key word when using Reality Discipline.* The child misbehaves and you must deal with it. If you deal with it in too permissive a manner, the child will soon decide that he is running the house, but if you deal with it with too much of the authoritarian approach, the child will feel that you are trampling him and bide his time until he can get back at you in one way or the other. "Getting back" can run the gamut from being sassy or disobedient, all the way to running away to suicide. The tragedy that I see repeatedly happening is rebellious children who literally destroy their lives as they seek to retaliate against parental authoritarianism.[1]

As you attempt to walk the fine line between permissiveness and authoritarianism, you must be consistent and always be ready for action (another principle I'll describe in detail below).

In other words, *don't keep score.* When you keep score, you save up your resentment and anger and finally when you do let it out you are likely to be severe and unloving. Instead, when children misbehave, keep short accounts. Deal with it now, not later or "when your father gets home."

Dealing with it now may sound as if I'm suggesting the only way to handle misbehavior is with a swat or a spanking, but that isn't so. In fact, as I will explain later, swatting and spanking should be the last resort, not the first. Many other ways to discipline are far more effective in reaching your long-range goal, which is to help your children become accountable, responsible people who know how to be self-disciplined—who can live with self-control and consideration for others. To teach children to be considerate and responsible, practice this second principle of Reality Discipline:

Hold Children Accountable for Their Actions

When I tell parents that children "must be held accountable" for what they do, they sometimes mistakenly think I mean they must be punished. Again, let me underscore the fact that *Reality Discipline is not punishment.* For example, you're on the telephone and your little five-year-old keeps pestering you—wanting your attention, of course. You try to remain calm, but your five-year-old will not be denied. The racket gets so loud you can't hear the person on the other end of the line. What should you do?

If you want to use punishment, your solution is simple. You tell the caller that you will be back in a moment, put down the phone, grab your five-year-old, turn him over your knee, and give him three good whacks and send him to his room. You have "taught him a lesson," or have you? Now he's hurt, resentful, and not at all sure you love him. After all, all he wanted was you, and he really didn't really understand what your phone call was all about.

How can you turn this scene around and use Reality Discipline? The answer is equally simple. It will take a little more effort, perhaps, but not that much. Again, you tell your caller that you have something that needs to be done and will be back in a moment. Then you take your little guy by the hand and lead him to another room in the house, or even outside the house if the weather is cooperative.

Kindly but firmly you tell your son, "I'm talking on the phone right now and I can't play with you this very minute. As soon as I'm through in a few minutes, I'll come and help you with your puzzle" (or game, or book, or popping in a different video, or a snack). And then you leave your little boy to himself while you go back to your phone conversation. There has been no hitting, no angry hissing through clenched teeth—only eye-to-eye contact and a firm word from you about what you want your child to do.

Now I know what you're thinking. What if your little five-year-old doesn't listen and comes back to keep pestering Mom while she's still on the phone? Again, she will have to tell her caller to wait a few minutes while she guides (or carries) her five-year-old to his room and leaves him there, saying, "Because you have chosen not to allow Mommy to talk on the phone, you will have to spend some time alone in your room and come out when Mommy is through talking."

The key to handling this kind of pestering-Mom-while-she-is-on-the-phone situation is to remove the child from the scene. Do not allow the child to remain while you try to pacify him and still carry on an intelligent conversation with the person calling. The only reason your child will keep coming back to bug you is that he knows persistence will pay off. He knows that eventually Mommy will "give in."

But Mommy must not give in. As the parent, you must remain patient, calm, but resolute. Keep removing the child from the situation and letting him know that he is accountable for his actions and that you will not tolerate rudeness or irresponsibility.

Granted, it takes a little longer to hold children accountable for their actions, but it's worth it. Punishment may get "faster results," but it doesn't help children develop the kind of conscience that will help them be responsible. They may learn to be fearful, wary, and even clever, obeying Mom or staying out of her way when she's around, but not being self-disciplined when she's out of sight. A healthy conscience comes out of being held accountable and learning to follow the rules, because it is the most satisfactory way to operate in life, whether you're five or fifty.

USING MONEY TO TEACH ACCOUNTABILITY

One of the best tools for teaching children to be responsible and accountable for their own thinking and actions is money. Recently we dedicated an entire one-hour "Parent Talk" broadcast to the topic of children and money. We asked parents to call in and tell us how they handle money in the family. Did their children receive allowances simply for being part of the family, or did their children have to "earn" any money given them for the doing of certain chores?

We learned that either approach can work successfully in a family as long as children are still held accountable in one way or the other. For example, Bob, our in-studio guest and the father of three children ages five, eight, and ten, gives both of his older children the same two-dollar allowance each week. No particular chores are tied to the allowance, but the children are taught that, along with the privilege of benefiting from the family's total income, everyone in the family has obligations that include respecting other family members, keeping one's room clean, personal hygiene, and the like. If the two older children wish to earn additional money, they may do optional tasks if they wish.

One thing Bob and his wife do is give their children careful guidance in how to be good managers of their money. They let the children decide on the amount of money they want to give in the church offering and they also are invited to contribute 25 cents a week to what is called the family's "capital equipment fund." The parents match this 25 cents and in this way the fund builds up for each child. Later, if the child needs a bigger item, such as a bicycle, a basketball, whatever, he can go to his share of the capital equipment fund to buy that item.

Bob and his wife work hard on teaching their children to make good shopping decisions. They are constantly asking their children one basic question whenever they want to buy anything: "Is this a good deal or not a good deal?"

In one case, their eight-year-old daughter wanted a giant panda bear that was almost as big as Bob. Bob voted against the panda bear, saying it was simply too big to have around the house and it was too expensive a purchase for his daughter to make. Her mother, on the other hand, thought the panda bear would be a wonderful toy for her daughter because she knew how much the daughter was in love with it and would take good care of it.

The decision was to "wait and see." So the daughter watched and waited for a couple of months, and then one day she saw the panda bear on sale at 30 percent off. At this point she brought up the topic again and pointed out she had enough to pay half of the price of the reduced price of the bear. So, the decision was that the parents would pay half and the daughter would pay the other half out of her share of the capital equipment fund.

"I think all of us learned something from the panda bear," Bob observed. "My daughter learned to be patient, something about shopping, and watching for a sale. And I learned to respect her opinions and personal tastes concerning what she wants in her own room."

The other approach to children and money was represented by Kris, mother of four, who called in to tell us that she and her husband paid no allowances to their four children. Instead, the children have required chores that they must do, such as emptying the dishwasher, vacuuming, emptying wastebaskets, and the like. If they wish to earn any spending money of their own, they can do certain optional chores, such as cleaning up "dog flops" in the back yard, sweeping out the garage, and others. The principle Kris and her husband work on is "No work, no money. You must earn any money you get in life. You do not get money simply for being alive."

Both approaches have merit, but I prefer Bob's plan, which makes allowances an economic benefit of being part of the family. I also believe that by giving each child an allowance of his or her own to manage more or less independently, the child learns much more quickly about how life will hold us responsible and accountable for our decisions.

And don't forget that an allowance is a great builder of self-image. There is something about having a few dollars—or even a few cents—in your pocket to give you feelings of positive self-worth, particularly in this society where money talks so very loudly.

HOW ALLOWANCES WORK AT THE LEMAN HOUSE

At the Leman house, each child begins getting an allowance at age five. In addition to the allowance, all children are assigned responsibilities that are theirs to do each week as being part of the family. If the chores aren't done, however, then the children will have to pay someone else in the family to do them—Sande, myself, or a brother or sister. This approach provides an excellent lever for helping the child learn the importance of doing chores on a regular basis.

Not too long ago our junior high age son, Kevin, was having difficulty completing his weekly chore of taking the garbage from the garage out to the curb for pickup by the trash service. I called Kevin in for a chat and simply said, "I'll give you six days to think it over. If you don't want to take the trash out to the curb yourself, you can pay your sister, Krissy, to do the job. I've talked with her and she'll be more than happy to earn the extra money."

Kevin's eyes narrowed a bit, but he didn't say anything. Instead, he decided to think it over. On the sixth day, just before the trash man was due, he announced his decision. He would always take out the trash himself. The thought of having his older sister collect some of his allowance was really more than he could bear.

With younger children who are just beginning to understand the value of money, the typical scenario may see little Sally and Jimmy blowing their entire allowance in the first day or two of the week—probably on candy, although there could be any number of other tempting items, such as trinkets, a special comb, baseball cards, or a neighbor's garage sale.

As the week goes on, the kids are broke. When they are out shopping with Mom, they come across something in the store they really want—a triple-decker ice cream cone, perhaps.

"Can we have one?" they ask blithely. "Well, I think so," Mom might reply. "You ate a good lunch and it's quite a while until dinner. Just pay for them out of your allowances and they're yours." A typical allowance for a five-year-old is $1.50 per week—in the Leman household we add just 25¢ per week.

The kids faces fall, and Sally says, "But I spent all my allowance three days ago. And Jimmy did too." Here is where Mom must be firm. There will be a strong temptation to buy the children their treats, particularly if they have been good, being especially cooperative, eating all the right foods, and being helpful with little brother, Harley, who is only three. But if Mom wants to truly make the allowance a teaching tool, she will say, "That's too bad, kids, I guess you'll just have to wait until Saturday. I'm sure I'll be shopping here again next week. Maybe you can come along and get those treats then."

In this simple little scenario, we see the power of accountability as well as the power of money. Children who get anything they want, any time they want it, with no regard for spending an allowance carefully, grow up to be Yuppies who simply do the same thing with their earnings on a larger scale. But children who learn the rudiments of budgeting and saving for a rainy Friday have a much better chance of growing up knowing how to handle the responsibility of a budget, at any age, from five on up into adulthood.

THE CASE OF THE FOOLISH FRESHMAN

One mother called our "Parent Talk" show to tell us that her daughter, who was a freshman in a private college located in another state, had been dipping into her college fund. The nineteen-year-old freshman had ready access to this money and was responsible for spending it wisely throughout the year. Unfortunately, she had overspent and found herself $400 short for the next quarter's tuition. Her options at that point were: (1) Come home and go to a local state school for the next semester; (2) Borrow money and pay the difference herself; (3) Because the parents hadn't monitored her properly, let them make up the difference in this case.

We pointed out that number (3) was no option at all. Nineteen-year-olds should not have to be monitored by their parents for anything. We strongly urged this mother to let the daughter remain responsible for her own problem. Instead of coming home, she could borrow the money from the college financial aid office, learning all about what it means to sign on the dotted line for a student loan and then having to repay that loan on a future date.

One other point is worth making. When teaching accountability, the discipline should always fit the infraction. Overspending one's allowance results in not having money for your treat when you want it. Interrupting Mom while she's on the phone results in being asked to leave the room so she can have peace and quiet.

As we saw in Chapter Three, Reality Discipline is a simple strategy for practicing the first of the Six Magnificent Rules for having a functional family—Be Firm But Fair. When applying Reality Discipline, there are no lectures or sermons. There is no haranguing children with verbal abuse, which is coming to my attention as an increasingly serious problem in many families. Instead, you respect children even though they may have made a poor decision that needs correcting.

The key is to *always keep responsibility squarely on the shoulders of the children*. Do as little decision making for them as possible. Whenever possible, avoid telling children exactly what to do. What you want to do is tell your children what you expect and then let them figure it out from there. You let children learn from their mistakes, which is far better teacher than a parent's voice saying "I told you you should have saved some of your money." ". . . How many times have I said not to interrupt Mommy when she's on the phone? . . ." Instead, you are using a third important principle of Reality Discipline:

Let Reality Be the Teacher

The technical term for letting reality discipline your children is natural or logical consequences, concepts developed extensively in the writings of Rudolf Dreikurs and others. One of the things I hear parents say the most is "If only little Jonathan would be *responsible*." I reply that you don't teach children to be responsible; you give children responsibility and let them learn how to handle it through trial and error. When they make errors, natural or logical consequences usually come into play, *if you allow them to do so*. But if you're going to give children responsibility, you will have to make several commitments:

1. You will have to back off and let children do things for themselves, even if what they do is not always perfect or up to "your standards."

2. You will have to set aside time to train your children. Rushing in to take responsibility away from children because you're behind schedule will not work.

3. You will have to learn to ask or request instead of order and demand. Parents naturally feel they can order their kids around. They may do it nicely, but what they say is still in the form of a demand, not a polite request. There is a world of difference between snapping: "Get in here and get this cleaned up!" and saying, "Harley, honey, I really need your help. Can you give me a few minutes of your time?" Then, when he does help, you can say, "Thanks, Harley, you were really a big help and you made my day go so much easier."

You will have to learn to use natural or logical consequences as a teaching tool, not as a weapon to punish. Instead of lecturing, badgering, or nagging, you let reality do the teaching when your children fail to carry out one of their responsibilities. The best approach is to say as little as possible and simply withdraw from the situation and let the children experience the consequences of their own irresponsibility. That may sound complex and even a little ominous, but it's really quite simple.

For example, if little Mikey habitually forgets to take the lunch Mom packs to school, Mom has two basic choices: one, she can keep harping at Mikey and bawling him out for his forgetfulness after she trots down to the school to make sure the lunch gets to his classroom. Or Mom can simply put the lunch in the refrigerator and let Mikey go hungry.

Undoubtedly, Mikey will be upset when he can't get Mom to perform her usual services, but Mom can just smile and say, "It's your responsibility. I'm sure you will figure out a way to handle this." Mom may, of course, have to let the people at school know that no one is to lend Mikey lunch money. If he fails to bring his lunch, he simply has to do without.

Or suppose Mikey tears up one of his favorite toys. Again, Mom has two choices: She can replace the toy, or she can simply tell Mikey, "That's too bad. You loved that toy. If you'd like another one like it, you can save up and buy one out of your own allowance."

The key to both of these examples is in the way Mom talks to Mikey—not only what she says but her tone of voice. If she makes comments such as "Maybe this will be a lesson to you" or "Hereafter you'll be more careful," she has turned the natural or logical consequence into a form of punishment, and it will be less effective, or possibly not effective at all.

REALITY DISCIPLINE ALWAYS GIVES THE CHILD A CHOICE

The idea behind Reality Discipline is to give children a choice and let them decide if they want to be responsible enough to follow through. For example, suppose Billy is habitually late for dinner because he enjoys playing at a friend's house so much. Mom needs to let Billy know "We serve dinner at six o'clock. If you aren't here by six o'clock, I will assume that you have chosen not to eat tonight."

Of course Billy will test Mom and come home at six-forty wanting to know "Hey, Mom, what's to eat?" Then Mom has to say firmly but still in a friendly way, "Billy, it seemed obvious that you chose not to come home in time for dinner and now dinner is over. I'll fix you a good breakfast in the morning."

Note there is no lecturing, no talking about "being late again" and "going straight to bed without any supper." Billy is simply left with the reality that he did not get home in time for dinner and, therefore, he will not have dinner (or any snacks before bedtime) for the rest of the evening.

When you make reality the teacher, you balance the need for order against making it okay to fail or make a mistake. Order and organization are important in the Reality Discipline home, but if children choose to disregard the need for an orderly approach to life, they are not ridiculed and punished. They simply learn the hard way through personal experience that it's okay to fail and it's also okay to learn from your failures.

An important part of letting reality do the teaching is closely allied with a fourth basic principle of Reality Discipline:

Use Action, Not Words

While it's important to speak softly, quietly, and in a friendly way to your children when using Reality Discipline, it's equally important to keep arguing and debating to a minimum. The longer you dialogue with children about why something is being done or why something is fair or not fair, the more you enter into the power struggle conflicts described in Chapter Five.

You will get much better results if you simply act swiftly and decisively with a minimum of unnecessary conversation. My favorite way of putting it when I speak with seminar audiences is "Pull the rug out and let the little buzzards tumble." There is no attempt to hurt the "little buzzards." Your goal is to communicate the consequences of ignoring reality.

Suppose, for example, you have two children ages eight and five. As you are all sitting in the family room watching a TV program together, the five-year-old decides he is going to pester his older sister. The first time the five-year-old creates a disturbance, you take him aside and say, "Jeremy, you have a choice. You can sit quietly and watch the program with all of us or you can leave the room. You have to decide."

Return Jeremy to the family room. If he persists in pestering his sister, then you use action, not a lot of words. You simply say,

"I see that you have decided you want to leave rather than stay here with us. You can come back when you are ready to watch the program."

If Jeremy wails that he doesn't want to leave or that his sister caused him to make a disturbance, you simply say, "Do you want to go to your room on your own, or do you need some help?" If Jeremy does not want to leave, you firmly but gently remove him and place him in his room for a stipulated amount of time—ten or fifteen minutes should be sufficient. Then go and ask Jeremy if he would like to return to the family room. If he pouts and says no, let him stay where he is but tell him he may return of his own accord when he is ready.

This approach calls for swift, decisive action, but at all times you are under control, not badgering, lecturing, bawling out, or, possibly, swatting Jeremy for his misbehavior. You are simply letting him learn through logical consequences that he cannot cause a ruckus when the family is trying to watch a television program.

Sometimes, however, a child may start a disturbance and there just isn't time to negotiate or give the child a choice. For example, your three-year-old is having a temper tantrum right in the middle of the living room in front of your guests. You do not dialogue with her; you simply pick her up and remove her from the scene. At a time like that, action is always better than words.

Or suppose your thirteen-year-old picks up the extension phone in her room four or five times in less than five minutes while you are on the kitchen phone talking to a friend. You have clearly spelled out to your daughter that she is not to interrupt while other people are on the phone. You know that it would have been no hardship for her to come out to the kitchen to wait to see when you had hung up, then go back into her own room and use the special extension that you had installed just for her a few months ago.

Instead, however, she has interrupted you impatiently four times. What will the consequences be? After you hang up, you go to the child's room and, without sermons, lectures, or yelling, you tell her that you will have to take her extension and put it away for a week.

"A week?" your daughter says. "What for?"

"For not living up to our agreement," you tell her cheerfully. "You know you aren't supposed to interrupt while others are on the phone, and you did it four times in just a few minutes while I was talking. So you're going to have to do without your own extension for a week. You may still make calls from the kitchen phone, but only when others are not using it."

Granted, Mom had to use some words of explanation as she invoked Reality Discipline in this situation, but the emphasis was on the action, not on doing a lot of lecturing or arguing.

And there are those occasions when the best action is no action at all. For example, suppose Becky, age nine, fails to do her homework and comes wailing to you for help just before bedtime or possibly just before the school bus is due to arrive. Instead of scurrying around madly trying to help Becky get her math in order or her spelling words alphabetized, you simply say, "Sorry, but you should have done your homework sooner. You'll just have to go to school without it being finished."

At school, of course, the child will soon experience the reality of the teacher's displeasure with undone homework. In this case, your "action" is refusing to help do the child's work.

WHEN IS SPANKING APPROPRIATE?

Some parents mistakenly think that when I talk about "action, not words" I mean swiftly moving in to spank or swat when children misbehave. While I believe there is a time and place for a swat or possibly a spanking consisting of several sharp swats in a row, I always emphasize that spanking is usually a last, not a first, resort and that it must always be done when you are under complete control of your emotions. Also, the best place to spank is on the bottom. Parents should *never* slap or hit a child in the face or upper body.

While it is difficult to put an absolute age limit on spanking, as a general rule, spanking is more effective with younger children, ages two to five or six. When children reach the age of seven and on up, spanking becomes less effective, and by the time they are preadolescents or early adolescents, spanking is totally inadvisable.

But when a two-and-a-half-year-old looks you right in the eye and defiantly says, "No, I won't!" after being asked nicely several times, it may be time for a good swift swat to let the little rebel know that you can still pull the rug. Then, of course, you follow up immediately with a hug and a kiss and an explanation of why you had to give the swat and how you love him or her very much.

Different children require different discipline but, as a rule, if you find yourself having to give a child a swat day after day, you may need to back off a bit and start asking yourself, "Is this really the best approach? Will this work in the long run?"

WENDY SCORNED REWARDS OR PUNISHMENTS

Some children are very strong-willed and powerful and constantly are seeking to engage in powerful behavior to get a parent into a power struggle with them. My colleague, Randy Carlson, and I devoted a recent program to the subject of spanking. Karen, the mother of a twelve-year-old daughter, called in to ask for help. Her daughter, Wendy, had been a strong-willed child from birth, very precocious and advanced. But after Wendy turned ten, she was almost impossible to motivate as far as cleaning her room and doing homework were concerned. Karen had tried every kind of punishment on the girl, from spanking to taking privileges away. She commented that her daughter was

"An excellent child with her friends and other parents, but she fights us every inch of the way on everything."

After pointing out to Karen that spanking a twelve-year-old would have little or no impact and could only make the daughter resentful (not to mention destroying her self-image), we asked her about the issue of control. Was Karen really trying to over-control (dominate) her child? Even if she wasn't consciously trying to do so, was this what the child was perceiving?

Karen explained that Wendy was not in open defiance of the rules and standards of the home, but for some reason balked over two things: doing homework and cleaning her room. It seemed that these two duties ate into Wendy's free time, and she just had no interest in them.

Karen also shared that her firstborn twelve-year-old did not respond well to rewards or punishment. The promise of either one did not get the intended results. "She either bucks us all the way," Karen explained, "or she will measure what the penalty will be and often take the penalty rather than do what she's supposed to do."

"Reward and punishment sometimes work with small children for a while," I commented, "but I don't advise using either one as a long-range principle of parenting. The goal of parenting is to produce children who are able to make responsible decisions because they want to, not because they are going to get a reward or be punished."

"Then what am I supposed to do?" Karen wanted to know.

"Use Reality Discipline—let logical consequences take over. The critical thing that you must do, however, is to find out what kind of consequences will really make a difference to Wendy. What does she really like to do? Does she have an activity she wouldn't miss no matter what happens?"

"Well, she likes her youth group at church, but we certainly wouldn't want to say she couldn't go to that."

"Why not? If that's what really makes a difference to Wendy, then that's a true consequence. If she misses a youth group meeting or two, it isn't going to be vital, but it will send her a message."

"But won't that be punishment?"

"Only if you invoke the consequences in a punishing way. The Reality Discipline equation in this case is: 'If certain work doesn't get done, then you cannot go to certain activities that you truly enjoy because you haven't carried out your responsibilities!' If Wendy understands this up front and you remain firm but friendly, then you aren't punishing her, you are simply allowing logical consequences to take their course."

Karen agreed to try a true Reality Discipline approach and let us know what happened, but I knew it wouldn't be easy. Working with headstrong, firstborn twelve-year-old Wendy would take patience, lots of patience. Reality Discipline doesn't guarantee some kind of quick and easy solution. But once Karen decided on the logical consequences that would be attached to certain misbehavior on Wendy's part, she had to be absolutely resolute. In other words, a fifth principle that must always be used without fail if Reality Discipline is to work is:

Stick to Your Guns

In a very real sense, the entire Reality Discipline system rides on this principle. It will do no good to put your children in a place where they are accountable and reality can do the teaching if you step in at the last second to bail them out and let them off the hook.

Granted, it is hard to stick to your guns. Sometimes it is downright painful for you as well as the children. What Mom or Dad wants to see a hungry child go to bed without dinner? What parent enjoys seeing a child sitting dolefully in his room until he is ready to join the family on a peaceful basis? And what parent is really eager to send a child to school with homework undone —a reflection not only on the child but on the parent as well?

But unless you allow children to suffer the pain involved in the consequences for being irresponsible, they will never learn accountability. You will simply go right back to the same inconsistent seesaw of being permissive on one hand and then authoritarian on the other. How can you psych yourself up so you are able to stick to your guns without feeling like a heartless ogre?

First, always look at the big picture—that is, what will your child be like down the line when he or she is an adult? It may be hard to enforce Reality Discipline at the moment, but remember that you're doing it because you don't want your kids growing up and throwing temper tantrums in front of professors or employers some day.

And along with that thought of your children growing up, think also of the whole area of operating an automobile. If children of sixteen or seventeen are irresponsible at home or in school, there is no way they should be allowed to drive the family car (or any other car, for that matter) for any reason. Any parent who allows children to grow up without developing a responsible attitude is asking for something terrible to happen in the future.

Also, remind yourself that your goal as a parent is not to solve every problem for your children immediately. Actually, they should be solving their own problems. There is no instant maturity, no instant happiness. In fact, it is a rule of life that we cannot be "happy" all the time. I run into so many parents who feel the opposite is true—that their mission in life is always to "make their kids happy." The truth is, Reality Discipline may sometimes bring unhappiness for a brief period, but it helps children develop the maturity that leads to true happiness and satisfactory living later on.

On the walls of gyms and workout centers across the world you will find the slogan No pain, no gain. This is equally true for the home. If there is to be real emotional growth and development, there has to be some pain. Parents must prepare their children to deal with the reality that, in life, we don't always get what we want. The home should be a proving ground for this very profound truth. And what better place for children to learn about reality than in the protective boundaries of their own family, where there is love, concern, and support?

You may have noted that all of these tips point in the direction of a final principle of Reality Discipline. Some parents raise an eyebrow when they hear this principle, but I still wholeheartedly advocate it because it is the best guarantee I know to build a healthy self-image in every one of your children. The key to the balance between love and limits is:

Relationships Come Before Rules

Josh McDowell, who speaks to thousands of young people on college and high school campuses every year, has a favorite saying: "Rules without relationships lead to rebellion." He's right. Invoking limits without communicating love not only erodes a child's sense of self-worth, it drives a bigger and bigger wedge between the two of you.

Quite probably the best thing Karen can do with her headstrong daughter is try to build a better relationship. Ideally, parents start building a good relationship with their children from the day of their birth, but no matter where you are in raising your children—whether they're two or twelve—you can always work on strengthening the relationship between you.

In Karen's case, her best bet might be to sit down with Wendy and talk about homework and keeping her room clean. Instead of lecturing or accusing, Karen could ask Wendy, "Tell me how it is. I don't have to do homework practically every night. What's that like for you?" In regard to keeping the room clean, Mom can certainly relate to Wendy there. Mom has to keep several *other* rooms in the house clean, and she knows something about the tedium of housework. Letting her daughter know that she doesn't enjoy cleaning either might help.

"LIGHTEN UP, NOBODY'S PERFECT!"

Also, if Karen wants to build a better relationship with her daughter, she will do well to remember one thing: *Wendy is still a kid.* Yes, she is twelve and is heading into adolescence. Yes, she should be more responsible than her seven-year-old brother, Tommy. Nonetheless, she will not do things perfectly. A cardinal rule for parenting is to remember that you are not dealing with robots or machines. You are dealing with people, and that means you are not always going to get a 100 percent effort or success rate. As the old baseball cliché says: "Nobody bats one thousand." (Of course, that even includes you, the parent.)

Always have healthy, realistic expectations for your children, but balance those expectations by fully expecting them not to always meet your standards or desires. In other words, *take things in stride.* I don't mean adopting a permissive or laissez-faire attitude. But I am saying that it probably won't hurt to lighten up a bit.

Now I realize that it's easy for a laid-back baby of the family like Dr. Leman to give such sage advice, but what about the parent who just isn't that relaxed for one reason or another? Maybe you're a firstborn or only child, and you learned to be a little uptight from the cradle. It isn't natural for you to put a relationship ahead of the rules because the rules are *very* important. Sure, you try to take things in stride, but there is always that little voice whispering in your ear "Watch out! If you let your kids get away with this or that, are you really teaching them to be *responsible?*"

I have dealt with literally thousands of parents who have felt "I can't let down now. If I do, the whole family will fall apart."

If lightening up just doesn't come naturally for you, I suggest that the next time your child misbehaves, that you ask yourself one question: "What difference is this going to make seven, or ten, or fifteen years from today?" If you think about it, growing up is really a trial-and-error affair. Children make lots of errors, and the parents feel it is a trial.

But Karen, for example, should try to look at the big picture. She shouldn't focus on the undone homework or the room that is messy—again. She should discipline her daughter as best as she can, always communicate her love and forgiveness, and then move along with life and make the best of it. You *never* give up on teaching the right standards. You *never* stop expecting, but you also don't let imperfection or even downright rebellion get to you. Remember that you're out to build psychological muscles in your kids—the kind of muscles that will hold their self-esteem high and prepare them for a world that is not exactly user-friendly.

Another good tip that I like to share with parents is to always be willing to share yourself and your own mistakes. It seems natural for most parents to be afraid to share their real selves. They don't ever want their kids to know that they used to get in trouble when they were young. Maybe they even got drunk once in high school, or possibly lost their license for a while because they got a little bit too enthused over the gas pedal.

Try sharing with your child personal struggles you had as you grew up. You may be amazed at what it will do for your relationship—and for an improved attitude in your child concerning the rules of the family.

TAKE THINGS IN STRIDE, THEN PULL THE RUG

To put Reality Discipline in a nutshell, learn to take life in stride as you hold your kids accountable. It does work. Recently the father of an eight-year-old, who had been very irresponsible at home, came to me and told the following story:

> Dr. Leman, I did exactly what you suggested. Billy disobeyed and didn't do his usual weekly chores. Then later he

wanted to go see the University of Arizona Wildcats play baseball. I pulled the rug and told him that because he had misbehaved, he couldn't go to the ball game that day. Billy fell on the floor and lay on his back screaming, and for a moment I couldn't believe I was doing this horrible thing to him. But I stuck to my guns. I told him that I loved him very much, but that a deal's a deal. When chores don't get done, we don't get special privileges. The next week he did his chores right on time. I could see a real difference. I think I'm finally understanding what it means to discipline my kids in love.

That's what Reality Discipline is all about. To paraphrase that note my daughter, Holly, wrote to me when she was only seven, "Even when you discipline your kids, they still know that you love them just the same!"

Words to Remember . . .

- To build a child's self-image, there must be a balance between love and limits.

- Six basic principles of Reality Discipline are:

  1. You are in healthy authority over your kids.
  2. Hold children accountable for their actions.
  3. Let reality be the teacher.
  4. Use action, not words.
  5. Stick to your guns.
  6. Relationships come before rules.

- Fear and defensiveness are the seedbed of rage and anger. Healthy authority rejects wrong behavior but always conveys love to the child.

- A key to Reality Discipline is always to keep responsibility squarely on the shoulders of the child.

- You can't teach your children to be responsible; you give your children responsibility and let them learn how to handle it.

- Reality Discipline gives children a choice and lets them decide if they want to be responsible enough to follow through and obey.

- Reality Discipline is short on lectures and harangues, quick to take action.

- Spanking is a last resort, not a first choice for action to take. Never spank a child before age two and seldom if ever after age five or six. If you can't be totally controlled while spanking, don't spank. One or two swats on the bottom is usually sufficient to get your point across. Follow up any kind of spanking with plenty of hugs and kisses and assurances that you love your child very much.

- As much as possible, give your children opportunities to solve their own problems.

- It is not your job to "make your kids happy all the time."

- Reality Discipline will not work unless you stick to your guns and make your children be accountable, even if it is somewhat painful for both of you.

- Rules are important, but relationships are more so.

- As much as possible, take your children's misbehavior in stride. Discipline them, but lighten up and do it with love.

Actions to Try . . .

- The next time one of your children tries to get you into a power struggle, stop and ask yourself: "Am I in healthy authority over my child?" Then use Reality Discipline to diffuse or avoid the power struggle.

- Following the example of the mother who disciplines her five-year-old when he misbehaves while she was on the telephone (see pages 138–140), use the same general approach to hold your child accountable when he or she misbehaves. Work on keeping your cool and speaking firmly but softly. No shouting or hissing through clenched teeth. Use eye-to-eye contact and firmly explain to your child what you want done or what must happen because he or she has misbehaved.

- If you are not doing so already, use your children's allowance as a way to teach them accountability. Use the examples in this chapter or develop your own approach to help your children learn how to be a good manager of money. If your children waste money and want more before the next time you pay allowances, *stick to your guns* and don't give them any loans or bail them out in any way.

- If you have more than one child and one is not fulfilling a responsibility, such as doing a chore, try the Leman approach by paying another child to do the chore out of the negligent child's allowance. This may help the negligent child shape up in a hurry.

- Make a conscious attempt to use fewer orders and make fewer demands on your children. Instead, work at asking them politely for their help.

- Apply Reality Discipline Principle #4, "Use Action, Not Words," by doing less arguing with your children and more acting—to apply logical consequences or whatever is necessary. Remember that when children seek a power struggle, their chief goal is to get you into a verbal exchange and to keep it going.

- If you have a hard time "sticking to your guns" when invoking logical consequences, use the tips on pages 180–182 to remind yourself of why doing so is absolutely necessary. Keep in mind that you are looking at the Big Picture—what your children will be when they are adults. And always remember that your job is not to solve problems for your children and make them happy. Your job is to help them learn how to cope with reality and fulfill responsibilities.

- If possible, talk with your mate about the approach both of you are taking toward disciplining your children. Are you together or far apart? Do you both agree that your relationship to your children is more important than "the rules of the house"? Do you both understand that making relationships important does not mean that rules aren't important? Does either one of you or perhaps both of you need to lighten up on your approach to raising your kids? How good is each of you at taking things in stride?

___

Chapter Seven

THE CRUCIAL DIFFERENCE BETWEEN PRAISE AND ENCOURAGEMENT

■

How to Build Your Child's Self-Image over the Long Term

It's time for a quiz, and there is only one question:

The most important aspect of raising children is:
a. Love
b. Encouragement
c. Discipline

Now, it would be easy enough to check off "a. Love" because nothing can be more important than love, right? Not necessarily. We've already looked at the fact that if all you try to do is love, love, love little Buford, you can wind up with a monster on your hands. From all I've been saying in the last chapter or two about discipline, maybe "c" is the right answer. After all, that's what makes love real love. You can't have real love without some limits.

The correct answer, however, is "b. Encouragement." Rudolf Dreikurs, the father of logical consequences, wrote:

Encouragement is more important than any other aspect of child raising. It is so important that the lack of it can be considered the basic cause for misbehavior. A misbehaving child is a discouraged child. Each child needs continuous encouragement as a plant needs water. He cannot grow and develop and gain a sense of belonging without encouragement.[1]

If you want to discourage your children, there are all kinds of weapons at your disposal: criticism, scolding, cutting remarks, doing everything for them (or doing it over because they aren't big enough, smart enough, or capable enough to do it right— according to *your* standards). But if you want to be a little more subtle as you discourage your kids yet be every bit as effective, try praise.

Yes, I said praise discourages children. You may be thinking that Leman has really lost it this time. What's wrong with a little honest praise and its first cousin, rewards? Doesn't praise work with just about everyone? Isn't this a sound way to motivate children and build their self-image?

Perhaps you'll think I want to split semantic hairs, but I don't believe praise is the right thing to use on anyone, especially on kids. In short, I have not come to *praise* Buford, but to *encourage* him. Believe me, there is a world of difference.

Ironically enough, a lot of people think praising their children is just what they need. In truth, it can be very discouraging and damaging to children's self-image in the long run. I often tell parents who call our "Parent Talk" radio show, "Encouragement, yes; praise, absolutely no."

WHY PRAISING LITTLE HARLAN DOESN'T HELP

Let's look at some examples to see why praise, which seems like a perfectly loving and good idea, is not that loving and good at all.

Picture the scene. We're on Any Street, Any Town, U.S.A. Mrs. Smith walks into her eleven-year-old son's room and discovers that he has cleaned it from stem to stern. She can actually see the rug, the top of the desk, and, wonder of wonders, the bed is made!

And to top it off, little Harlan is over in the corner, doing his homework.

"What a good boy!" Mom gushes. "Mommy didn't even have to ask you. You are the greatest. I love you so much for doing all this without even being told."

Now what's wrong with what Mom said? She told her son he was a good boy, that he was the greatest, and that she loved him a great deal. Don't all kids need to hear that?

Yes, our kids do need to hear that we love them and that we think they are the greatest. But in this situation, Mom isn't using the best terms at all because they're couched in the language of praise. And children can interpret praise any number of ways. When we use praise to stimulate kids into right or better behavior, their reactions can be anywhere from gloating, to "So what?" to "Well, finally!" to the other end of the spectrum, which can leave them on the brink of panic.

In this case, little eleven-year-old Harlan's typical reaction to Mom's gusher of praise could well be that he would think to himself: *Hmmm, Mom loves me because I did my room and my homework. Would she love me as much if I didn't?*

Although praise seems innocent enough and even beneficial, it affects children's self-image in a drastic way. Children can easily get the impression that their personal worth depends on how they measure up to what Mom wants. When she praises them, their personal worth is up. But if their rooms were messy and she had scolded them, their personal worth would have plummeted.

Down the line, when little Harlan becomes an adult and gets out in the high-tech, fast-track world, his ability to cope and function well will depend a great deal on how he believes he stands as far as the opinions of others are concerned. When they tell him he's done well, his self-image will be up, and when he is criticized or ignored for doing something well, his self-image will go down. He will live on an emotional elevator.

Also, note that in this particular scene, Mom's praise centers the attention on little Harlan rather than on what was needed—cleaning his room. Harlan is prompted to think: "How did *I* measure up? I guess *I* did real good because Mom is happy." Praise teaches a child to think: "What's in it for me?"

PRAISE SEEMS TO GO WELL WITH REWARDS, BUT . . .

But let's take one other example of how praise can be more damaging than helpful, particularly when it is linked to a reward. Let's go a few doors down from the Smith home and listen in. Mrs. Jones, who has just gotten home from a hard day at work, discovers that her nine-year-old daughter has folded and put away an entire week's worth of laundry, even though it isn't one of her assigned chores for the week. Mrs. Jones meets her daughter in the hallway and says, "What a great kid you are for doing all that laundry! Did you do all that by yourself, or did your older sister help you?"

"All by myself, Mom," little Cindy replies.

"That's wonderful! I just wish your brother could be more like you. Tell you what, for all that wonderful work, here are two extra dollars for your allowance. You're the one I can always count on to give me some extra help."

What can be wrong with this picture? After all, little Cindy has gone above and beyond the call of duty—putting away an entire week's washing—all by herself when it isn't even part of her usual chores. Why shouldn't Mom tell her she's wonderful? And who could blame her for letting slip that she wishes Cindy's older brother could be more like she is? And what's wrong with slipping a couple of extra bucks into her allowance for all that extra work?

Again, we see Mom centering on Cindy and linking her doing of the work with her being wonderful. Let me repeat: It does not help to praise children by telling them that they are wonderful *because* they do something. Soon children come to see praise as their right—something that is due them for any little effort they make. And what if they don't receive that praise, which is the far more typical situation in life? Then they will see life as unfair and start holding little pity parties, telling themselves "Poor me, no one appreciates me."

But let's stop a minute and consider the meaning of the extra two dollars for Cindy's allowance. This teaches Cindy that if she makes an extra effort, she gets a reward. This seems to fall in line with the great American work ethic: "Work hard and get rewarded with a bonus at the end of the year." The trouble is, what happens the next time Cindy does a load of laundry and Mom may not have the extra two bucks for her allowance? And what if Mom is so busy (or tired) she forgets to notice that Cindy did the laundry? Cindy can quickly deduce that she has no obligation to perform extra duties, such as putting away laundry, if there is no praise or reward in it for her.

This is what I often call the "carrot syndrome." We turn our kids into little carrot seekers, and they go through life saying "Hey, I did something good so give me my carrot." But is life really a place where you get carrots at every turn for every "good thing" you do? Are you due a reward for everything that you do in life?

When you raise carrot seekers, you are teaching your children that they count in life only when they gain the attention and approval of others. Doing so is not equipping them for life as they will really have to live it. Although praising and rewarding them may give you a warm glow at the moment as you see the look of delight on their little cherub faces, you are really crippling them for coping with real life later on.

That's why I say praise can be damaging instead of helpful. When children are praised regularly, they soon figure out, "Hey, this is a good deal. Mom and Dad are pretty big on this stuff"—doing chores, eating my peas, washing hands before dinner, whatever. Pretty soon children expect praise for everything they do, and when they don't get it they'll start assuming that whatever they do isn't good enough. They decide that "it isn't worth the effort" and they simply give up.

PRAISE CAN CREATE A PERFECTIONIST

Another problem with praise is that it can easily create a perfectionist mentality. Children decide that what they do is who they are and that they've got to do it better and better and better. Even young children can set exceedingly high standards for themselves. But what happens when a perfectionistic child does a drawing and her mother gives her usual gushing assessment? To a child locked into perfectionism, gushing praise may sound like mockery or scorn, not something encouraging or helpful.

Be especially careful with firstborn children who may be driven toward perfectionism. If your firstborn is being pushed very hard by a very competitive and capable second child, be even more careful.

Frank, who is ten, has a lot of interests but is famous for starting things but not quite finishing them (the sure sign of a perfectionist). Frank's younger brother, eight-year-old Ralph, competes constantly with him, getting good grades and finishing any projects that he manages to start. One evening Frank is out in the garage working on a birdhouse when his dad walks in and says, "Hey, Frank, that is really looking good. You are a super carpenter."

Frank gets a strange look on his face and, then to his father's utter astonishment, throws the birdhouse on the garage floor, smashing it into pieces. "It isn't any good at all!" Frank shouts. "Ralph can probably build a better one." Then he runs out of the workshop and up to his room and doesn't come out for the rest of the evening.

Frank's dad is totally dismayed and can't figure out why a little honest praise would set his son off in a minor rage. What Dad doesn't realize is the extent of Frank's feelings about his younger brother and, more important, about himself. Frank always sees himself as never quite measuring up to what his parents expect or what he expects of himself.

To praise a boy like Frank is to walk into the lion's den. Frank doesn't need praise; he needs very tactful encouragement, done with full awareness of what's going on in his life.

EXAMPLES OF ENCOURAGEMENT
IN PLACE OF PRAISE

What then does it mean to encourage a child? Encouragement does not focus on children and how "wonderful" they are. Encouragement centers on what the children need to do and the satisfaction they get when they do it.

To be honest, encouraging rather than praising is a tricky business. You won't always get perfect results, but certain principles and techniques can work wonders.

Let's double back and replay the scenes in the Smith and Jones homes to see what might be done. As you will recall, Mom Smith has discovered that her eleven-year-old son, Harlan, has cleaned his room and that he's busy with homework, all without being prompted. What can Mom say that would be encouraging instead of praising?

"This room really looks great, and I'll bet that really makes you feel great too."

"I'm so glad to see that you're starting to enjoy studying, Harlan."

Or, for a little humor—which I admit can sometimes backfire —Mom might say: "Well, there is a rug in this room after all! I appreciate knowing that. I'll call and cancel the fumigation man right now!"

Note that in each example, Mom has centered on what has been done. The room looks great. She sees that her son enjoys studying. She has noted that all the clutter has been picked up off the rug. In the last example, she has tried to inject a little humor. Humor should be used sparingly. It all depends on your children's sense of humor and how much they appreciate being kidded a little while being encouraged at the same time. In none of these examples, however, has Mom told Harlan he's "wonderful." Instead, she has commented on the work that has been accomplished. She has encouraged Harlan instead of praising him.

One way to state the difference between praise and encouragement is this: Praise says "You're great *because* you did something." Encouragement says "It's great that something was done and I appreciate it."

The difference is subtle but very important. Giving encouragement isn't simply a matter of praising what children do. Every parent must be aware of the very fine line here. Many people —adults and children—believe that "Unless I perform, unless I achieve, unless I do things people like, I won't be loved or approved of. I'll be a nothing."

The key to encouraging your children is their own perception of what you are saying. When they do something right, good, or productive, you want to focus on what they did, but *how* you talk about what has been done is absolutely crucial.

For example, suppose twelve-year-old Harold has cleaned the garage without being asked. Dad comes out and says, "Harold, the garage looks great!" Dad has made no mention that Harold is "a good boy" for doing the garage. Instead, he has made an observation. Granted, it is a warm and enthusiastic observation, and Harold can see that Dad is pleased. From this he can deduce *for himself* any of the following: "Mom and Dad value what I do. . . . They appreciate my work. . . . I am a capable kid. . . . I can pitch in. . . . I am a contributor to the family. . . . I can figure things out on my own. . . . I can do it!"

When you encourage your children, you are helping them feel that they are *accepted*, that they *belong*, that they are *capable*— the A-B-C's of self-image. Encouraging remarks enforce the A-B-C's of self-image. Praise—which is a form of conditional love— undermines the A-B-C's of self-image.

Praise tends to recognize the actor. It is often couched in the form of a "you" message that says *"You* are wonderful, *you* are great, *you* are outstanding." On the other side of the coin, encouragement is couched in the form of an "I" message that acknowledges the act without passing judgment on the value, quality, or worth of the person who did the act. Encouragement says, "Nice work, I appreciate your thoughtfulness and effort." When properly encouraged, children are left feeling that whether they succeed or fail, they can always try without fear of being criticized, scolded, or expected to jump a little higher next time.

Now let's go down the street a few doors to the Jones house. There nine-year-old Cindy has just accomplished the improbable task of folding and putting away an entire week's worth of laundry. In our first example, Mrs. Jones not only praised her, but she tipped her with a couple of extra dollars in her allowance—a pure and simple reward for service above and beyond the call of duty. To be encouraging instead of praising, however, Mom Jones might say

"Cindy, I really appreciate having all that laundry folded and put away. That's going to make my day go a whole lot easier. Thank you."

"Cindy, you didn't miss a thing when you folded that laundry and put it away. I couldn't have done it any better myself. I appreciate the help."

Note that we don't have Mom saying anything about how she wishes Cindy's brother could be more like her. Nor does she say "You're the only one that I can depend on for help." Both these remarks are the kind that can only give a child the wrong ideas and, quite frankly, puffed-up perceptions of her own importance. Although someone has said that we should never say "never," I will say this: *"Never* compare one of your children to another."* It is a surefire way to cause self-image problems.

But what about Frank and the smashed birdhouse? Let's recreate that scene and put it on stop action as Frank's father walks in and finds Frank putting on some finishing touches. He wants to encourage Frank but not irritate him with what seems to be false praise to a perfectionist firstborn son. What can Dad say?

> "Frank, I see that you really enjoy woodworking. Have you been working on that birdhouse long?"

> "That bird house seems to be coming along. What do you think of it so far?"

Frankly, if it is a given that Frank feels very threatened by his secondborn brother, even these remarks may cause him to react negatively, but that's the kind of thing that Dad needs to find out and talk about with his son.

THIS MOM GOT RESULTS WITH TOKENS

It's true that praise can sound good and, in some cases, it can get good results. A mother called our "Parent Talk" program to tell us about her token system, which was working very well with her son, Brandon, who was six. He had been having all kinds of struggles—getting up in the morning, getting dressed for school, being at the breakfast table on time. He was also having real problems with cleaning his room each Saturday and even getting frustrated with his homework, particularly his spelling words.

Every day seemed to be a trial, so Mom came up with what she called a "token reward system." The rules were simple. Every time Brandon spelled a word right, he got a token. Every time he got dressed on time, he got a token. Being at the breakfast table on time earned him another token each day. On Saturdays, if he cleaned his room, he hit the jackpot—ten tokens for that one.

The pay-off to the token-giving, of course, was what Mom called the "grand prize." When her son acquired forty to fifty tokens, he got to go to the toy store and pick out a new toy or some other kind of reward. Just before Mom had called, Brandon had earned enough tokens to buy a new Lego game, but because he hadn't cleaned up his room yet, Mom's ruling was that he couldn't play with the game until he had finished his weekly chores. When he got home from the store, the first thing that Brandon did was tidy up his room. Then he got to play with his new game.

All of that sounded very positive. Mom was getting results with her tokens, and what more could she ask than that? I asked only one question: "What would Mom do when Brandon was sixteen?"

"I don't know," Mom replied, "but tokens are working right now." With the token system, Brandon was responding well to simple little deadlines such as, "Brandon, I've set the timer— you've got ten minutes to get up and dressed for breakfast." Brandon would appear ahead of schedule, saying, "Is it time yet, Mommy?"

In a way, Mom's token system seemed almost miraculous. The little boy who couldn't get up, couldn't get dressed, couldn't get to breakfast on time, couldn't get his room cleaned, couldn't spell very well had done a total flip-flop. Tokens definitely seemed to be working!

I explained that tokens *do* work. You can use tokens, prizes, rewards, money, and oodles of praise to get kids to do things, but the question remains: Do you want your kids to grow up looking for tokens ("carrots"), or do you want them to learn to be responsible and independent, capable of fully functioning in a world that isn't too big on handing out tokens or rewards for every little thing they do?

Yes, there are all kinds of ways to bribe children to get up on time to eat their breakfasts, but a better approach is Reality Discipline mixed with plenty of encouragement. It might be more painful for Brandon to learn that if he doesn't get up on time for breakfast, he will have to go hungry, but in the long run he will benefit. And when he does start getting up on time, that's when Mom can say "You're up and ready for school! I really appreciate that. It makes serving breakfast so much easier."

I'm not sure I convinced this mother to give up her tokens and try encouragement instead. As we hung up, she sounded a bit dubious. She may have opted for getting short-term results with her tokens, which seemed to be working so well. But what I wanted her to think about was the long run.

You see, her praise and her tokens will cause Brandon to fashion attention upon himself. In the long run, he won't get a lot of satisfaction or self-fulfillment, because sooner or later he'll start wondering what else he has to do to receive more praise, or why he doesn't get a token for every positive thing he does at home or out in the world—school, for example.

It's what has been called "the Saturation Principle."[2] Any time you motivate people with rewards, sooner or later they "saturate on the reward." In other words, they "get their fill" of the reward and their interest in it declines along with their performance.

Then, to pump up the interest and the performance, you have to make the children another offer better than the first.

The bottom line is that, with rewards, children really don't take responsibility for their performance, the parent does. Instead of learning there is great intrinsic satisfaction in being cooperative, obedient, and productive, children simply learn "If I do this or that, I'll get my reward."

WHAT ABOUT DEALING WITH FAILURE?

Before leaving the subject of praise and reward versus encouragement, we need to take a good look at competition and failure. It's a competitive world, and children find this out soon enough —usually down at the day care center, or maybe in the sandbox the first time they go to the park. For that matter, they find it out at home through the simple process of being siblings.

The major problem with living in a competitive world is that you constantly are experiencing one of two things: success or failure. But what happens when children seem to fail all the time? Whose fault is it?

One thing parents must evaluate is their expectations for their children and what kind of pressures they are putting on them. When children aren't competing very well at all, it can often be traced back to parents who have set standards that are too high, or perhaps they criticize and blame too much. The children's self-confidence quickly erodes away, and they get on a downward spiral from which there is no escape. One loss or failure leads to another and their self-image plummets.

I can recall a mother who came in very concerned about her five-year-old's self-image. Whenever she corrected him or reminded him of anything he was supposed to do, he would get the "long-jaws" and say he was dumb, stupid, or that he never did anything right. He would stand there and shuffle his feet, looking like the most defeated little five-year-old in all the world.

"What do you do then?" I asked Mom.

"Oh, I try to say things like 'Now, honey, you know you are

not stupid and you certainly aren't dumb. Mommy loves you and you're a good boy.' "

"I know you say those things out of love, but they are the worst possible things you can say to your little guy," I told her. "The bottom line is that this kind of talk doesn't do any good whatsoever, but it's very typical for parents to say these things to their kids when the kids come up saying things like 'I'm dumb, I'm stupid, and I never do anything right.' "

I went on to explain to Mom that her child was pulling her chain. She would do much better to say, "I'm sorry you see yourself that way, honey, I don't feel that way about you at all." In that kind of remark, there is no pay-off for the child when he uses the "poor me," victim-type behavior that you can see so often in young children who feel a little threatened by life.

Unquestionably, this five-year-old had a self-image problem. The only way his mother would turn it around would be to encourage him, not baby him or help him hold his little pity parties. I explained to Mom that what she needed to do was set her little Buford up for success. She needed to give him something at which he could not miss. Then, when he succeeded, she shouldn't gush all over him and tell him how wonderful he is. Instead, she should say things like:

> "Thanks for the help . . . You're on the right track. . . . Now you're getting it. . . . I bet that makes you feel better about yourself. . . . It looks as if that extra practicing is really paying off."

Any of these are encouraging words for a five-year-old to hear—or a ten-year-old or a fifteen-year-old, for that matter.

Whenever children fail, it's important to separate *what* they did from *who* they are. It's the old hate-the-sin-but-love-the-sinner syndrome, but it's all too true. Instead of saying such things as "You blew it that time. What's the matter with you? Don't you remember the rules?" try making comments similar to these:

"Too bad it didn't work out. . . . It's hard to remember everything all the time. . . . Maybe you forgot—I forget things too, I know how that feels."

What's important is to help your children understand that a "failure" simply means a lack of skill and experience. What failure does *not* mean is that the one who fails is of less value as a person. Failure is simply a means to an end—to learning and eventually succeeding. As Anthony Robbins, a human development specialist who appears frequently on television, puts it:

There Are No Failures—Only Outcomes

We need to teach our kids to have the courage to be imperfect —to make mistakes and then learn from those mistakes and failures instead of having their self-image undermined or even destroyed. When children fail or make a mistake that looks like carelessness or thoughtless behavior, it's so easy to lose our cool and come down on them with all four feet, which only makes them feel worse and more of a failure than ever.

For example, Dad finds his tools spread from one end of the workbench to the other. He can see that little Jason has been trying to fix his bike, but now the place is a disaster and little Jason is nowhere to be found. After storming into the house, Dad finds Jason playing with Nintendo. He grabs him by the arm, marches him out to the garage, and says, "What is all this? How many times have I told you to put away the tools when you use them?"

Little Jason is mortified (not to mention petrified). Now he remembers. He had been working on his bike when Mom called him into the house to answer a phone call from a friend. After hanging up, somehow he never got back to the garage. He had forgotten about his bike and decided to play Nintendo. But how can he tell Dad that? Instead, Jason just tells himself, "I made Daddy mad. I guess I just can't do anything right."

But let's change the scenario a little and have Dad find the messy tool bench, go in and find Jason playing Nintendo, and then have Daddy ask Jason, "Jason, would you come out to the garage with me a minute?"

Once in the garage, Daddy and Jason survey the messy workbench and Daddy says, "It looks as if you were trying to fix your bike."

"Yeah, I was," says Jason, rather embarrassed. "Then I went in the house for something and I forgot to finish working on the bike—besides, I couldn't quite make it work anyhow."

"Well, let's see what's wrong with your bike," Dad can say. And then Dad can help Jason make the adjustment he wasn't strong enough or experienced enough to make himself. And while he is at it, Dad might add, "Now let's remember to put the tools away, okay?"

From this experience Jason can learn that fixing his bike isn't impossible—all he needs is a little help and instruction. He can also learn that Daddy isn't going to bite his head off if he forgets to put the tools away. Granted, all of this has a rather idyllic sound, and it depends almost entirely on Daddy keeping his cool. Nonetheless, it's the kind of thing that parents need to do if they want children to learn from mistakes, and not just to feel they are more and more of a failure.

I like what my friend and colleague, John Rosemond, said in one of his parenting columns, which appear in newspapers throughout the country as well as in *Better Homes and Gardens* magazine. Rosemond observes that self-esteem (a healthy self-image) is not instilled, it is discovered. Children can realize that, despite their fears, frustrations, and failures, they are capable of surviving. They can learn to deal successfully with the setbacks that come to all of us every day.

When Rosemond's daughter was in the fifth grade, her teacher asked her if her parents would allow her to be tested to determine if she was eligible for a gifted and talented program. The Rosemonds told Amy that it was up to her. As they looked at the pros and cons, they discovered on the pro side that there would be interesting, challenging work and possibly a more impressive academic record for Amy. On the negative side, the work would be much more difficult and there would be a lot more homework that would take up Amy's time.

But most important, they told Amy that as far as they were concerned, it wasn't important to them whether or not she was in any gifted or talented program. As Rosemond saw it, Amy was a gift herself, and her parents were well aware of her talents. Whether or not those talents showed up on a test was irrelevant.

Amy took the test and she didn't make it. Was she devastated? Not at all. She went on with life, and eventually enrolled at one of the nation's top colleges where she got A's and B's. Most important for Rosemond, Amy knows that "failure isn't forever. What's forever is the determination to succeed."[3]

As Sande and I parent our own kids and as I talk with parents in counseling sessions, on "Parent Talk," or at seminars throughout the country, I have become increasingly convinced that praise sets children up for failure while encouragement teaches children how to cope with failure. But as I have said earlier in this chapter, as you try to encourage your children, you must know them and what they will perceive as phony praise and real encouragement.

For each child, the equation is just a little bit different. It's up to you, the parent, to figure that out. But a broad guideline is that children should not be left thinking "What am I?" That is, don't say things that always have children deciding, "Am I good? Am I bad? Am I poor? Am I terrific?" Instead, help your children think about how they are contributing to the total situation in which they find themselves. Whatever you say, always aim for helping children understand that they are parts of a functioning unit and that they can contribute, cooperate, participate, and help things go better.

Encouragement focuses upon each person's capacity to be part of the group, the team, the whole family. Praise causes the tail to want to wag the dog. With encouragement, children learn they are part of something bigger than themselves and that they can be part of making that something bigger, stronger, and better. In that they will discover that life can indeed be fun.

That's the kind of encouragement kids need so they can learn they are good enough *as they are*. They don't have to be perfect, they just need to see that there is great personal satisfaction in simply trying. That's what a healthy self-image is all about.

A growing trend in public education has been the establishment of programs and curricula to help students build self-esteem. These programs are now in place in such states as California, Florida, Hawaii, Kentucky, Louisiana, Maryland, New York, Ohio, and West Virginia. A recent survey of over one thousand teachers found 73 percent agreeing that instilling self-esteem and personal growth "is the one aspect of teaching most important to helping students learn."[4]

Robert Reasoner is a retired school superintendent who now spends his time helping develop self-esteem programs in schools. According to Reasoner, research shows people need to feel successful about what they're doing at least 75 percent of the time if they are to sustain their motivation. If their success rate drops to 50 percent, they begin to get discouraged and even feel despair.[5]

Whenever we fail—adults as well as children—we typically berate ourselves with negative self-talk that says such things as:

"Well, that was really a total flop."

"See? You really can't do it."

"You stink. No wonder nobody likes you."

But as you encourage your youngsters, they can learn to accept failure and mistakes as part of being human. Instead of negative self-talk, they can tell themselves:

"I missed that one. But I'll have other chances."

"I blew it that time, but I know I can do it and next time I will!"

"Anybody can make a mistake. My friends understand that and they still like me."

Or, as one eight-year-old who was getting self-esteem instruction in his school put it, "I may not be *perfect*, but I am *awesome*."[6]

In this chapter we have focused on the crucial difference between praise and encouragement, and why encouragement is a much better tool for helping children cope with life, which has to include a certain number of failures. But there is a lot more to be said about how to use encouragement to build your child's self-image. In Chapter Eight we look at discouragement as well as other feelings and emotions, and learn how to talk to our children in ways that build their confidence instead of tearing it down.

Words to Remember . . .

- Every child needs encouragement as a plant needs water. Nothing is more important.

- Praise and rewards often discourage children rather than encouraging them.

- Praise can make children think their personal worth depends on how they measure up to what their parents want.

- A "reward" can be a thinly disguised bribe. Giving rewards can turn children into carrot-seekers. They will believe they deserve a reward for anything positive they do in life.

- Be especially careful of praising firstborns who are often perfectionists. To them, praise may sound phony, like mockery.

- Encouragement focuses on what the child has done and emphasizes your appreciation.

- Praise says "You're great because you did something." Encouragement says "It's great that something was done and I appreciate it."

- Encouragement causes children to think: "I can do it. . . . I am capable. . . . Mom and Dad trust me."

- Praise may trap you into comparing one child with another. True encouragement never makes comparisons.

- If your child is failing more than he or she is succeeding, check your own expectations and how critical you are.

- Never let children's failure reflect on their self-image or self-worth. Failure is a means to an end—learning and eventually succeeding.

- Encouragement helps children know that they are good enough *as they are.*

- Rewards, prizes, tokens, and lots of praise work for the short term, but they do not help children develop the maturity needed to cope with life.

Actions to Try . . .

- Try to keep track of how often you use praising words and phrases with your children. You may be surprised.

- To help children who feel like failures, set them up for success, then encourage them: "Now you've got it. . . . That's great! Keep it up!"

- When your child does something right, use any of the following phrases to encourage him or her:

  "Good job! I appreciate your efforts. . . . That's it! You're on the right track for sure. . . . The garage [or whatever] looks tiptop. You didn't miss a thing. Thank you! . . . I'm happy to see you're enjoying your work. I'll bet you're happy too. . . . Wow, look at this—this is a real improvement. I'll bet you feel good about that. . . ."

Chapter Eight

DEALING WITH THE FEELING FACTOR

■

How to Really Listen and Then Respond to Your Children

Another day dawns and, as you survey your children who are still snoozing in their beds, you vow that it will be a better day than yesterday. In place of rivalry, there will be harmony; in place of rebellion, there will be cooperation. Kindness and love will quench the fires of bickering and jealousy. Instead of ending the day in a frazzle of frustration, you will be serene and at peace.

If a problem does arise, you will deal with it swiftly and efficiently by putting Reality Discipline into action. Instead of stooping to power struggles, you will soar above it all, remaining firm but fair, disciplining but never preaching, walking that fine line between permissiveness and authoritarianism. In fact, you will be so caught up and in control you will read today's newspaper *today*!

And then two things happen. The children wake up and so do you. Your dream of what the day could be is over, and reality arrives like a bucket of ice water in your face.

"I hate you!"

"I can't do it—I'll just die if I have to go."

"I have a stomachache, I can't go to school today."

"It's not fair, he always gets his way!"

"I wanted the red one, why does *she* always get the red one?"

"I did *not* punch him, he bugged me and I just gave him a little push."

Most of these phrases are familiar to parents. They are all typical words uttered by children who have one thing in common: discouragement. Every child (and every parent, for that matter) is a bundle of feelings. A secret to bringing your kids up without tearing them down (or having them tear you apart) is to understand how to handle the Feeling Factor—their feelings and yours.

If discouragement leads children to being out of sorts and misbehavior, it follows that encouragement will help them deal with what the day has to offer. Rudolf Dreikurs maintains that as a child goes through a typical day, he is

> exposed to a sequence of discouraging experiences. Deliberate encouragement is essential to counteract them. The child misbehaves only if he is discouraged and does not believe in his ability to succeed with useful means. Encouragement implies your faith in the child. It communicates your faith in the child. It communicates to him your belief in his strength and ability, not in his "potentiality." Unless you have faith in him *as he is*, you cannot encourage him.[1]

Now, most parents I know are all for encouraging their children, and they claim that they try to do it constantly. But their good intentions are often quickly diffused, if not washed away, by having to put up with a child's negative feelings expressed in such trigger phrases as "I hate you. . . . This is yucky. . . . Why do I have to do it? . . ." and on and on.

It is incredible how quickly the climate can change. Before you realize it, you are no longer the benevolent encourager; you have suddenly become the one who must lay down the law, keep the peace, and try to administer discipline with Solomon-like wisdom. In one way or another, a parent winds up having to apply pressure to get children to behave. But as Don Dinkmeyer points out:

Pressure from without rarely promotes desirable behavior. One can seldom "make" a child behave, study, apply himself, if he chooses not to do so. Pressure from without has to be replaced by stimulation from within. Reward and punishment do not produce this inner stimulation or, if they do, it is short-lived and requires continuous repetition. This is different from inner stimulation. Once a child moves voluntarily in the right direction as the result of intrinsic motives, the chances are that he will continue to do so without any outside influence.[2]

It's getting them to move in the right direction that's a challenge. Why is it children don't want to get up in the morning? And strangely enough, why is it that the same bed they find it so hard to leave in the morning becomes very uninviting at night? Why won't kids eat properly—or eat at all? Why won't they put their belongings away and stop fighting with their brothers and sisters? And why can't they be on time and do at least a little bit to help around the house? Can all of this *really* be attributed to discouragement? A lot of parents would say, "Hey, it's not the child who's discouraged, *I'm* discouraged! And if my kids would just shape up, we would all be happier."

But admonishing kids to shape up or asking them "Why can't you be a little more cooperative?" is not how encouragement works. While we all agree we want to encourage our kids, encouragement is a fairly complex process. We need to learn how to do the kind of encouraging that really can help children feel that we do understand and know what it's like to feel discouraged and be out of sorts, irritated, and even angry with the world. After almost twenty years of counseling, I've decided that the best place to start with encouraging children is to:

Acknowledge Their Feelings

Strangely enough, many parents think it is their business to deny children's feelings.

A child says he hates his brother. Our typical response is

"You don't really feel that way," or "You shouldn't feel like that."

The child says she isn't going to school, and we respond, "Oh, you're just saying that because it's Monday."

An older sister chases a younger brother out of her room screaming that he has no right to be there. We admonish her and tell her, "Just because he went in your room is no reason to get so angry."

The truth is that a lot of our parenting centers on correcting our children by refusing to accept their feelings. In fact, we teach them that certain feelings (anger, especially) are unacceptable. They quickly determine that when they have these feelings, *they* are unacceptable as well.

It's a vicious cycle. Just dealing with life's pressures, deadlines, and demands is enough to bring children plenty of discouraging situations. But when they react with certain feelings and are denied those feelings, their discouragement only increases. Following are just a few examples of how parents deny their children's feelings. You may recognize yourself as you read these examples, or you can easily think of something similar that you've said to your child.

CHILD: "Cindy is always getting into my things, I hate her!"

PARENT: "How can you say something like that about your own sister? You do not hate your sister and I want you to apologize right now for ever saying anything like that."

CHILD: "The picnic was boring—it wasn't any fun at all."

PARENT: (after spending all kinds of time and money to make the picnic a success): "How can you say the picnic was boring? It was a perfect day and you had three hot dogs. I thought everybody had a great time."

CHILD: "I don't want to wear that dress—dresses are for babies! Besides, it's ugly!"

PARENT: "It's a perfectly good dress. All the girls your age wear dresses. It's very much like the dresses your friends wear."

CHILD: "My coach is an idiot. Just because I was two minutes late for practice, he made me run laps."

PARENT: "Don't call your coach an idiot. And rules are rules. If you are late for practice, what do you expect? A medal?"

These are typical examples. I could give dozens more, but let's look at these four scenarios to draw some conclusions and develop some principles for a better approach to the Feeling Factor. In each example, the parent is making two basic errors.

First, the parent isn't really listening for the child's feelings. For that matter, the parent isn't listening very well at all. The parent hears the child's negative word or phrase, and the immediate reaction is: "My child is wrong and I have to correct him."

Second, in being so quick to correct what is perceived as error or a bad attitude, the parent does not acknowledge how the child feels. In fact, any feelings the child has are totally ignored and treated as if they aren't there. Whenever your feelings are ignored and treated as if they aren't there, it's the same thing as if *you* aren't there, and what can be more discouraging than that?

What's the answer? Obviously, your first task is to stop and *really listen* to what your children are saying. Stop listening with the typical half an ear tuned in only to the frequency labeled "What's wrong *now*? What do I need to correct this time?" Instead, listen carefully, not only for the so-called facts, but for the children's feelings. Communication specialists call this kind of listening "active listening" or "listening with empathy." The idea is to project yourself into what the children are saying—to put yourself in their shoes, so to speak.

This kind of listening is *not* easy. Most of us do not do it naturally or very well. We are too busy in our own little world, with our own thoughts, or, quite possibly, we are tuned in to the tube and, of course, our child has approached us just as the game, scene, quiz show, or newscast is getting good. Kids can always tell if we're really listening. If we try to do it with both eyes on a TV screen and not on them, and one-and-a-half ears tuned to the TV audio, it's no wonder the child feels unheard, not to mention insignificant and discouraged.

To listen with total attention, try the following:

1. Stop what you're doing. Turn to your child with full eye contact and listen, not only for the details the child wants to convey, but for the feelings. Frankly, the details won't always make a lot of sense to your adult logic, but that's not what really matters. Feelings are what really count.

2. Try to acknowledge the child's feelings with just a word or two. You may or may not be able to identify the exact emotion the child is experiencing, but what's important in the initial exchange is to at least let the child know that you are hearing him by saying something such as "Oh . . ." or "Uh-huh" or "I see. . . ."

One other helpful technique as you attempt to listen to your children actively and with empathy is to try to give the feelings they seem to be having a name. For example, "It sounds as if you are very angry," or "My, that must have been very embarrassing."

Parents sometimes think that if they identify children's feelings out loud, it will only make them feel worse. Of course, exactly the opposite is what really happens. For example, I was talking to a grandfather whose ten-year-old grandson had received a very expensive cockatiel as a birthday present. About two months after receiving the bird, the boy came to his grandfather and said, "My bird is dead!"

"Oh, that's too bad, that's terrible," the grandfather said. "You loved that bird, I'll bet you feel very sad."

"I don't know why he died," the boy went on. "He had food and water, and I checked on him all the time."

"Yes, you took good care of him," Grandfather said. "It must hurt to lose your little friend."

The grandpa was actively listening for the boy's feelings and was willing to give those feelings a name. If the grandfather had denied the boy's feelings, he would have said such things as "Now, don't get so upset. Birds die. There's nothing you can do about it. Maybe you can get another one soon."

Those kind of remarks would probably gain this response from the boy: "I don't want another one. I liked this one."

And at this point it's typical for an adult to respond, "Now, don't be unreasonable, you can't have this one, he's dead, and you'll just have to live with it."

Another good technique is one recommended by the late Haim Ginott, who was one of our foremost authorities on child guidance psychotherapy and author of such best-selling books such as *Between Parent and Child* and *Between Parent and Teen-Ager*. I attended a colloquium where Ginott was speaking and heard him say that one good way to acknowledge children's feelings is to "grant in fantasy what you can't in reality."

For example, suppose the rain is keeping your five-year-old in all day. He is becoming a miniature caged lion, and he finally bursts out: "The rain is ruining everything. I wanted to play with Tommy today and I have to stay inside! Can't I go outside for just a little while?"

The parent who fails to acknowledge feelings will respond, "You know you can't go out in the rain and get wet. It has to rain sometimes—besides, we need the rain. You can play with Tommy tomorrow."

This kind of moralizing and matter-of-fact logic will only make your five-year-old feel rejected and maybe a little angry.

He can easily respond, "I want to go out. You never let me have any fun!"

More explanations from Mom will only get more protests, and the little guy might wind up pounding fists on the floor in a full-fledged temper tantrum.

Instead of logic and the rational explanation, what children need to hear is that Mom knows how they feel. When her five-year-old comes to complain about the rain, Mom can say, "You really are tired of staying inside because of the rain, aren't you? I know you love playing with Tommy and it would have been fun. . . ." Then Mom might try granting her child's wishes in fantasy by saying enthusiastically: "I wish I could just stop the rain and make the sun come out with blue sky and clouds. Then you and Tommy could have so much fun!"

This approach doesn't provide a surefire guarantee that your little five-year-old will suddenly decide he loves staying in when it's raining outside, but it's very possible that he just might respond, "Yeah, then we could play army in the backyard. Can I have some cookies and milk? Would you play Sorry with me?"

Obviously, you can't stop the rain and you can't control the appearance of the sun, blue sky, and clouds, but sincerely telling your little guy that you wish you could so he could have a better time is all that he is looking for. It will make his reality—having to stay in because it's still raining cats and dogs—a lot easier to deal with.

Let's circle back and look again at the four illustrations of how parents can easily deny children's feelings. Our aim is to apply these four techniques, which are designed to encourage, not discourage, children. To recap, the four techniques are:

1. Pay complete attention to what your children are saying and listen for feelings as well as facts.

2. Let your children know that you are hearing them by giving simple one-word replies, such as "Oh," "Uh-huh," and "I see."

3. As you identify your children's feelings, name each feeling out loud so your children know that you know how they feel. ("No wonder you're upset . . . that must have really hurt.")

4. When appropriate, grant the children's wishes in fantasy, even though you can't do much about the reality of the situation.

Let's take each of the four "denial of feelings" illustrations and see what we could do to turn them around.

Example #1
"Cindy Is Always Getting into My Things. I Hate Her!"

In this case, Mom denied her daughter's feelings by wondering how she could say anything like that about her own sister. Then she admonished her that she really didn't hate her sister and she'd better say she was sorry right now.

But if Mom wants to acknowledge, and not deny, the feelings of the older daughter—let's call her Amy—she could use any of these three sample responses:

1. "You sound very angry."

2. "Nobody likes it when other people get in their personal things—I can understand why you're upset."

3. "Sometimes little sisters can be a pain. I'd bet you'd like to put a great big padlock on your door to keep Cindy out."

Now, granted, in each one of these replies, Mom hasn't "corrected" Amy's anger against her sister, and she may not be quite sure where the conversation might go from here. A key to acknowledging feelings, however, is not to have the hidden goal of eventually correcting the child for being angry or depressed or bored or whatever the emotion might be. In order to make the active listening technique work, Mom has to be committed to the principle that feelings are neither good nor bad. They simply *are*.

Amy needs to know that acting on her feelings—smacking little Cindy, or worse—is something that is not allowed. But by using response 1, Mom gives Amy the freedom to feel angry and she also starts in motion processes that will help Amy cool down and eventually even forgive little Cindy for her trespasses.

Responses 2 and 3 are particularly useful because they include a note of empathy. Any time Mom can communicate to her children that she knows how it feels to be in their shoes, she is doing a great deal to build their self-image. In this case, it also will diffuse Amy's anger toward her little sister. Being lectured and preached to about being angry will only make Amy feel more angry and resentful. Being understood and heard in her anger will help her to calm down and deal constructively with the situation.

Later Mom can let Amy know that she will be talking to Cindy and telling her that, if she persists in getting in her older sister's things, there will be logical consequences for doing so.

Example #2—"The Picnic Was Boring!"

In this case, Dad had spent a lot of time and money to make the picnic a good one, and he denied his son's feelings by wondering how the boy could even think it was boring. It had been a perfect day, his son had eaten three hot dogs, and obviously everyone had had a great time.

At this point, little Rosco will probably retreat into his room or some other safe spot because now he has his father on his case and he knows he is outgunned. Besides, he may even realize that his dad is "right." It was a perfect sunny day and he did eat three hot dogs. But he still felt bored, and that's the feeling he was trying to convey. If Dad wanted to help him deal with that feeling, he could have used responses such as:

1. "So you didn't have such a great time? That's too bad."

2. "So you were bored? Tell me about it—what was boring?"

3. "That must have been disappointing. You had really looked forward to that picnic too."

With any of these remarks, Dad has succeeded in avoiding the trap of feeling parental indignation because an ungrateful child doesn't appreciate his efforts. When children say they are "bored," they can sound impertinent, ungrateful, and irritating. It's easy for a parent to think "That kid doesn't know how lucky he is. What right does he have to feel bored?"

The truth is, Rosco had every right to feel bored, if that, indeed, is how the picnic made him feel. To repeat, feelings are neither good nor bad, they just are. Maybe little Rosco can't explain why he felt bored, but he is being honest enough to share his feelings. By acknowledging those feelings with responses like 1 and 2, Dad is doing a great deal to build a better relationship with Rosco, instead of making him feel discouraged, alone, and misunderstood.

Again, there is no magic guarantee that Rosco will immediately launch into a long explanation of why he was bored. All he may say is something such as "Oh, I just think playing Frisbee is dumb" or perhaps "We always go to the same park every year." On the other hand, with a little more prodding, Rosco may reveal the hidden reason why he thought the picnic was boring. He brought his best friend, Jason, who played with someone else and ignored him the whole day, which was a real downer.

Note that response 3 is designed to show Rosco empathy. His dad is letting him know that he realizes that it's no fun to be disappointed. Rosco may just grunt or, possibly, he might just reply, "Yeah, I usually do like picnics. Maybe next time we can go to the beach instead."

Example #3: "Dresses Are for Babies!"

In this case, Mom denied her daughter's feelings with a typical adult response to the idea that a perfectly good dress is for babies. All of the other girls wear dresses, so why can't her daughter?

The child's typical response to this kind of adult logic is: "Oh, you just don't understand—I hate dresses." Now, it may be true enough that tomorrow, or next Monday, dresses will be back "in," but today dresses are out and that's what Mom is failing to hear. If Mom wants to acknowledge her daughter's feelings about wearing a certain dress, she could use any of the following responses:

1. "It sounds as if you really don't care for this particular dress this morning. Would you like to tell me why?"

2. "You seem to be saying you're too old to wear dresses, but your older sister wears them and I wear them. Maybe you'd like to wear pants and a top today instead."

3. "You seem to hate this dress. I wish I could wave a magic wand and create a dress that you would just love."

In responses 1 and 2, Mom is acknowledging her daughter's feelings and asking for clarification. It could just be that there is something about this particular dress she doesn't like. Or it could be that she is down on dresses right now because of what a friend said at school or some other reason. By asking her daughter to explain and give her a preference on what she'd like to wear today, Mom is giving the girl a certain amount of freedom of choice. She is allowing her daughter to have her own opinions and tastes—and, obviously, her own feelings. Furthermore, she is trying to work out a compromise that will be satisfactory to both of them.

In response 3, Mom is trying to grant in fantasy that which she can't provide in reality. It might be better for Mom to lead up to this kind of remark with a couple of preliminary probes to acknowledge feelings (as in responses 1 and 2). Depending on the child's response, Mom might want to suggest that she wishes she could create the perfect dress for her today. On the other hand, if the girl is really down on dresses, speculating on the perfect dress may do little good at all.

The point is, whenever you try to actively listen to your children, you can't depend on certain stock phrases or responses and expect the children to respond perfectly each time. You need to probe and to discover what is really on their minds. What you say is important, but your attitude is what counts. You are trying to convey empathy and real interest in what the children are saying, even though they may be insulting and irritating.

Example #4: "My Coach Is an Idiot!"

Dad set his son straight very quickly in this exchange. Children are never to call adults idiots or any other like names. Furthermore, his son broke the rules and didn't get to practice on time. Did he really expect the coach to smile and say "That's okay"? Doesn't the boy realize that life doesn't work that way and that if he isn't careful he'll be fired some day for not being on time?

All of this kind of logic may make excellent sense to a dad, but it won't help his son too much because the boy is smarting over being embarrassed by having to run laps. Maybe he also fears the coach won't let him start the next game. Dad could have gotten a lot further with his son if he would have used any of the following replies:

1. "You've always liked your coach but now it sounds as if you are really upset with him."

2. "It must have been embarrassing to run laps in front of the other guys—no wonder you're angry."

3. "Running all those laps must have been a bummer. . . . I can remember having to do the same thing when I was late for practice."

In response 1, Dad is simply acknowledging his son's feelings. If it's true that he's always liked his coach up until now, Dad is leaving the door open to learning more about why his son is so angry with being disciplined.

In response 2, Dad is probing to see if his son's real emotion isn't embarrassment for having to run laps in front of the other members of the team. If, indeed, he was the only one who had to run laps, this could be the key to what is making him so angry.

In response 3, Dad shows empathy because he too knows what it is like to run laps after being late for practice. The son may want to know more about what it was like when his dad played ball. On the other hand, if his son is really smarting over his experience with the coach, he may not be that interested in what his dad went through many years ago. He's still involved in what happened to him just an hour or two before. It helps to show empathy, but guard against going off in a tangent, which may make your children think you aren't really interested in their experiences and you only want to talk about your own "good old days."

THE FEELING FACTOR IS ALWAYS PRESENT

Parenting includes a lot of things, but one of your major tasks is learning how to handle the Feeling Factor. In a sense, you are challenged to recognize and acknowledge your children's feelings every day. What you are trying to learn is just what is discouraging them. Then you will know why they are feeling anger, embarrassment, or any other number of emotions. Once you learn that, you must decide on what you can say or do that will encourage them to go back to the battle of life and try it again.

Dealing with the Feeling Factor is more of an art than a precise science, and you never get to know it all, even if you have a psychologist's shingle hanging on your wall. With four kids who range from the second year of college down to a five-year-old, I get my share of opportunities to deal with feelings.

As she started her last year of high school, our daughter Krissy came home after the first few days with what I call the "long-jaws." Finally she burst out crying and said she wasn't ever going back to school; that she wanted to transfer because she hated it.

I waited until after dinner and found Krissy in her room, already tucked in bed and looking more glum than ever.

I sat down on the foot of the bed and asked Krissy, "What's wrong?"

"Nothing's wrong!" she snapped.

"Well, I'll just sit here for a couple of hours until maybe you'll want to talk."

Traces of a smile played around Krissy's mouth. She knew that she couldn't hide that something was bothering her. In fact, the whole family knew something was wrong, she had made that plain enough when she had gotten home from school. Finally she let it all out.

"I don't have any friends," she wailed. "Everybody I hung out with last year is in college, along with Holly. My boyfriend is back in New York and I probably won't see him again until next summer at camp. No one will even eat with me. I'm not going back to school. I want to transfer from that place now!"

"Nobody to eat with—that must be rough," I observed.

"Everyone is mean and unfriendly. I'm going to transfer, I just don't want to go back."

"I think I can see why you would feel that way. I'd feel the same way myself."

"I'm not going back, and that's final!"

After having acknowledged Krissy's feelings and trying to show her some empathy, I seemed to have hit a stone wall. Krissy wasn't snapping out of it. She really didn't want to go back, she wanted to fix everything in one fell swoop—a swoop right out of the school. She was going to some other school where—in her mind—everyone would instantly be more friendly.

Because I knew Krissy pretty well, I had a strong hunch it was time for a little friendly advice. I might run the risk of turning her off, but I thought it was worth it.

"Honey, I understand. I'd feel the same way you do, but I learned a long time ago when you have trouble at school, you've got to face it—preferably at eight o'clock A.M. the next morning. The longer you stay away and don't face it, the worse it gets. Switching to another school isn't any real answer. You'd be more of a stranger there than ever."

"I don't care. It would be worth it!" Krissy snapped.

"Just go to school tomorrow. At lunch, find yourself a table— by yourself, and don't try to kiss up to the kids who are turning their backs on you. Don't set yourself up for failure. Just wait it out."

"Okay," Krissy said with a glower. "I'll give it one more try, but I still want to transfer."

Krissy came home the next afternoon from school, looking neither upset or happy. But she didn't say anything about transferring.

The next evening she mentioned that a couple of kids had sat with her at lunch. By the end of the week, she had at least two good friends and several other kids she was hanging around with.

Meanwhile, Sande called another private school in the Tucson area and learned that if Krissy truly did want to transfer, she could do so with no problem. We made that call not because we were permissively humoring Krissy's angry outburst, but because we wanted to show her we respected her feelings and, if the problem was going to increase, then she could decide whether to transfer. But I had a hunch there would be no need for transferring, and I was right.

As Krissy headed out the door for a football game that Friday night, I stopped her and said, "Krissy, Mom made some calls and found out that you can transfer if you really want to. There would be no problem. Do you still want to do it?"

"Transfer? Transfer to where?" Krissy said with a sheepish grin. "Why would I want to transfer? I've been going to the same school for the last four years. Everything is cool now, Dad, so don't worry."

I share this real slice of life in the Leman family as an example of how an active listening conversation may not go perfectly, but how you can still get your point across and then let your children work on their own problems. That first night when I tried to acknowledge Krissy's feeling, she was adamant. She hated her school and she was going to transfer, period. But Krissy is a naturally friendly, social type, and I knew that she would make friends quickly if she gave it half a try.

All Krissy was looking for when she came home and told us "I hate school—I want to transfer" was a friendly, listening ear that would acknowledge her feelings. Because she was seventeen and sensible, I felt I could go on to give her a little friendly advice as well. It was free and there were no lectures or sermons. But, even while "giving advice," I let Krissy feel she was in control and able to make her own decisions.

WHY KEVIN GOT "FRIDAY-ITIS"

Kevin, our other teenager, presented an opportunity to do active listening not long after school got under way when he went into eighth grade. The first several weeks of the term went well. In fact, Kevin was elected president of his eighth-grade class. Not long afterward, however, he developed "Friday-itis" and began staying home from school on Fridays, claiming he didn't feel well. After he missed the third Friday in a row, I decided to have a little talk with him.

"It's interesting that you seem not to feel well lately only on Fridays," I said casually. "Could you help me understand this strange coincidence?"

Kevin looked at me and knew the jig was up, so he decided to come clean. "Dad, P.E. class is on Fridays and I hate P.E. I'm not as good a jock as the other guys and they tease me. And besides that, the teacher has it in for me."

It would have been simple enough to blow Kevin away with a typical nonlistening comeback that didn't acknowledge his feelings. I could have said, "Nonsense! You've got to attend P.E. class along with everything else. You be sure you're in that class next Friday."

Instead, I tried to run through my mind what Kevin was really feeling and thinking. He's not your typical athlete. He is into art and is a master cartoonist. He also loves magic and is always spending his allowance on the latest magic trick, which he performs for us with great enthusiasm and surprising skill.

"It must be hard to feel that you're not equal to the other guys," I replied. "Sometimes I bet it gets a little embarrassing."

Kevin looked at me with relief in his eyes. "You don't know the half of it, Dad," he said. "I hate P.E. and I just don't want to go."

"I can understand how you feel. It's true you're probably not one of the better athletes in the class, but you know, some of those athletic kids in your P.E. class are also in your art classes, and they can't draw a stick but I'll bet they still give it their best shot and do the best they can."

"Well, yeah, there are two or three guys I can think of," Kevin admitted, "but I don't pick on them because they can't draw."

At this point I decided Kevin was mature enough to take a

little advice, just as his sister had about "hating school and wanting to transfer." I said, "It's no fun to be teased, and I know how it feels to think the teacher has it in for you. I always thought a lot of teachers had it in for me, but you know, we've got a problem. I don't think you have any physical reason why you can't do P.E., and if you're popular enough to be elected class president, *everybody* can't be teasing you. Maybe your best choice is to give it another try. Problems like this don't go away, and I'd like to see you go back to class and give it your best shot, whether some of the guys tease you or not."

Kevin looked a little dubious. Finally he said, "I guess I can try, but I won't like it."

I put my arm around his shoulders and said, "You don't have to like it, I just want you to take your licks and try. I think you'll feel better if you do. Life is full of things that we don't like but we've got to try to do them anyway."

The next Friday Kevin attended school and went to P.E. class. Later when I asked him how it went, he said, "Okay, Dad. No big deal."

Many of the problems kids have seem to be a big deal one day, but they turn out to be "no big deal" if the children are willing to face the problem and deal with it. But the last thing children want to hear—and this certainly includes teenagers—is that their problem is "nothing at all and why can't they get with it?" Teenagers, especially, need plenty of active listening and acknowledging of their feelings. The smallest things can become blown out of proportion when you're a teenager. I'm not sure about the *real* reason for Kevin's Friday-itis. Maybe somebody *had* teased him. Maybe the teacher *had* spoken sharply about getting in line quicker. Whatever happened, it was enough to cause him to think of all kinds of ways to duck the problem. But once he faced the problem, it was "no big deal."

Some key points to remember the next time your teenager comes to you with a "big deal": (1) Listen carefully and hear your teenager out. (2) Keep cool and don't immediately pooh-

pooh your teenager for feeling that way or start lecturing because he or she should "shape up." (3) Keep your balance and help balance your teenager by acknowledging the feelings that you're hearing expressed. Let him or her know that you understand and you know it isn't easy. (4) Don't try to solve your teenager's problems. If advice is warranted, give it in a casual way, as a suggestion, not as an order.

HANNAH FELT THREATENED AND THEN SOME

Listening for feelings with little Hannah, our preschooler, is a different ball game. At age three, Hannah was already a good communicator of feelings. Whenever she wanted a nap, she would come to Sande, grab her hand, and say, "Tired now." Then Hannah would lead Mommy to the bedroom so Mommy could tuck her in.

When Hannah was four and having her first experience in preschool, she told Sande on the way home one day, "I'm not going to preschool tomorrow!"

Puzzled, Sande said, "You're not going to preschool? What's wrong?"

Little Hannah just shrugged her shoulders and wouldn't say. Sande dropped the subject, deciding to let Hannah tell her when she was ready.

Later than evening Kevin came to Sande and said, "I know why Hannah doesn't want to go to preschool."

"Yes?" Sande replied, "what did she say?"

"I think she should tell you," Kevin said.

Kevin went and got Hannah and she cuddled up to Sande, who got things going by saying, "Sometimes school can be pretty scary—is that why you don't want to go tomorrow?"

"Sarah and I were playing on the playground and this boy came up and told me he was going to get a gun and shoot my eye out," Hannah said with a very serious look on her face. "Mommy, I'm scared."

"Oh, my," Sande said, "no wonder you're upset. That sounds scary, honey, but don't you worry. I'll talk to your teacher and see what I can find out."

The next day Sande took Hannah to preschool as usual and immediately went over to Mrs. Tuttle, the preschool director. After hearing about the problem, Mrs. Tuttle thought for a moment, then said, "There is one little boy who interacts quite often with Hannah. I'll check into it."

Later that day, when Sande picked Hannah up, Mrs. Tuttle took her aside and said, "I talked to Jimmy. I guess he was just feeling out of sorts yesterday. He told Hannah he was sorry and gave her a big hug."

Let's look back at this little drama and see what happened. First, note that when Hannah didn't want to say what was wrong, Sande didn't bombard her with question after question. I often advise parents to ask as few questions as possible because being interrogated by an adult usually causes children to clam up. It's as if the children vow to themselves, "Mom and Dad aren't going to hear about this from *me*." Sande wisely backed off for the time being and decided to let Hannah come to her, when she was ready.

Also note that Hannah "tested the water" by telling her big brother first. Then, with his gentle urging, she came to Mom, but the battle wasn't over. How Mom would talk to her had everything to do with how much she would say and her reactions.

Some adults might feel that in the sandbox world of preschool, threats don't mean much, but what they forget is that a threat is very real to a small child. Little children take things very literally, and Hannah actually believed that the boy would harm her. By acknowledging her feelings, Sande was able to calm Hannah down and get her to go back to school. Then she followed through and found out what was wrong, something that made Hannah feel even more secure.

WHEN YOUR OWN FEELINGS GET IN THE WAY

It's one thing to talk about coolly and calmly acknowledging your children's feelings when they have a problem with something at school, a playmate—something outside of your personal relationship to the children. But suppose they really let you have it with an angry accusation or remark. A favorite one that mothers often ask me about is "I hate you!" What's a mother to do when a child screams, "I hate you!"? Lectures and admonishments only make children more angry—and they often threaten to run away as well.

If your child screams "I hate you!" try to take a step back from the situation and realize what's going on. First of all, you are undoubtedly in some kind of power struggle. Your child wants to do one thing and you want her to do something else. Because the child feels outgunned and without any other weapons, she has finally resorted to using what she might see as her last resort. If she tells Mommy she hates her, maybe Mommy will knuckle under to the pressure.

Instead of knuckling under or dropping to the child's level with anger of your own, you need to take the wind out of her sails by refusing to get angry. After all, the child really doesn't hate you. She is simply trying to control you and let you know she wants her own way.

Even though you may feel a little anger yourself, you'll get a lot further by responding to "I hate you" with: "You sound pretty angry with me—tell me what's wrong," or "Well, I don't hate you and I wish you'd tell me more about why you feel that way."

Whenever you have to deal with children's anger or even rage, it's best to be transparent, open, and vulnerable. After all, you are the parent—the adult—and being able to take some heavy shots across your bow (or directly amidship) comes with the territory.

As I counseled with one couple who finally decided to go

ahead with a divorce, they told me about their thirteen-year-old son who had reacted with all kinds of acting out—refusing to do his school work, getting in fights at school, screaming at both parents, and so on.

"Obviously your son is expressing how he sees life right now," I said. "He sees everything as very unfair and he's fighting back."

"But he claims he just doesn't care," the mother said. "He says it doesn't bother him that we're getting a divorce."

"You know very well it bothers him. It's tearing him apart, and he doesn't know how to deal with it emotionally. The world is hitting him and so he is striking back."

"So what can we do?" the father asked.

"Have your son come in with you next time. We'll all sit down and talk together about what's going on in your lives. You have to be up front with him as best you can. Help him understand what is happening—don't keep him in the dark about anything."

"I realize now I should have gotten to know my kids better," the father admitted. "I should have spent more time with them and less time working."

Inwardly I shook my head as I heard another father realize too late that he had neglected his family and paid the price. During counseling, his wife had told me bitterly that his main priority had always been money. Ironically enough, one of his major goals was getting enough money together to provide college educations for his kids.

We went ahead with that meeting and, while it was very emotional and very hard for everyone, it was very beneficial. The boy had a few things to tell both parents, and they listened quietly and undefensively. And then they explained that the divorce was going to happen. They realized that it was shattering, but they wanted their son to know that somehow they would still be a family and that they loved him.

One of the hardest things for an adult to grasp is that children have their perceptions and quite often their perceptions don't match an adult's. And because Mom and Dad are quite sure that their perceptions are superior to their children's, they discount what the children say. This can be so true in regard to children's fears. A child complains, "I don't want to go to the doctor. He'll hurt me."

And what is Mom's typical answer? "Of course he won't hurt you! He's there to help you. Don't be such a baby!"

How much better to say to a child "I understand that you're a little afraid of going to the doctor. You may have to get a shot, and a shot will hurt. But it will only be for a few seconds and then you'll feel better."

With this simple remark, you acknowledge the child's feelings of plain old simple fear. Who hasn't feared going to the doctor or the dentist? Who hasn't felt uneasy as the doctor has come through the examining room door? Is it really that hard for us as adults to project ourselves back and understand the child's perception of the doctor and how the child associates doctors and dentists with pain and hurting?

Telling the child "It won't hurt a bit," "Big boys don't cry," or even "I'll get you a sucker afterward" won't do as much good as letting the child know that you understand how it is, but you'll be right there alongside helping him or her get through it.

A final rule to tuck into your memory bank is:

Always Trust Your Children's Perceptions

I can hear what you're thinking. What if the children's perceptions are *wrong*? Yes, that's possible, but the point is, they are the *children's* perceptions, and it's your children's feelings that you are trying to acknowledge in order to communicate better.

Keep in mind that there are times—more times than adults may care to admit—when the children's perceptions are *right*.

While writing this chapter I was talking to Krissy and Kevin and said, "I could use a good illustration of a time when you tried to tell me how you felt and I *didn't* listen."

"Well, Dad," Kevin teased, "that ought to easy. How many examples do you need?"

"Just one will be fine," I said, not sure being vulnerable was always that enjoyable.

"What about the time that you and I went out to dinner with your friends, Tom and Wendy, and I told you I didn't feel so good. You just said, 'Oh, you'll be okay. Let's just have dinner.' "

My memory flashed back to a Christmas when Kevin was eleven. Sande had to be somewhere to meet Krissy, and so Kevin had gone along when I invited Tom and Wendy, old friends who were house guests at the time, to eat at one of my favorite restaurants. Kevin had indeed complained of not feeling well as we walked into the restaurant, but I was busy talking with Tom and Wendy and had ignored him.

A few minutes later, after we had all ordered, Kevin complained of feeling cold. Tom was wearing a sport coat, and he took it off and put it over Kevin's shoulders, but it didn't seem to do any good. Kevin got that green-around-the-gills look, but I still didn't want to make a big deal out of the problem. Kids often feel a little sick and then it passes quickly.

But Tom's wife, Wendy, wasn't so sure. "Do you mind if I take Kevin to the rest room?" she asked me.

"No, if you think it's necessary, but I'm sure he'll be okay," I replied, and then, still preoccupied, I turned back to talk with Tom.

Wendy and Kevin left the table, but they didn't get more than a few steps when Kevin's feelings came out in full force. He hurled a "five-footer" that covered the front of Tom's jacket and a good portion of the restaurant floor. All the waitresses stopped in midstride and stared at the mess. I stared too, wondering why I had ignored Kevin's clear-cut warning about how he felt.

As I helped clean Kevin up, I apologized to him profusely for not paying more attention to how he felt. This was a graphic reminder of something I already knew but had forgotten because I was preoccupied with "adult concerns": *Never discount a child's perceptions of reality.* There are plenty of times when children's perceptions are right on target, as Kevin's were in the restaurant.

Yes, there are plenty of other times when children's perceptions may be off, due to a lack of experience or maturity, but listen carefully anyway. If you are concerned about a child's feelings, whether your child is right or wrong is not the issue. A parent's first job is to deal with the Feeling Factor. There is no more important way to build a child's self-image and sense of self-worth.

Words to Remember . . .

- Every child who complains, protests, criticizes, argues, or just plain "lips off" is a victim of the same problem: discouragement.

- To encourage your children, learn how to handle the Feeling Factor—your children's feelings and yours.

- Pressure from without (you) rarely promotes lasting desirable behavior by your children. They need stimulation from within.

- The best way to encourage your children is to acknowledge their feelings. When you deny a child's feelings and say such things as "Stop that, how can you say such a thing?" you only add to the child's discouragement.

- Whenever a parent ignores children's feelings in order to "correct an error or a bad attitude," it's the same thing as treating the children as if they aren't there. Nothing is more discouraging than that.

- Listening to your children involves two things: really being there, not tuned out and thinking of other things, and listening with empathy—putting yourself in the children's shoes.

- When trying to actively listen to your children, don't depend on stock phrases or responses and expect the children to respond with the perfect answer every time. Gently probe to discover what is really on their minds.

- Dealing with the Feeling Factor is more of an art than a precise science.

- Always trust your children's perceptions. In many cases they may be right.

Actions to Try . . .

- For the next week (the next thirty days would be even better because active listening takes lots of practice), try checking yourself on how often you discount your children's feelings. When you find yourself tempted to discount their feelings, stop and try to acknowledge those feelings.

- Over the next week try to keep track of how often you say to your children "You don't really feel that way," or "You shouldn't talk like that."

- Instead of discounting your children's feelings, use the four techniques discussed in this chapter to acknowledge them:

  1. Pay complete attention to what your children are saying and listen for feelings as well as facts.

  2. Let your children know that you are hearing them with simple one-word replies, such as "Oh," and "Uh-huh," and "I see."

  3. As you identify your children's feelings, state them out loud so the children know that you know how they

feel. For example, say, "I can see why you're angry," or "That must have really hurt."

4. When appropriate, grant the children's wishes in fantasy even though you can't do much about the reality of the situation. ("I wish I could stop the rain and bring the sun out and have it shine especially for you.")

- Use the many examples in this chapter of how to show empathy to your children. Feeling understood, especially by one's parents, helps build the self-image immeasurably.

- When active listening and acknowledging feelings doesn't seem to work (you get a blank look or the impertinent reply), don't give up. It takes time to learn how to acknowledge *your* children's feelings. Some things will work better than others.

- The next time your children scream "I hate you!" use the suggested techniques to take the wind out of their sails by refusing to get angry.

PART III

What to Do When Reality Discipline Runs Smack into Reality

. . . From potty training to temper tantrums and much, much more . . . troubleshooting and specific suggestions for weathering the "wonder years," from birth to age five

■

. . . When the parenting game starts to get really interesting . . . guiding your children through the "blunder years," ages six to twelve

■

. . . Conquering the canyon of inferiority . . . helping your teenagers survive the "thunder years" with their self-image in one piece

Chapter Nine

CREATING THE IMAGE

■

Questions and Answers:
Parenting Infants to Age Five

Parenting preschoolers is the nearest thing to "Double Jeopardy" that I know of. First you have the awesome responsibility of nurturing and training your child in the most critical period of his or her life. Whenever I think of small children I'm reminded of the title of a charming book on child training written by Anne Ortlund, *Children Are Wet Cement*. She's right. The small child is impressionable and malleable—capable of being shaped, formed, and influenced in thousands of ways.

A child's personality, life plan, and life-style are 85 to 95 percent formed by age five. By age seven it's all over and the grain of the wood is completely set. All this would be challenging enough, but add the realization that moms and dads of preschoolers are, as a rule, new at the parenting game, and the stress level mounts even more.

To their firstborn, parents can offer *no* experience. They learn by trial and error, and their little firstborn learns along with them. I have a special concern for all the firstborns of this world. Sometimes I think it's a miracle that they survive.

After "learning on the first child," parents generally decide to have one or two more. Then they get another rude awakening.

What they learned from having the first child doesn't always work. Parents often think, *Our next child will be just like the first.* Good luck! They quickly learn that every child is different— sometimes amazingly so. What works with one will be a sure-fire failure with another.

I recall talking to one mother of three toddlers who recalled having "romantic ideas" about parenting. She planned to have "perfect kids" who would seldom, if ever, misbehave. She envisioned orderly organized days, with the children down for their naps while she caught up on the bills or perhaps had a few moments of "quiet time" for herself.

Then her first child arrived. He "came out screaming" and continued to scream for the first several months. Welcome to reality, which is often followed quickly by the vicious combination of guilt and fatigue that can erode a parent's self-image and sense of self-worth in a hurry.

What mother of a toddler hasn't ground her teeth (at least mentally) when little Festus throws his soup or spaghetti all over her newly mopped and waxed floor? Mom thinks (or perhaps screams), "I can't believe you did that! All over my clean floor!" And then, trying to keep her cool, she says, "Okay, Festus, let's wipe it up." Inside, however, Mom is battling frustration, or even rage, and the very real desire to wipe the floor with Festus.

Later she feels guilty about her anger and her self-image drops another notch. Ironically, those who are supposed to be building a healthy personality and self-image in their little ones are often stunned by realizing that raising those little ones is destroying *their* self-image.

Mary, mother of three children under five, explained that her worst attacks of frustration, guilt, and low self-image would come, ironically enough, on Sunday mornings when she tried to get everybody ready for church. Her husband, who served as an usher and officer of the church, always left early to help open and prepare the building for two worship services that would be held that morning.

Mary, feeling "like a single parent," was left to get the children up, dressed, fed, and ready to go in time to make it to the 9:00 o'clock service. As each child arrived in the family, Mary found that it was necessary to get up another thirty minutes earlier to help everyone be ready to go.

The worst part was arriving at the church and trying to find a parking place fairly close to the door. Then Mary struggled up the walk, carrying baby, Bible, diaper bag, and other odds and ends while the two older children either clung to her skirts or tried to wander off.

Mary admits to feeling "like an idiot," out of control and helpless. "I'm sure I looked like a fool." Perhaps you've known the same feelings—at church, the supermarket, the mall, or just when trying to get everyone to the corner park to play on the swings for an hour or so.

Nadine, mother of toddlers ages four and two, struggles with plenty of guilt feelings. She said, "Children push you to limits you don't face with adults. After all, adults don't lie on the floor, screaming, kicking and provoking you . . . all those things that are part of being a toddler."

When asked if she missed adult conversations during the day, Nadine laughed and told me of the time she went to a weekend women's retreat. As soon as she arrived at the retreat grounds, she "went crazy" and started talking to other women—anyone who would listen.

"I was just so hungry for adult conversation, I talked practically nonstop for forty-eight hours," she admitted. "When I got home, I was exhausted."

We may smile and sympathize with this mom, but I'd like to go back for a moment to a phrase she used—"part of being a toddler." The frustrating negative parts are easy to remember, but there is another side to toddlers and almost all moms would be the first to tell you they love and enjoy their kids and wouldn't trade them for the world (most of the time). And let's face it, having toddlers usually provides many moments of priceless humor.

I heard of one mother who tried to slip away from her little one to get a few moments of quiet time. She was, in fact, trying to pray for wisdom to be a good mom when her little girl came in. Mom tried to ignore her daughter and kept on praying, but her four-year-old would not be denied. She cuddled up to Mom and started to rub her leg. Suddenly she said loudly, "Oh, oh, Mommy! It's time to shave!"

Mom cracked up laughing and then decided to give up trying to pray. She just thanked God for her little girl and went on with her day.

In several places I've mentioned our little surprise package, Hannah, who arrived when Sande was forty and I was forty-four. Having Hannah has renewed my empathy for parents of small children, but at the same time she's reminded me how funny little kids can be. Holly, who was a freshman at college at the time, had arrived home for Christmas vacation and, while I was talking with her one morning, we heard noises in the master bedroom. We walked in to find four-year-old Hannah jumping up and down on the king-size bed. As any good father and family psychologist would do, I quickly took charge and said, "Hannah, honey, don't jump on the bed. Beds are for sleeping, not jumping on. You can fall and hurt yourself."

Hannah stopped jumping for a moment, but I could tell by the look on her face that the wheels were turning. Suddenly she began jumping up and down once more and I said a bit more firmly, "Hannah, stop jumping on the bed."

In midflight, Hannah said, "But, Daddy, I'm jumping on *Mama's* side!"

Holly and I broke up laughing, and then I regained my composure and managed to say, "Hannah. No more jumping." Hannah stopped jumping, but, to be honest, I couldn't stop chuckling the rest of the day.

As you go about creating the self-image your child will carry for life, you need to remember the funny and charming moments along with the frustrating and maddening ones. It's all "part of being a parent to a toddler," which is, perhaps, the most important task in all the world—forming that lovable package of "wet cement" into a healthy personality and sound self-image.

Instead of being dismayed by the awesome responsibility of raising a child, I believe most moms and dads are determined to do it as best they can. The rest of this chapter will cover common (and some not so common) problems and concerns faced by parents of children who are anywhere between birth and age five. The answers I suggest to these questions come from my own parenting or from counseling other parents. Not all of the following may work for you. Parenting is an imprecise art, but I do hope that you get some ideas that will help you bring your kids up without tearing them down.

Q: Our two-year-old daughter is usually very loving, but lately she is baffling her father and me by saying things like "I don't like Dad," or "I don't want to sit by Dad" (at dinnertime, for example). We wonder why she expresses herself like this. My husband and I both hold full-time jobs, and we wonder why our daughter shows such a strong preference for me but opposition toward him right now. Is this normal?

A: It is very normal. It is unwise, however, for parents to read too much into this kind of a statement by a two-year-old. Little children are extremely attached to their mothers, and the fact that you are working outside of the home makes you even more of a premium in the eyes of your two-year-old daughter. Age two is a very clingy stage, with Mom as the favorite.

At the same time, you see your child beginning to exert some independence ("I don't want to sit by Dad"). She is going through a very natural stage and, before long—in a year or so— you will see that your daughter is going to show a preference for being around her father. Little girls of three or four often become very attached to Daddy, and it's important for fathers to establish a good relationship with their daughters.

Dad is the first teacher of his daughter concerning what men are all about. Daughters who grow up having a healthy relationship with their fathers usually do much better at picking a husband. The best thing your husband could do right now is to be loving, patient, and gentle with your two-year-old daughter. His time to be "popular" will come.

Q: Our daughter is three and unusually bright for her age. She has a large vocabulary, is very articulate, and can express her wants quite effectively. Some friends keep telling me I should enroll her in a very popular preschool in our community that specializes in "bright children." What do you think? Is our daughter ready for this?

A: Because your daughter is "articulate" and unusually bright, don't be tempted to go out and get her enrolled in some prestigious "kiddie kollege" or "urchin university." Remember that for firstborn children, parents are the main models and setters of examples. Therefore, it's not unusual for a firstborn to pick up language skills earlier than later-born children.

Beware, however, of preschools that are known for their work with brighter children ("Superkids"). David Elkind, author of *Our Hurried Children*, has sounded a clear warning against the popular modern concept of "Superkid." Elkind writes:

> Like Superman, Superkid has spectacular powers and precocious confidence even as an infant. This allows us to think we can hurry the little powerhouse with impunity. . . . Today's child has become the unwilling, unintended victim of overwhelming stress—the stress born of rapid, bewildering social change and constantly rising expectations.[1]

Be cautious as you shop for a preschool. Try to stay away from the fast tracks where competition can be fierce. We enrolled our youngest daughter, Hannah, in a preschool when she was three, two morning per week, three hours per morning maximum. Some preschools will take children from 9:00 A.M. to 3:00 P.M., but I feel that is too long for most children. Regarding Hannah's preschool, we waited until she was well past her third birthday to enroll her. To enroll a child any younger than that is also asking for problems. And we checked the preschool out carefully to be sure it was low key and stressed social adjustment over academic skills. I'm not against preschools, but I am against high-powered ones that stress academics.

My general advice to parents of preschoolers is to let them take their time in growing up. There is no proof that kiddie kollege or urchin university really helps children when they get into first grade and beyond. In fact, as David Elkind points out, after a generation of high-powered preschools, we see teenage pregnancy rates higher in the United States than any other Western society. Our suicide and homicide rates among teenagers are triple what they were twenty years ago. High school students are getting lower SAT scores than ever. And on the other end of the spectrum, 15 to 20 percent of young children are "flunking" kindergarten. As Elkind says, "Clearly, the Superkid conception has not been a boon to children."[2]

I suggest that you back off, relax, and enjoy your little girl in these precious preschool years. She will be into the educational rat race soon enough.

Q: Our little boy is sixteen months old. Almost from the day he was born, my wife has been buying him every conceivable "educational toy" and gimmick she could find. Now she is bringing home toys labeled "For ages three or four and up." I'm waiting to find a small computer in his crib. I tell her kids can be happy with a wooden spoon and a saucepan, but she

gets upset, especially when I point out that all this stuff is getting expensive. Is it really necessary?

A: It sounds as if your wife means well, but she has overdone things. Brightly colored mobiles and other simple toys are good for infants, but parents sometimes get carried away and start bringing home every toy they can find. I agree with you and I suggest you open up the cupboard and get out the pots and pans and spoons, and the like, particularly now that your child is moving into the eighteen- to twenty-four-month range. I'm not saying you can't buy any toys and educational products, because there are some excellent items on the market. But study carefully what you're buying and don't emphasize toys that do all the work. Instead, give your child the simple toy that he can play with *in order to amuse himself.*

It's important to let kids discover and create by themselves rather than being passive observers of toys, television, what have you. When children have to create their own entertainment, it helps them achieve confidence in their ability, which is a key factor in building a healthy self-image.

Q: Our three-year-old daughter is an only child. When we ask her to do something, such as put her toys away, she asks, "Why?" After telling her about three times, I get up and get the paddle and then she immediately does what I ask. I'm wondering if I should go ahead and spank her to show her that she should have listened to me the first time, or should I just put the paddle away and continue letting her think that she can push us right to the limit before she has to do what we ask?

A: You have trained your three-year-old to believe that she doesn't have to do anything until you ask her at least three times and then reach for the paddle. It appears that she is what I call a "powerful little buzzard," and she is more than willing to test your limits. There are several ways to handle this situation.

First, when you ask her to put away her toys, ask her just once. Give her an appropriate time to react and, if you see her wandering off to do something else, go pick her up or take her by the hand and take her to the toys. Sit down with her on the floor and say, "Let's put the toys away now."

By doing this simple act, you have already disciplined your child. But you have made it a learning situation, not punishment.

In all likelihood, if you sit down on the floor with the child, the child will begin to pick up her toys. Keep in mind that with three-year-olds, you must take the time to train them. You cannot expect a three-year-old to salute and do everything you ask at first command. That isn't typical of three-year-olds whether they're powerful firstborns or happy-go-lucky babies of the family.

The key is that Mom and Dad must make the commitment that they will not tell their children to do things more than once. If the job isn't done, they need to take action, such as I have just outlined.

But suppose you are in a situation where toys need to be picked up and you are late for a doctor's appointment. You ask your three-year-old to pick up the toys because you're leaving in a few minutes for the doctor, and your child stalls around and refuses to do so. Instead of repeating your request several times, lecturing and getting into a power struggle, simply take the child, get in the car, and go to your appointment. When you return home, let your child know that she has a chore to do. She has a choice: Pick up her toys or sit in her room for a while. Make it clear to your three-year-old that her toys need to be picked up before she is allowed to do any more playing, watching TV, and the like.

If your preschooler has big brothers or sisters who are favorite playmates after they get home from school, try building in the consequence that toys must be picked up before big brother and sister come home from school—no playing with either one until all toys are picked up.

Still another approach is that you tell your daughter that she has to pick up her toys before dinnertime or she will not be allowed to come to the dinner table. The principle you are teaching is that work must be done before play or even before eating. It is an age-old solution that usually works beautifully with young children (and older ones, for that matter).

A final principle to apply is "Treat children in a way that you expect them to behave and chances are they will behave exactly that way." Although children may sometimes act as if they're in a conspiracy to drive you crazy, their natural desire is to please their parents. Holding healthy, reasonable, and reachable expectations is an excellent way to give your children opportunities to please you and build their self-image and sense of self-worth.

Q: Our four-and-a-half-year-old firstborn son always wants to be "the boss." He's even starting to boss us around. How do we use Reality Discipline and let him feel he belongs without letting him run the show?

A: It sounds as if your firstborn son has developed a life-style motto that has him telling himself, "I count only when I'm in control." You must be firm but do it gently, in a way that helps him learn that he can't always have his own way and that in life none of us "always runs the show."

Remember, Reality Discipline Principle #1: "You are in healthy authority over your children." This means that they do not tell you what cereal to buy, what restaurant to go to, or what TV shows to watch. They have a vote, true, but it is only that—a vote, not final say. Whenever possible, give others in the family opportunity to voice their opinions. That includes you, your spouse, and any brothers or sisters. On some occasions it would be very healthy to let younger brothers and sisters "outvote" an older child. In other cases, you and your husband may want to outvote him.

In all situations, be gentle, firm, and fair with everyone concerned. Don't "gang up" on your four-and-a-half-year-old to "teach him a lesson." In fact, he should get to stay up longer than his younger brothers and sisters and have other privileges that are normally allowed to the firstborn. What you are after, however, is balance. Your firstborn should realize that he is special, but not better than anyone else. If you allow him to develop a controlling or bossy life-style, you are setting him up for a lot of future conflict later in life. You want your oldest child to have a good self-image, but at the same time you don't want him believing the myth that he must always have his way and always run things.

Q: Our five-year-old firstborn son is very intelligent. If a western is on television, he goes and gets his rocking horse. If the movie is about cars, he gets his MatchBox cars out and lines them up carefully in a row. If there is a dog show, he makes our dog watch! What does all this mean?

A: Basically it means that you have a bright firstborn son on your hands. You may also have a perfectionist. Note that lining up the cars carefully in a row and matching whatever he's doing with the theme of the TV show he's watching can be early signs of perfectionism. Some ways to curb the tendencies of a budding perfectionist include:

1. Don't overcorrect your child. Check your own tendencies to be perfectionistic. Whenever possible, share your own imperfections with the child as he grows up. Let him learn from his adult role models (remember, firstborns always see adults as role models) that you are imperfect and that you have flaws. Let him know it's okay to have flaws and be imperfect.

2. Avoid praising your child for his "clever ways" when he lines up his cars, brings in his rocking horse, or makes his dog watch dog shows. Downplay these activities and encourage your child in other areas. (See Chapter Seven.)

3. Don't be drawn into making judgments about what your son does. He may ask you in his five-year-old way: "Do you like this? What do you think of what I did?" Whenever possible, turn his question back to him: "Honey, how do you feel about it? Which do you like the best?"

In every way possible, send your child the message, "We know you're capable. You decide. You don't always have to please us or do exactly what we want." It may seem contradictory at first, but by encouraging your son to decide things for himself, you actually curb his perfectionism, because you no longer play the role of "all-knowing role model."

Q: Our two-year-old daughter is the baby of our family. (We have three children.) She is so outgoing and friendly that sometimes she embarrasses me (probably because I'm the shy type). Also, I'm concerned about her being too friendly to strangers. What can we do to help her understand that not every stranger is necessarily a friendly person and that she needs to be aware of "Stranger Danger"?

A: Teaching a two-year-old about Stranger Danger is difficult if not impossible because her conceptual processes aren't ready. If you are worried about Stranger Danger for your two-year-old, my best advice is: "Never leave your child unattended." I often cringe when I see mothers leaving two-year-olds, and even older children, alone in shopping carts while they busy themselves picking out products that may be forty to fifty feet away, and even around the corner of an aisle where the child is out of sight for a few minutes.

Beginning at age four and give—certainly by age six—gently begin talking to the child about Stranger Danger. Explain that there are people who aren't nice—everyone is not like Mommy and Daddy. The child must learn to be careful. Never get in cars with strangers. If a car pulls up along the sidewalk, never let it get closer than fifteen or twenty feet. (Show a child how far that is.) Always be ready to run to a safe place (her own yard or a neighbor's front door, for example).

Because your daughter is the precocious, outgoing, friendly type, it will be important to teach her about Stranger Danger, but right now, while she is only two, relax. Many parents would be extremely pleased to have an outgoing child who meets people well. Realize that this is a social skill that she is already making part of her basic personality and life-style. Some day, down the road, she may put it to good use by becoming skilled in sales or public relations. For the present, sit back and enjoy your daughter; teaching her about Stranger Danger can come later.

Q: My five-year-old son goes over to his friend's house and gets along beautifully throughout the day. When I come to pick him up, however, he starts throwing a fit. Sometimes it gets so bad he starts crying and saying hurtful things to me and to his little friend. What kind of discipline would be appropriate?

A: First, take comfort in the fact that kids can be absolute angels at somebody else's house and when Mom comes in they can go slightly bonkers. The question is, why? It could be a sign that you are too controlling of your child when he is at home with you. It could also mean that your child wants attention—or power. He enjoys—and apparently succeeds at—getting you into power struggles.

When you walk into the home of your son's playmate and your son starts to act up, it means that your child is used to having power struggles with his mother, and when Mom shows up he goes into his Jekyll and Hyde act.

As for what you can do about this, the specific Reality Discipline needed is to simply pick up your child (and I mean that literally, if it is at all necessary) and leave immediately. Don't negotiate, bribe, or argue. Leave—now.

Then the next time your five-year-old asks to go to the house of his little friend, you tell him no and remind him of the scene he caused. A few days later he will probably ask you again if he can go to see his friend and you can tell him that you're willing to let him try again, but that you expect better behavior when you come to pick him up.

If your son does handle himself better the next time you pick him up, you can say on the way home, "You know, it was really fun to drive you over to your friend's house today and then come and get you later. Today wasn't like the last time at all. I think you can go see your friend again very soon."

In this way you reinforce in a very positive way the responsible behavior your five-year-old has displayed and you encourage him to do more of the same in the future.

Q: My child is four years old and she won't go to bed by herself. She always wants me to lie down with her because she says she's afraid even if I leave the light on and the door open. What can I do to get her to go to sleep by herself?

A: I'm afraid that, like many well-meaning parents, you have taught your child a bad habit. As I often tell parents, don't start habits you don't want to have your children continue until graduate school and beyond.

Your daughter's protest that she's afraid and you must lie down with her before she can go to sleep is a means of gaining attention. The more you placate her and reward her for irresponsible behavior, the more her appetite for such unnecessary attention is going to grow. The solution is simple, but it will be difficult, at least for a little while, because your daughter will resist having her control of you challenged in any way. Do not lie down with your child. Just kiss her good night, tell her that you love her very much, and you know she can go to sleep by herself from now on. Then *stick to your guns!*

When your daughter realizes that you are serious, she will probably try to negotiate. She may say she will stay in bed as long as you leave her night-light on and don't close the door. You can try this, but if your little girl is truly a powerful child—and it sounds like she might be—she will pop right out of bed and be out looking for you in no time. You see, a powerful child just keeps coming. The powerful child is not interested in going to sleep, only in exerting control over you.

If this is the case and leaving a night-light on and leaving the door slightly ajar doesn't help, then you must go to "Plan B." You must let the child know you are in healthy authority over her and that you do have the power to make her stay in her room. Lovingly and gently tell her again that she must stay in her bed and that now, because she has not done as she said she would, you will leave the night-light on but you will shut the door.

At this point, you must be patient—and keep a good grip on the doorknob. Your child will scream and cry and try to get out, but you must simply hold the door shut and be patient, strong— and a little bit deaf. The unofficial world's record for screaming and crying by a small child who isn't getting her way is something like two hours and forty-seven minutes. But be patient, your child *will* stop.

To some parents, "holding the door shut" sounds cold and brutal, *but you do this only when you are quite sure the child is using powerful behavior to control you.* The good news is that you will have to do it only once or twice. For a change, you will get your child's attention and your child will learn to go to sleep by herself with the door closed and the light out, or perhaps with a night-light on.

If your child is like most, you will need to hold the door shut for only a few minutes. The child will fall asleep, perhaps just on the other side of the door, lying on the rug with her "blanky" tucked under her arm like a football. Pick her up, tuck her in, and leave. If she awakens, you may have to go through the whole routine again, but for an even shorter time. Keep your major goal in mind: letting the child know that you hold all the aces and that, in a showdown, you can and will win.

While your child is learning that she must sleep in her bed while you sleep in yours, it may be hard on your nerves, but do not let her get the upper hand in this power struggle. If you do, you are being trapped into thinking your child "needs you." If you let that happen, perhaps you need to question your own dependency needs as a parent. Perhaps you "need to be needed." The rule is: Children and adults stay in their own beds.

Of course, while rules shouldn't be broken, they can bend sometimes. For example, the child may have a nightmare, or perhaps you have moved into a strange house where curtains aren't up yet and black windows frighten the child. At times like that, you comfort him or her, but then the rule goes back into effect as soon as possible—everyone stays in his own bed.

Of course, kids have an incredible skill of getting around the rules. Among our four children, Krissy was perhaps the most talented. As a small child—around four or five—she would sometimes get in bed with us at night without our realizing it. The next morning I would wake up with a little bum-bum in my face. But we still hung firmly to our standards and Krissy soon learned that she had to sleep in her own bed.

Q: A professional counselor tells me that I expect too much of my children (ages three and five) by insisting that they respond to my requests the first or second time I ask them to do something. He claims they are not developmentally ready to obey adult requests. Is this true?

A: No, it is not true. At age three and five children are quite capable of responding to many requests. It is true that before age two, children are extremely limited in their conceptual abilities and are unable to obey most simple requests. In fact, around eighteen months the typical child is what is called "oppositional," meaning, for example, if you go toward the child, the child will back up. If you want the eighteen-month-old to come to you, you try backing up.

But at ages three and five, and even at ages two to two and a half, the child is quite capable of fulfilling many responsibilities when patiently and gently instructed. As the list on pages 246–249 shows, children ages two and three can pick up their toys and put them away, put books away, and help set the table by placing napkins, plates, and silverware in the correct place. They can also learn to clear the table and even wipe up their own spills! Four- and five-year-olds can learn to put groceries away, polish their shoes, help do yard and garden work, or help make the beds and vacuum. See the lists for additional ideas.

Q: We moved recently and my four-year-old daughter cries and carries on terribly whenever I try to leave her in her weekday preschool class. I thought it might be because of the move, but even months before our move she cried and carried on when I tried to leave her at Sunday school. How should I handle this?

A: You are in a power struggle with your daughter and she appears to be winning. She began this power struggle back when she was three and you lived in your other home. Now that you've moved, she's continued it on into her new preschool situation.

If you have any other younger children coming up, you might want to consider doing the following to prepare them for any preschool or kindergarten experiences. Several months ahead of when the child is to go to preschool or kindergarten, take the child to that school for an "observation day." Let the child meet the teacher and spend some time with the other children. Of course, you stay in the room the entire time on this particular occasion. When your child comes back several months later, it will not be to a completely strange environment. For example, you may want to have your child visit the school in May, but you don't plan to enroll her until September.

Also, as you prepare your child for preschool, don't overdo it with all kinds of remarks such as "My goodness, you're going to have so much fun in preschool," or "You're just going to love kindergarten." Your child may not be that sure and you could be setting her up for failure. It is best to wait for the child to say something, such as "I'm a big girl and pretty soon I'll be going to preschool (or kindergarten)." And you can say, "Yes, that's coming after summer is over with, honey." Take preschool in stride. Then the child is more apt to do so as well.

But all of these preparatory ideas don't help you with your current problem, which is a crying and complaining four-year-old who begs you not to leave when you try to take her to preschool class. In this case, what you must do is avoid being drawn into battle. Kiss your child, assure her you will be back soon, hand her to the teacher or attendant, and leave *quickly.* In the vast majority of cases like this, the child stops crying almost as soon as the parent is gone. Some children may cry a few minutes, and occasionally one may cry for an extended time for the first one or two times the mother is firm in leaving quickly. After that, the child adjusts and is fine.

There are cases, however, where a child may continue to balk and protest when you try to leave her at preschool. If this is the case, perhaps your best solution is to withdraw the child from preschool and keep her home for another year. (It's possible that withdrawing the child from preschool for a few days or a week or two may do the trick; and she may be willing to stay on her own after that.)

One thing that many parents must face is that putting their child in preschool is for their convenience, not the child's. If the child is truly unready for preschool, leaving her there is a form of abuse. It is better to take the child out of preschool and try again next year.

Q: Our son is three and a half and we want to know how to handle his anger, particularly the anger he shows when he is disciplined. He will scream, hit, and refuse to talk to us. Is it a good idea to isolate him at times like this? Is it okay for children as young as this to express such strong anger?

A: Parents should make sure their children have the opportunity to express anger, but the key is to help them express it correctly and in a way that helps them resolve their feelings. In this case, the first thing I would check is how I am disciplining my son. His anger indicates that you may be coming on too strong—you are too harsh and too authoritarian in your methods. The saying goes: "If you have a powerful angry child, the chances are you have a powerful and probably angry parent.

You say that he gets very angry after being "disciplined." If disciplining him almost always means punishing him with a swat or a spanking, you need to reconsider. Or if your discipline revolves around trying to use logical consequences, you need to analyze how you are invoking those consequences. What is your tone of voice when you talk to your child?

Q: My children (three and a half and five and a half) have neighborhood friends their age who are not good influences. Should we forbid our children to play with these neighbor

kids, or should we simply try to curb their time with them and concentrate on counteracting the things that come up, such as bad language, bad attitudes, disobedient actions, and the like?

A: Most mothers are concerned about who their children play with and the influence that their friends have on them. You can try to forbid your children to spend time with these neighborhood friends, but this can lead to awkward situations, bad feelings with your neighbors, and other problems. I would prefer that you concentrate on counteracting what your children are hearing from the neighbor kids. One of the best ways would be to enroll your children in any number of programs that are available in your immediate community. I'm thinking of the YMCA, the YWCA, church children's programs, Brownies. If you can afford it, you might try to get your children into gymnastics, dance, or activities of that nature.

The idea, of course, is to expose your children to what you hope will be more wholesome companionship, but even then you can't be sure of what they will see and hear. The truth is, your children will constantly be meeting friends their age who are not good influences. Your best way to counteract this is through staying close to your children, communicating with them, letting them know that "our family is not like Johnny's family. You don't have to be like the other kids. You can choose to be different."

Q: My three-year-old daughter keeps trying to do things she can't really handle, and I have to keep telling her, "No, you're not quite ready for that." I don't like this, but I don't want her to hurt herself. Any suggestions on what I can say?

A: One of the first signs that a small child is developing properly is the attitude: "Want to do it myself." This usually starts around age two, when the child starts pushing the adult's help-ing hand away. My advice is to find as many safe things for your three-year-old to do by herself as possible. Don't put her at risk, but be willing to risk perfect order or perfect cleanliness in order to allow your child to learn that she is capable. Nothing helps a child's self-image more than this.

Admittedly, taking risks can be messy and even expensive. One night we had the grandparents over for dinner and Sande made spaghetti and meatballs, one of four-year-old Hannah's favorites. Our older children served up generous portions of spa-ghetti and meatballs on plates that would be carried into the dining room several feet from the kitchen counter. Sande started to pick up Hannah's brimming plate when Hannah insisted, "I do it myself!"

Sande and I looked at each other and I winked reassuringly. "Okay, honey," she said, "now hold on to the plate tightly. That's a big helping of spaghetti and meatballs."

Hannah made it across the kitchen floor, but two steps into the dining room and onto the beige Berber carpet she lost her concentration and let the plate tilt. The entire helping of spa-ghetti and meatballs slid off, down the front of her white outfit, hitting the floor and spattering a good two to three feet in all directions. The look on Hannah's face was priceless. She was sure she had committed the unpardonable sin. The rest of us all stood there in shocked silence, but only for a few seconds. I quickly responded by saying, "Honey, that's okay. We'll wipe it up."

Sande got a roll of paper towels and everyone pitched in to clean up the mess, including Hannah. What was really gratifying to Sande and me was that our older children, Kevin and Krissy, reassured Hannah that it was okay. "We all spill stuff," they said. "It happens." Unfortunately, beige Berber carpeting does not wipe up that easily when the spill is rich, red spaghetti sauce. We did our best and went on with dinner, but the next morning the carpet cleaner arrived and $36.00 later the spot was totally removed.

But I say it was worth it to let Hannah try. And I believe it's worth it to let your three-year-old try everything she can. When she wants to do something you feel is too dangerous, go easy on using the word no. Instead say, "Why don't we do this instead?" Or perhaps you can say, "Mom will do this much and you can do the rest." The general principle is to always give your small child every opportunity to learn that she is capable, that she can do it. This is what will help her develop a healthy and confident self-image.

Q: My wife is expecting our first child in a few weeks and the sonograms tell us it will be a boy. I not only want to be a good father to my son, I want to be his best friend in every sense of the word. How can I start developing this kind of relationship from the very beginning?

A: If you want to be your child's "best friend," don't try to be his pal, be his parent. For the next eighteen years or so, you are to be in healthy authority over your child. As he reaches adulthood, your role will change from parent in authority to parent who is a friend and advisor.

Being in healthy authority means taking out plenty of image insurance on your child, spending the time it takes to provide a functional family, and striking a good balance between love and limits. All this is discussed in detail in Chapters One through Six.

By the way, you are to be commended for wanting to be so involved in your son's life. You are among a small but growing number of fathers who realize that parenting children is not just "women's work." A father has a key role of primary male role model to play in the life of his child, and if he's not there to play that role, it leaves a hole in the child's self-image.

Q: My husband thinks I baby our five-year-old son too much by protecting him from his older brother and sister (nine and seven). They often pester or bully him. What am I supposed to do? Sometimes the older children can be really mean.

A: The first thing I would check on is whether or not your five-year-old is "setting up" his older brother and sister. In other words, is he pestering them, bugging them in subtle and not-so-subtle ways to get them to come down on him because he knows Mom will come to his rescue, punish older brother and sister, and so on? Talk separately with your older children. Throw out leading comments, such as "Sometimes little brothers can be real pests," or "You're angry with your little brother a lot lately. Tell me about it."

Then sit back and actively listen your older children to see what you can learn. (For a review of the active listening technique, reread Chapter Eight.)

Obviously, if the two older children are really hurting the young one without any provocation on his part, you need to step in and intervene, but the chances are the younger boy is part of the problem. In this case, "It takes three to tango."

Another approach is to bring the younger brother together with his older brother or sister and talk through what he does to bug them. Let him know what he needs to stop doing and then try to stay out of the squabbles as much as possible. Beware of always snowplowing the roads of life for your five-year-old. He needs to learn how to deal with his older brother and sister, as well as the rest of life, and in the long run he needs to learn it on his own if he is to develop a healthy self-image.

Q: My husband and I have one child who is now two and a half. Many of our friends are opting for only one child, and we are considering doing the same. It is just too expensive to raise children these days. I have heard there are dangers in having an only child—what are they and how can they be counteracted?

A: Back in the 1950s in the days of the "nuclear family," only children were in the definite minority. In recent years, millions of couples have decided to have only one child, usually for economic reasons.

One woman put it this way: "It's tough raising a family in this economy, and I don't feel I can work full time and give another child the time and attention he would deserve."

Her husband added: "Our child is only three and we're already thinking about how we're going to pay for her college education. . . . We both have to work, and things would be crazy if there were more than one child. The mornings are a real rush: You have to feed and dress the child, get ready for work and take her to day care. She wants to be with us, we want to be with her, and it takes an emotional toll."[3]

But is being an only child a good deal? Talk to adult only children and you get mixed answers. One might tell you he felt deprived and lonely, and another might say it gave her confidence to take leadership roles because she got more attention. According to one woman who as an adult is self-reliant, confident, and independent, she wouldn't change her only childhood, but she admits there were compromises:

"When it's just one, you can be . . . sucked into your parents' lives and whatever they're dealing with," she said. "You're very focused on pleasing them."[4]

As a counselor, I am in favor of having more than one child if you have any choice at all. Only children are fated to become perfectionists. From what I see, we are moving more and more toward being a perfectionistic society. Many people are living life at a breakneck pace and biting off more than they can chew or cover as they are driven by their desire to be first, best, fastest, prettiest, and "have it all."

In my experience, when only children grow up and get married, they do not have only one child. They seem to sense instinctively that they missed something (someone?) while growing up, and they opt for at least two or three kids to make sure each of their children has the "brother or sister I didn't have."

Another problem that can occur is that out in society, particularly the school system, only children sometimes get a bad rap. They are considered uncooperative, self-centered, not able to blend in with the group, and the like. Undoubtedly, there are only children who fall into these classifications, but so do many children who have siblings. I have met and counseled a number of only children and have found them to be likable people—competent, loyal, and with a strong sense of responsibility.

If you do opt for an only child, be aware of the need for a good balance between love (getting all that attention) and limits. As soon as possible (from eighteen months on up), get your child in situations where he or she can play with other children and learn the fine art of "give and take." A preschool that emphasizes social adjustment and learning to get along with the other kids would be advisable, but don't start that until age three.

And whatever happens, do all you can to discourage your only child from becoming a driven perfectionist. Help your child see the difference between perfectionism and "doing the best you can."

Q: I read an article by Dr. Joyce Brothers who said that spanking erodes a child's self-esteem and resentment can build up between the parent and child. Do you agree?

A: I do not agree with Dr. Brothers. The permissiveness that reigns in America today in so many homes is what is really eroding self-esteem and relationships between parent and child. Responsible parents who, at certain times and under full control of their emotions, correct their children by spanking (not beating) are not eroding the child's self-image; I believe they are strengthening it because they are giving the child a loving lesson in reality.

I do agree that brutal, authoritarian use of spanking (which I call beating a child) can severely harm the child's self-image and lead to a poor relationship with the parent who does the beating.

We have all met teenagers and adults who "need a good spanking," but, of course, it's too late. If any spanking is to be done, it needs to be administered early. By early I don't mean before two years old. Spanking the child under two is rather pointless because the child doesn't comprehend what's going on. But from two years on up, to at least six or seven, spanking can be a helpful method, depending on the situation and who is doing the spanking.

I realize that Dr. Brothers and a large number of other psychologists, counselors, and child-rearing experts would draw a sharp breath at hearing "one of their own" advocate spanking. I have been on any number of talk show panels where I was the only one who was in favor of spanking, as long as certain definite guidelines are used.

As I said in Chapter Six, spanking is a last resort, not a first choice of discipline. The time to spank is when you and your child are eyeball to eyeball and he or she is saying, in so many words or actions: "No! I *won't* behave and *you* can't *make* me!" At this moment, the parent faces a choice! Communicate who is in charge or let the child believe he or she is in charge.

Second, when I say spank, I mean one or two swats on the bottom, administered with an open hand while in reasonable control of your emotions. I do not think spanking means taking a spoon, switch, paddle, belt, or "rod" of some kind and striking a child fifteen or twenty or more times—in other words, a good old-fashioned "whipping." Whipping is not even a good idea for horses or dogs, and it certainly doesn't make sense for children.

Spanking should be done by a parent who is capable of doing it correctly, not as a means of punishment but as a way of correcting the child and letting him know "Yes, I *can* make you because I am your parent and I am in loving authority over you."

Critics of spanking often point their finger at a misquoting of the Old Testament, "Spare the rod and spoil the child." There is no such wording in the Bible. What it does say is: "He who spares the rod hates his son, but he who loves him is careful to discipline him."[5] As I have pointed out in Chapter Two, I believe that when the biblical writers used the word "rod," they had correction and guidance in mind, not hitting and beating.

For example, the Bible is full of the imagery that pictures the Lord as our Shepherd. We are His sheep, and we need guidance. If you know anything about shepherding, you know that the shepherd uses a rod not to beat on his sheep but to guide them and even rescue them from danger. The Twenty-third Psalm, one of the most well-known pieces of literature in the world, clearly says, "Your rod and Thy staff they comfort me."[6]

I counsel a lot of people who don't really believe that. They have been raised under authoritarianism and they think God wants to wale on their heads and their bottoms at every wrong turn they make.

But all this begs the question. Joyce Brothers says even a "mild spanking," which is what I advocate, damages a child's self-esteem and the parent-child relationship. Yes, that could be true, if that's all the child got day after day. A swat or two sets limits, but those limits must be balanced by love. If you are using Reality Discipline at all, it should be seldom necessary to spank, but when you come to those times when a swat is necessary, sit down with your child immediately afterward. Just hold him or her close for a few moments. Tell the child how much you love him or her and then say, "I am very sorry. I don't like it when *we're* like this. I don't like to spank, but this time I had to. Now, let's go do something fun!"

Obviously, that kind of speech is for the younger child in the "preschool" range. For an older child of six, you could say, "I'm sorry, but you went too far. I want you to know that I love you very much and that's why I couldn't let you be irresponsible. But life's going to go on and let's go on together, okay?"

What you say is really not as important as your attitude. Before you spank, stop long enough to ask yourself three questions:

1. Is this a time for spanking or would some other method work as well or better?

2. Am I under control or am I really very tired, frustrated, and angry?

3. Am I giving this swat to nurture my child or to control and punish my child?

Your answer to that third question is the real answer as to whether a spanking damages a child's self-image or strengthens it.

Q: I am stepfather to a four-year-old. When trying to discipline my stepdaughter or even ask her to do simple things like take a bath, she will retort, "My mommy says I don't have to." How do I handle this?

A: You are facing the most common missile fired in stepparent families. The child is telling you, "You aren't my *real* parent and I don't have to listen to you."

Your best approach is to go get Mom and come back *together* Then *you* say, "Honey, it's bedtime. Mom and I want you to take your bath now."

If Mom wants to put in a word that she backs you up, that would be very much in order. But you should still keep your role of parent, even though you are a stepparent and not the "real" Daddy. Don't just bail out and just let her mother handle it.

You can never be the child's "Daddy," but you do need to be

her "father," and you and your wife must work together in raising the child.

Q: The other day my five-year-old took a Tootsie Pop from the grocery store and I didn't notice until we got to the car. I took her back in the store, made her apologize to the clerk, and then paid for the pop. Because I felt facing the clerk was punishment enough, I let her keep the Tootsie Pop and eat it on the way home. My husband says I should have thrown the Tootsie Pop away. Is he right?

A: Yes, your husband is definitely right. By letting the child keep the Tootsie Pop, you didn't do a thorough job of helping her learn from her mistake. She should have apologized for taking the pop and then, with your guidance, thrown it into a wastebasket, whether she had started licking it or not. Not only that, but if your child gets any kind of an allowance, she should be docked and made to pay you back out of that allowance.

Q: We are expecting our second child in about two months. My friends have been telling me about how first children get jealous when a second baby is born. Is there anything I can do to avoid this?

A: Before little baby brother or sister is born, prepare your first-born for the blessed event (which he may not see as so blessed). Say "You know something? In a few days, Mommy is going to the hospital and you are going to have a new little brother or sister. I think it would be a great idea if you would put your best toys up on the shelf so the baby won't be playing with them. You'll want to keep your favorite toys safe."

This kind of talk may not make much sense to adults who believe they need to teach children to share, not be "selfish." But the remark makes perfectly good sense to a three-year-old. Then, to balance things off, say "You know, honey, you have some toys you are getting just too big to play with anymore. Maybe you'd like to give one to Baby."

While it's true little children can be selfish and possessive, it's also very true that they like to give. In addition, they want to please their parents, and I'm sure your firstborn can find a toy that he wants to give to new little baby brother or sister.

After "the Thing" (from your firstborn's perspective) comes home from the hospital, get him positively involved with his new brother or sister so he won't feel there has been some tremendous intrusion on his "turf." Let your firstborn help with the baby as much as possible. Beware of the natural tendency to tell your firstborn, "Careful, don't touch the baby." As soon as little firstborn sees "the Thing" is labeled "hands off," the battle lines will be drawn. Instead, involve your firstborn in helping with baby in every way he can. For example, let him go and get a new diaper and even help change the baby if he's at all capable. By "capable" I mean at least he gets the diaper on the lower part of the baby's body. If the diaper is covering the baby's face, you might have to point out, "Wait a minute, honey, I think your aim is a little high."

Seriously, respect your firstborn's efforts. Redo what he does only if necessary (and when he's not there, if at all possible). Another thing you can do after baby comes home is sit down with your firstborn and tell him how big and strong and capable he is in comparison to the baby. Let him know how important he is as you tell him what babies are like: "You know, you take one nap a day, but baby needs to take six naps a day. [Hold up six fingers.] You're so big and strong and take care of yourself so well. You are Mommy's best helper."

Another tip is, when you are holding or nursing the new baby, *never* turn down the firstborn if he wants to sit on your lap. It can get pretty crowded, but he wants to know that he still has access to you. So let him climb up, give him a hug, and he will be assured that you still love him. He won't want to stay long and will get off your lap on his own accord.

The important thing to a firstborn when a secondborn invades his life and his territory is to go out of your way to make the firstborn feel accepted, that he belongs, and that he is capable (the A-B-C's of self-image). Read Chapter Seven again with this question in mind.

Q: Our baby, who is now three months, has been a crier since birth. We are both hollow-eyed with lack of sleep and near the ends of our respective ropes. Any suggestions?

A: An obvious guess is that your baby has colic (continuing stomach problems), and for colic there are no easy answers. Hannah, our fourthborn surprise package, arrived when we were both in our forties, and for six months all her waking hours were spent crying. Sande and I took turns walking her through the night and we somehow got through it. At six months Hannah's crying suddenly stopped and after that we had no problems. In fact, at age two and three when it was time for a nap, she would come and get us, take us by the hand, and say "Tired now," and then go down for her nap.

Something like colic is physiological and should not be confused with an infant crying for attention. If you have checked to be sure baby isn't hungry, isn't being stuck by a pin, isn't needing a diaper change, or all the other obvious things that might make a baby cry, then you have to analyze if you may be jumping too quickly when she lets out the faintest yelp. In other words, watch for extremes in how you respond to baby's crying. If you do, the baby will eventually learn that crying gets attention and will keep you needlessly running back and forth.

The basic principle applies: balance and good judgment. Obviously, a newborn baby needs more comforting than an older infant. Sometimes waiting the baby out five minutes or so will result in a baby falling back to sleep and even learning to sleep through the night.

Q: What is your opinion of playpens? My eighteen-month-old daughter is extremely mobile and she gives me not a moment's rest or peace. Some days I can't get anything done. I have a good friend who says playpens are "medieval." What do you think?

A: Playpens are not medieval. They are very modern and extremely useful. I've known of cases where a playpen has saved some mothers from going totally bonkers. In other cases, playpens have saved babies' lives. They are extremely safe places to put baby, particularly when you're cleaning, fixing dinner, answering the phone or doorbell, and just can't give him or her attention every second.

Obviously, the use of a playpen can be abused, which means you are abusing your baby. A playpen isn't an answer for all day or even several hours a day. It is an answer when at certain times you need to be handling other things and can't give full attention to your child.

Q: My daughter's third birthday is coming up and I'm planning her first full-fledged party, complete with several little guests, decorations, games, the whole works. What is your counsel (besides having lots of aspirin ready)?

A: You don't need aspirin, you just need a good plan, and one of the best suggestions I've found comes from Melanie Kirschner, who works for a toy company in New York City. Her ideas include:

1. *Plan the festivities with your child.* Keep in mind that the party is your child's and involve her in the decision making. Even a three-year-old can help choose the theme, make up the guest list, and send the invitations.

2. *Have the party at home, if possible.* It'll be more personal.

3. *Make it age-appropriate.* Children aged three and a half and older have fun mingling with friends. But before this age, kids lack the language and social skills to enjoy a party.

4. *Keep the guest list small.* Invite as many guests as the age of your child. But if the entire preschool class must come, don't panic. A few more guests can be accommodated easily, as long as you have enough help.

5. *Make it short.* Allow no more than two hours for a preschool party that includes lunch.

6. *Spend moderately.* A great party needn't be expensive.

7. *Enlist help.* A good ratio is one adult (besides you) for every five children.

8. *Plan ahead.* Relieve the pressure by giving yourself a few weeks to plan the party.

9. *Prepare for the unexpected.* If you're having an outdoor party, for example, decide what you'll do if it happens to rain.

10. *Develop a schedule of events.* Map out the beginning, middle, and end of the party, making sure you have more than enough activities to fill the time allotted. Start with a quiet arrival activity. When the guests have assembled, begin the main events. (Alternate between quiet and boisterous games and deemphasize winning and losing.) Wind down with food and a quiet game. Distribute the favors as the final treat.[7]

Q: **I thought I had my three-year-old fully potty trained (he didn't really learn until he was almost three), but lately he's been coming in the house from play with wet pants. He tells me he "forgets" to come in and go to the bathroom. I've tried spanking him and making him stay in his room, but he still continues to "forget." Any ideas?**

A: I have a standard answer for this type of problem. Tell your son that he gets one dry pair of underwear and pants a day. If he gets them wet, he comes into the house, takes off his soiled clothes, puts on his pajamas or bathrobe, and his day of play comes to an end. My guess is that having to spend one day, possibly two, indoors when he could be out playing should do a great deal for his memory.

TIPS FOR TEACHING RESPONSIBILITY

Parents are usually all for having children "be responsible." They often wonder, however, what assignments they can give children to teach responsibility. Following is a list of responsibilities that small children can do in the home. Go over the list and decide what might work with your child.

Some of the suggested assignments may seem fairly formidable for someone as young as two and three years old. Get together a list and talk with with your child. Have the child pick the jobs he or she wants to do. Three or four tasks will be enough to start. Be sure the child never has to do more than one chore at a time. (That is, don't make a child do several things right in a row.) Emphasize that once the child accepts a responsibility, he or she is, indeed, responsible to do it. This isn't something the child can do "when he or she feels like it."

Home Responsibilities for Two- to Three-Year-Olds

1. Pick up unused toys and put in the proper place.

2. Put books and magazines in a rack.

3. Sweep the floor.

4. Empty ashtrays.

5. Place napkins, plates, and silverware on the table. The silver is on but not correctly at first.

6. Clean up what they drop after eating.

7. Select from a choice of two breakfast foods. Learn to make simple decisions.

8. Clear own place at the table. Put the dishes on the counter after cleaning the leftovers off the plate.

9. Toilet training.

10. Simple hygiene—brush teeth, wash and dry hands and face, and brush hair.

11. Undress self—dresses with some help.

12. Wipe up own accidents.

13. Carry boxed or canned goods from the grocery sacks to the proper shelf. Put some things away on a lower shelf.

Home Responsibilities for Four-Year-Olds

1. Set the table—with good dishes too.

2. Put the groceries away.

3. Help with grocery shopping and compile a grocery list.

4. Polish shoes and clean up afterward.

5. Follow a schedule for feeding pets.

6. Help do yard and garden work.

7. Help make the beds and vacuum.

8. Help do the dishes or fill the dishwasher.

9. Dust the furniture.

10. Spread butter on sandwiches.

11. Prepare cold cereal.

12. Help parent prepare plates of food for the family dinner.

13. Make a simple dessert (add topping to cupcakes, Jell-O, pour the toppings on ice cream).

14. Hold the hand mixer to whip potatoes or mix up a cake.

15. Share toys with friends. (Practice courtesy.)

16. Get the mail.

17. Tell parent whereabouts before going out to play.

18. Able to play without constant adult supervision and attention.

Home Responsibilities for Five-Year-Olds

1. Help with the meal planning and grocery shopping.

2. Make own sandwich or simple breakfast. Then clean up.

3. Pour own drink.

4. Prepare the dinner table.

5. Tear up lettuce for the salad.

6. Put certain ingredients into a recipe.

7. Make bed and clean room.

8. Dress on own and choose outfit for the day.

9. Scrub the sink, toilet, and bathtub.

10. Clean mirrors and windows.

11. Separate clothing for washing. Put white clothes in one pile and colored in another.

12. Fold clean clothes and put them away.

13. Answer the telephone and begin to dial the phone for use.

14. Yard work.

15. Pay for small purchases.

16. Help clean out the car.

17. Take out the garbage.

18. Decide how to spend his or her share of the family entertainment fund.

19. Feed pets and clean their living area.

20. Learn to tie shoes.[8]

If a child fails to complete any assigned responsibilities, you need to use Reality Discipline to follow through with what you've been trying to do in the first place—teach responsibility. In most cases, the consequence for failing to carry out a responsibility would be withdrawal of privileges, of something a child really likes to do.

Chapter Ten

STRENGTHENING THE IMAGE

■

Questions and Answers:
Parenting Ages Six to Twelve

If the preschool years are the "wonder years," the next stage, ages six to twelve, are the "blunder years." Now children get out into life in earnest and start learning at new levels what trial and error is all about, especially error. Kids can get into the darndest situations. One of the most memorable in my files concerned an eleven-year-old boy who mistakenly walked into the girls' rest room at school. Immediately he noticed he was considerably outnumbered by the female gender and he asked incredulously, "What are *you* doing in here?"

Almost as a chorus, several eleven-year-old girls replied, *"What are you doing in here?"*

And then the boy noticed something else: There were no urinals on the wall in their usual place. In one horrible moment he realized his error. Like a flash, he bolted out the door, the titters of the girls ringing in his ears, and he kept right on going —straight home.

"I'm *never* going back to that school—*ever!*" he told his mother. And he didn't. He was so embarrassed that he could not even think about facing the teasing and razzing that would have awaited him when he returned.

I heard this story from the boy's parents, who came to me for advice when he absolutely refused to go back to school. We talked for a while and they decided that the best thing to do was to honor his feelings and let him transfer to another school. I believe they made the right decision and saved his tender self-image from taking a severe beating.

THE CEMENT ISN'T COMPLETELY HARD—YET

In Chapter Nine I described infants to five-year-olds as "wet cement" who are easily formed, shaped, and influenced. By age five, most of the child's personality and life-style are developed. By age seven I said, "It's all over." That's true for the most part, but I'd like to modify that a bit and say "*Nearly* all over." The cement is beginning to set, yes, but it can still be moved around quite a bit. This is the time for strengthening the child's self-image, helping him or her cope with an ever-widening world that is not just challenging; it can be intimidating and sometimes mean and painful.

There is much to be done by parents during this important span, when the young child grows into the preadolescent. The game is a long way from over; in fact, it's just getting interesting! Now the little person your child has become starts to interact with the world in earnest. The good and the bad (unfortunate terms) come out. I prefer to say the life-style—how the child demonstrates his or her perceptions and personal values—comes out. Children have decided that they have real significance only when they act in a certain basic way. Perhaps they have become budding controllers, potential pleasers, or maybe they are little comedians who need lots of attention.

Adlerian counselors believe that human beings develop a certain life-style based on certain flaws in logic. Very early on children may start telling themselves they're inadequate ("I'm helpless"). The children may even disparage themselves, saying "I'm no good, I can't do it, I'm hopeless."

They may get very pessimistic about their environment—where they have to do their living—and start telling themselves "This place is dangerous" or they might start saying "The world owes me a living."

And another flaw in logic that can develop very early is "I can't trust anyone, and unless people do exactly as I want, they're not being fair to me." Or, perhaps—which is very characteristic of babies of the family—children start telling themselves, "People are really here to serve me—I can get them to do what I want."

From these flaws in logic come certain life-styles. In truth, every individual who ever lived has his or her own "unique" life-style true only to him or to her. But there are several "general life-styles" that many people pick up to one degree or another. I call it "I count only when . . ." And some of these general life-styles include:

"I count only when I get approval."

"I count only when I'm in complete control—running the show."

"I count only if I'm superior—if I'm right and others are wrong."

"I count only when I'm taken care of by others."

"I count only when I'm used, put down, or abused." (This attitude can lead toward the child playing the role of the victim and, when it gets serious, the martyr.)

These are the years when the flaws in logic that have been part of children's thinking practically since birth begin to blossom into behavior problems. The great portion of my counseling of children has been done at the six-to-twelve level, followed closely by teenagers.

"DOCTOR, I'M NOT SURE THIS IS REALLY MY CHILD"

By the time parents bring a child to me, they believe the situation is serious, and it often is. These parents aren't just puzzled or frustrated by their child. They're wondering if they will survive! Perhaps their child has had some kind of behavior problem for quite a while. They may have asked the family pediatrician what was wrong. Some are sincerely wondering if their baby could have gotten switched with someone else's. This can't be *their* child, can it?

"Oh, I wouldn't worry," drones the good doctor. "Children usually grow out of this kind of thing."

The fact is, sometimes they do and sometimes they don't. As Don Dinkmeyer writes: "Unfortunately, there is now much evidence indicating that the child who is bad-tempered, nervous or uncooperative doesn't necessary 'grow out of the stage.' Instead, we find that behavior is patterned and predictable and that the child truly is 'father of the man.' "[1] And, I might add, mother of the woman.

The following questions and answers are keyed on some typical behavior problems facing parents and their children between the ages of six and twelve. As in Chapter Nine, my goal is to focus on how to help you build your child's self-image. As I say above, we want to strengthen the self-image of elementary-age youngsters, because these are the years when they discover just how competitive the world can be and how hard it is to please everyone.

Admittedly, they do make blunders as they explore, test, and experiment. Yes, they were exploring, testing, and experimenting when they were younger—back in those preschool years—but now they have the wherewithal and ability to range much farther afield. Now they can cross the street, go down the block, or even across town (if you are one of the fortunate few who still live in a small community). And now they have a vocabulary that can get them into all kinds of interesting predicaments.

Of course, ages six through twelve aren't all blunders; your child may be taking life in stride, getting good grades, and enjoying popularity among his or her peer group. If so, I offer my congratulations, but along with that, a caution. Every child at this level needs strengthening of his or her self-image, if not to cope with what life is throwing at him or her now, certainly to prepare for the onslaught of adolescence where, for many children, the bottom falls out. We'll be looking more closely at that in Chapter Eleven.

Right now, however, let's look at some typical problems kids at this level have and how to solve them. As I said in Chapter Nine, all of my solutions may not fit you and your children, but it's my hope you'll pick up plenty of ideas for strengthening and developing the psychological muscles in that tender precious self-image that children must carry the rest of their lives.

Q: We have a ten-year-old son who at times nearly drives me insane. This year we have already received four notes from the school principal for his: (1) making noises in class, (2) sliding down the banister, (3) verbally fighting with another student, (4) disrupting the school bus. I've tried all different kinds of discipline, but he is very strong-willed and nothing seems to work. Example: We have three trees in our yard and he's climbing one. I tell him not to climb that tree, and the next day he is in one of the *other* trees. His reply: "You told me not to climb *that* one," as he points to the tree he was climbing yesterday. He is the youngest of three boys. His older brothers are thirteen and fifteen, and they have been easy compared to our youngest. What went wrong?

A: This question hits close to home—all the way back to my childhood home, where I was the youngest of three children. I had an older sister who was almost perfect and an older brother who wasn't that far behind her. Sally got straight A's, was on the cheerleading squad, and was one of the most popular girls in her school. Jack got A's and B's, was quarterback of the football team, and also Prince Charming at the junior prom. The only route left for me (or so I told myself) was to go in another direction, so I specialized in being the best of the worst. My mother also got many notes similar to the ones you got recently.

One thing you might check on is if you have been raising your son on reward and punishment. In other words, reward and punishment have been your two basic means of controlling his behavior. The reason I say this is his clever way of "getting around the rules." Children raised on reward and punishment are masters at this. Tell a child "Don't drive that cement truck over the cliff," and the child will back it over or push it over instead. He will always find a way to "beat the system."

Another thing to consider is that you obviously have a very powerful ten-year-old. That reflects the strong possibility that you and your mate have been too powerful with your child. He is simply giving back to you what he has seen you model and use on him.

My suggestion is not to be so prescriptive in your rule-making. In fact, you might try making your son part of the rule-making process in your home. In other words, try being a little more democratic. This does not mean you give up your authority, you simply use it differently. For example, suppose your son requests permission to sleep over at his friend's house. You remember the last time he did this he started roughhousing and broke a very expensive vase. Rather than just giving him a yes or a no, say, "Well, why don't you think about this and tomorrow night at dinner you can tell us how you see this sleepover going. What do you want to take with you and what kind of rules will you set for yourself? Then we will talk about it."

If your son doesn't come up with much by the way of rules or goals for good behavior, simply tell him he can't go. If he demands to know why, tell him gently he hasn't developed his thinking enough. He doesn't seem to have the ability to decide how he will control himself and be responsible. Say "Before going to someone else's home, you need to think through—*How will I act? What will I say?* That's what being responsible is all about."

On the other hand, he may come up with an impressive list of rules that he plans to obey and how he intends to behave while he is at his friend's home overnight. It is at this point that you can develop some logical consequences—with his help, of course.

What will be the results if he does not obey his own rules? You can work out several "logical possibilities": If he gets into more trouble, he will not be able to go back to his friend's house on an overnight for an extended period of time. If anything gets broken or damaged, he will pay for it out of his own allowance. Not only can he not go back to his friend's house, but other things he enjoys (you can determine this yourself because you know your own son and each child has his or her own preferences) will be off limits for a stipulated length of time.

The idea behind Reality Discipline is to stay out of power struggles, which give a child undo attention. Instead, give your son some *responsibility* and let him try to handle it. If he can't, let logical consequences, which really hit him where it hurts, take over. Stop putting yourself in the position where you have to be the judge and jury of everything. Put responsibility on your son's shoulders.

Q: We have two boys, ages seven and eight. Whenever the younger becomes interested in what the older is doing, the older drops it and seems to just give up. This applies to all areas: reading, sports—even Nintendo. What can we do to en-

courage our eight-year-old? Shall we limit the seven-year-old in any way?

A: This is a common situation with children who are just a year apart. Your eight-year-old obviously "hears the footsteps" of his little brother. One of the reasons your eight-year-old is having problems in life is that he is spending too much time looking over his shoulder and not enough time looking forward to where he wants to go.

One thing you can try is treating the boys differently. This is particularly important to your eight-year-old's self-image. Give them different bedtimes, different allowances, and different responsibilities. Obviously, the eight-year-old should get to go to bed later. He should get a little more money in his allowance, and he should get responsibilities that are a little more demanding or "glamorous."

Also, keep them out of competitive situations. Try not to encourage them to go head-to-head. What your firstborn's behavior is really saying is this: "I'm afraid that my little brother is going to catch up to me and surpass me. And that is so frightening for me to think about that I would rather give up and go find another area where maybe he will leave me alone and not challenge me." The trouble is, little brother will always go find big brother and "challenge" him unless you move in to try to set up some boundaries and some firm guidance.

Q: My daughter, age seven and a half, dawdles every morning before school. I am constantly having to urge her to get up, get dressed, and I'm always having to remind her of the time. What would be good Reality Discipline for this behavior?

A: Take one of two routes: (1) Get her her own alarm clock and let her be responsible for setting it and getting herself up in the morning and ready for school. If she fails to do so, she faces several possible consequences for being irresponsible: She might miss breakfast, she might not look as nice as she normally does going out the door. Or she just might miss the bus and wind up late for school. One way to be sure she is late is to tell her you simply can't leave right now to drive her to school, you will be able to leave later when it's convenient and fits in with errands that you plan to do.

Your second approach is essentially the same but not quite as expensive. Instead of buying her an alarm clock, tell her that you will call her once in the morning and, after being assured that she has heard you and is awake, you will not call her again or remind her again of anything. She will be responsible to get ready, be on time for breakfast, then be out the door for the school bus.

With either approach, you get yourself out of the role of being your child's keeper. As long as you allow your child to dawdle and have you remind her of her responsibilities, she is in control in making you do things that are unnecessary. Instead, give her responsibility then back off and let her see what she can do. She may have to be late for school for a few mornings, but so be it. Write her no excuse notes. Let the school know by phone what you are trying to do and I'm sure they will cooperate. Being late is not the end of the world. The school will deal with that problem. I might add, having to explain to the teacher and possibly the principal why she is late will be the clincher in changing your daughter's behavior.

I have had to use this similar Reality Discipline strategy with all three of my older children at one time or another. The latest has been our son, Kevin, who, while in seventh grade, failed to get up on time and then wanted a note from me, explaining "Dad, I've got to bring a note of some kind or they won't let me in school."

"Okay," I said, "I'll write you a note. (I didn't say anything about an excuse.) The note read: "Kevin is late because he stayed in bed too long. He made himself late."

Kevin wasn't too happy with what my note said, but at least

it got him back into school where he had to deal with the discipline they handed out. As I recall, it was the last time he was "up late" for school that year.

Q: My nine-year-old daughter is jealous of her six-year-old sister who, frankly, is much prettier than she was at that age. Is being jealous a sign of low self-esteem? How can we help my daughter deal with her jealousy problem?

A: Jealousy is a sign of competition between children. And, yes, it is also a sign of a low self-image. I am quite sure the jealousy (that is, sibling rivalry) started much earlier in various ways.

A few years ago, Sande and I were looking at some videos made from old "Super Eight" movies of our children taken when Holly was three and a half and Krissy was eighteen months. It had been years since I had manned the camera as Sande had held Krissy on her lap while Holly stood next to them. We were amazed to see—for what seemed like the first time—that, while everybody kept smiling into the camera, every few seconds Holly would give Krissy a shot in the head or the face with her elbow. Krissy never cried, she kept on smiling with everyone else, and for some strange reason I was so busy taking the pictures I never noticed. But seeing it up there on the screen was a reminder that sibling rivalry has had its moments in our family, just as it does in most families.

In this case, one thing you can try is not giving the six-year-old so much attention. Instead, try to give your nine-year-old daughter compliments and attention that she is probably not getting at this time.

For example, have special one-on-one and even two-on-two dates with your nine-year-old. (If Dad takes her out alone, that could really be impressive.) Also try giving her special privileges in line with her age, for example, a larger allowance than her sister. Do all you can to make something of her oldest child's position in the family.

I know some parents might think that this might be unfair to the younger child because they believe every child should be "treated the same." My motto is "Treat each child differently according to need." I'm not saying to neglect your six-year-old; I'm only saying that you should make an effort to treat your nine-year-old in ways that will help her know she is totally accepted, that she definitely belongs, and that she is important.

In every way you can, teach your older daughter that she doesn't have to "measure up" or be prettier, smarter, faster, and so on, than everybody else in order to get your approval. She can just be herself. She needs to know that you love her just as she is, unconditionally. (See Chapter One.)

Q: How do you motivate a child to do what has been asked of him in a timely and cooperative way? Our six-year-old boy is unwilling to follow through on the simplest assignments or chores. What can we do?

A: The general rule is that you ask your child once and, if the child fails to fulfill responsibilities, follow through with discipline (not punishment). According to the Gesell Institute of Human Development, words to describe the typical six-year-old are *paradoxical* and *bipolarity.* In other words, your six-year-old may decide to do one thing one moment and then do the opposite the next. It's not surprising that your son doesn't want to cooperate. Right now, that's his nature.

I suggest that you go slow with your son and give him small goals that he can reach successfully. If he still refuses to do even the simplest chores, tell him that this means he will lose privileges that he really enjoys. Tell him that the rule at your house is "We work first, then we play." When he does get something done, encourage him and let him know how pleased you are. (See Chapter Seven.)

Make your own mental list of things that are important to your six-year-old—things that he really likes to do, places he really likes to go. Don't, however, hold these over his head by saying "Unless you do your chores, you'll not be able to do [whatever]." Give your son responsibilities and simply tell him you expect them to be done. If he fails to follow through, then let the natural or logical consequences result in a loss of privileges.

When using Reality Discipline, remember Principle #4: Use action, not words. Do no threatening, nagging, lecturing, or preaching. Simply take action and let your child learn from experience, which is a far more effective teacher than all the nagging and lecturing in the world.

Q: My seven-year-old daughter is very strong-willed and misbehaves often. After receiving a spanking, she will hit back and still refuses to behave. We have sent her to sit in her room, but that still doesn't resolve into good behavior. What now?

A: You and your husband are in a classic power struggle with your daughter. Here are some things you can try to avoid the power struggle and give your daughter a new outlook on what it means to behave.

1. Avoid spanking, which isn't having its desired effect. Spanking your daughter is only prompting more powerful behavior on her part.

2. Remember, a powerful child means powerful parents. Frankly, it sounds as if your daughter is being brought up by powerful authoritarian parents who are telling her "It's our way or the highway." Your daughter is learning to be powerful from you and she is fighting back. Her behavior is telling you "I'm not going to be everything you want me to be."

3. When your daughter misbehaves, let her experience the

reality of her decisions by withdrawing privileges she truly treasures and values. You will have to decide what those privileges are, but when you withdraw them, you must be careful not to make it sound like a punishment. Don't say "Because you misbehaved, you can't go to dance class" and so on. Instead, put it this way: "Privileges are granted when we fulfill our responsibilities. Because you aren't being responsible, that tells me you aren't ready to be granted privileges, and that's why you can't go to dance class."

Then stick to your guns and don't give in when your daughter protests that you're unfair and mean.

Q: My eleven-year-old son has been in at least ten fights at school during the past year. In the most recent one, he severely hurt the other boy with a punch in the face, and his mother filed assault charges. My son faces a juvenile court hearing. (The police tell me they really want to "scare him.") Is this what he really needs? We are still waiting for the letter telling us the date for my son's appearance in court.

A: It sounds as if you really don't have any choice. Your son is going to have to appear in court and face the music. Before I give some suggestions for how to help him do this, I want to observe that it sounds as if you are a single mother, or your son's father is too busy or preoccupied and is practically nonexistent in the boy's life. Your son obviously needs some male influence in order to work off his energy and hostility. The fact that he sees himself as a fighter tells me clearly that he believes life has kicked him squarely in the teeth, and, therefore, he has a right to strike back at other people. His life-style slogan is "I count only when I stand up for my rights and show people who's boss."

I suggest that you get in touch with the juvenile authorities and let them know that you want to cooperate fully in helping your son learn an important lesson. If possible, at the juvenile hearing, you should be there but try to stay in the background. Do not stand at your son's side while he faces the judge. This will preclude your speaking for him or trying to "explain" what happened. Your son is there because of his own behavior. He is the one who hit another boy in the face, and he is the one who must face the music. In my experience, juvenile judges are usually talented and insightful people who want to help youngsters, not punish them. Some straight talk from a good judge will undoubtedly help your son.

After the court hearing, on the way home, reassure your son that you love him very much. Let him know that you felt he had to face the consequences of what he had done and, while you stayed in the back, you were pulling for him all the way. If possible say something like "As we sat in the back, we wondered how you would handle yourself. Dad and I both agree that you handled yourself very well."

Once the court hearing is behind you, work with your son to help him develop a different self-image—one in which he doesn't see himself as a fighter and a hurter of others. Sit down with him and make a list of things that he is good at or some attributes that he sees in himself. Encourage him in these areas and he may decide fighting isn't worth all that trouble.

Also, as I have already suggested, get some adult male influence into his life. If his father is not living in the home or refuses to take his responsibility to be a real dad to his son, try to find a relative or a good friend—perhaps a teacher or coach at school—who will help.

Q: I have an eight-year-old stepson from my husband's previous marriage and he spends every other weekend with us. The boy is not particularly well behaved, but every time he misbehaves his dad backs down from giving him any real discipline. At the last minute he makes an excuse and lets Jacob walk away. I'm sure my husband is feeling guilty because of his failed first marriage, but he is not helping his son by allowing him to get away with bad behavior. What can I say to my husband that might help?

A: First, you might want to consider going into counseling because you have pinpointed your husband's problem. He is running on guilt. Keep in mind that guilt is the propelling force for most of the bad decisions in life. As you say, however, your husband is not helping his son by bailing him out every time he gets in trouble. It is the responsibility of the parents to hold a child accountable.

If it seems appropriate, sit down and talk with your husband about his attitude toward his son. Emphasize that you are not angry or judgmental, but you are very concerned about what you see. (If the boy is giving you a bad time with his misbehavior, you might want to share that with your husband.) You don't want to be a "wicked stepmother" but you do need some better guidelines for how Jacob can be disciplined while he stays with you.

Another thing you can do is watch for occasions when your husband does try to discipline Jacob. Comment on how well he handles it, even if he doesn't do as much as you had hoped for. Your husband needs encouragement so he can learn how to stick to his guns and give Jacob the discipline he needs to develop a good self-image.

Q: **Our eight-year-old son is a blend of discipline difficulties. He has a short fuse, several allergies, and pain due to related illnesses. When he is feeling well, standard discipline techniques work fine, but when his allergies are acting up and he is in pain, nothing seems to be adequate. What can we do?**

A: You obviously have an unusual situation, and there is no simple answer. Your child's health considerations are paramount and you must work around them, but at the same time you must try not to let the child use his health problems to make power plays.

I suggest that you be as consistent with your son as you possibly can, whether he is feeling good or lousy. If you say you are going to do something, follow through with it. If he flatly disobeys you (breaks a rule, refuses to comply with a simple request, and so on), he deserves consequences whether he is feeling sick or not. Try to let him know that you love him very much and are very concerned over his health, but you won't allow him to misbehave and use poor health as an excuse.

One more thing: When he is not feeling well, it makes all kinds of sense for you to be extremely low-key and not to overreact to things he might say or do. Also, if he's sick, keep your requests at a minimum. If he feels you are making demands on him, he will just refuse to obey because, "I'm sick." In other words, expect a good attitude, but don't expect him to do his chores with much enthusiasm until he feels better.

Q: All three of our children who are nine, seven, and three, are picky eaters. I made the mistake of usually fixing something each child likes. A lot of times I'm fixing three different things for the children and something else for my husband and myself. I've tried Reality Discipline and they just go without eating. What should I do?

A: Have you considered applying at Denny's restaurants as a short-order cook? Keep in mind your children were not born picky eaters. You are aware that you taught them to be picky, and now you must train them to eat what you decide to fix. Fixing three different meals for the three children, plus another meal for your husband and yourself, is ridiculous. You have to put order back in your home, and here is how to do it.

Don't just "try" Reality Discipline; *practice it until you get results*. Decide together with your husband that you will tell the children that you are fixing one dinner at night and that is *it*. If they don't want to eat it, they don't have to. But they eat nothing else until breakfast. Here is where it gets tough—sticking to your guns and refusing to give them snacks when they start wailing for something around seven-thirty or eight o'clock. Smile and say good-humoredly, "I'll bet you are hungry. Could it have anything to do with not eating your dinner? I'll fix you a good breakfast in the morning." I would think that one to three nights of being hungry would take care of the problem. Also, limit any afternoon snacks so they will be hungrier at dinnertime.

You must be strong and stick to your guns or Reality Discipline will not work. It is up to you.

Q: We have a little firstborn "Buford" (age nine) who always has an excuse or protest when he's being corrected. He never says "Okay," or "I'm sorry." He blames his brother or sister or gives us some reason why he's entitled to do the behavior he's being corrected for. How can we fix him?

A: "Buford" doesn't sound broken quite yet, but he does need a little fixing. Your best adjustment is to refuse to accept his cop-out attitude. Let him know that whenever he misbehaves, the problem isn't settled until he comes forward and acknowledges his part in it. For example, suppose he takes something from his brother's room and gets in trouble for it. Then suppose he says, "Yes, you found it in my pocket but I didn't put it there. Somebody else put it there. It is somebody else's fault."

Simply say to your son, "Honey, you can put it any way you want, but we don't happen to buy your explanation. Until we hear the truth, you are not going anywhere or doing anything."

Then make your promise stick. Buford doesn't get to play

soccer. He doesn't get to watch TV. He doesn't even get to go to Cub Scouts or church youth group. Nothing is sacred. Whatever he really likes should be prohibited until he comes clean with a true confession and a proper apology. Only then will the case be closed. If you do this just a few times, you certainly should get his attention and his behavior should improve.

Q: What can I do with my ten-year-old son? He is downright disrespectful of my initial commands. He makes faces at me or pretends he doesn't hear me and walks away.

A: Your son is exhibiting extremely powerful behavior. It sounds as if you have been very permissive and now you are reaping his disrespect. You have to start being firm but fair and also diplomatic. Don't give orders or commands; make requests and assignments. Obviously he will test you to see if you "really mean it."

You can't let him walk away or pretend he doesn't hear you. If necessary, follow him to his room and tell him that you realize he is acting "real cool" pretending he doesn't hear you, but you know that he has. Calmly but firmly repeat your request and tell him that you expect it to be done. Then leave him alone to decide what he wants to do about his responsibilities. Do not give him any deadlines or threaten him with any penalties if the work is not done. This simply puts you back in the realm of reward and punishment.

Later, if he has still refused to do what you asked, the consequences come naturally and logically when he asks to be driven to soccer practice or when he wants to do anything else he really likes. Say gently but firmly, "You did not do what I asked and that means you're not going to be able to do what you'd like to do. The rule in our house is 'We all pitch in and work together'— then we play or do things that are fun."

Q: My eleven-year-old daughter is strong-willed and constantly clashes with my husband, who is her stepfather and rather strict. To complicate matters, she is influenced strongly by her easygoing natural father, whom she sees several weekends a month. How can I get my daughter to obey our household rules and get along with her stepdad better? They are at odds most of the time.

A: Stepparenting is never a simple proposition. Your second husband sounds authoritarian in his parenting style, and your first husband, the girl's natural father, appears to be permissive, or at least a lot more flexible.

Talk with your husband about ways he can "lighten up" a little with the household rules. Tell him neither one of you has to let your daughter do as she pleases, but as long as powerful behavior is used on her, she will respond with powerful behavior of her own. That is why your husband and your daughter are at odds most of the time.

Another possibility is to work together as a family and invite your daughter into the rule-making process. For example, she undoubtedly has friends and they all like to go places and do things together. What does she suggest about where she can go and what time she should be back? Get a dialogue going with her and you may be surprised at the responsibilities she will take upon herself, *as long as she believes she is getting to make a choice.*

But, above all, your husband must learn to back off and not be so authoritarian in his approach. No suggestions will work so long as his attitude suggests "Listen, kid, I may be your stepfather, but I'm still in charge in this house and you'll do as I say as long as you live under my roof." If she senses that is how he really feels, you will continue to have problems.

Q: We have three boys and one girl. Our eight-year-old secondborn son has a strong need for approval and acceptance from his eleven-year-old firstborn brother, who constantly belittles him. By contrast, our eleven-year-old is nice to the two younger children, who are five and two and a half. How can we get our firstborn to show a more loving attitude toward our secondborn? The secondborn boy is beginning to show signs of frustration and anger toward his big brother.

A: It sounds as if you have a classic situation of a firstborn who hears his younger brother's footsteps and a secondborn middle child who is feeling squeezed and is beginning to wonder why big brother had to be born in the first place.

It may not solve your problem, but it's good to know that this situation is quite normal. In another book I tell of the time my older brother, Jack, who is my senior by five years, tried to lose me in the woods when we were kids. He wanted to go off with his buddy to the woods, and my mother told him he could go only if he took his little brother along with him. Well, what would any self-respecting sixteen-year-old do? He tried to lose his eleven-year-old brother in the woods, and he succeeded. Fortunately, I found my own way back.

There is nothing magical you can do to get your firstborn to accept your secondborn, but here are some suggestions:

1. Be sure to treat all the children differently. Be sure the oldest boy has privileges reserved only for the firstborn—he gets to go to bed later than anyone else, he gets to do things on his own that others can't, and so on. This will help him feel more secure about his younger brother, and if he doesn't feel as threatened, he may relax and treat him a little better.

2. As much as possible, keep the two boys out of competitive situations. This is particularly advisable if the eight-year-old shows signs of being more skilled (athletically, for example) than the eleven-year-old. Do all you can to bolster the eleven-year-old's self-image and always assure him that you love him very much and that his position as the oldest is secure. At the same time, help the eight-year-old not to feel so squeezed.

3. When the opportunity presents itself, talk separately with your eleven-year-old and eight-year-old and just sit back and listen for feelings. There might be a lot going on between the boys that you are unaware of. (See Chapter Eight for ideas on active listening.)

Q: Our firstborn son is nine, and he has developed the idea that I love his younger brother more than I love him. I try to explain that he had the same "quality time" when he was his brother's age, but now my time with him has to be worked out differently. Any suggestions?

A: I am curious about what you mean when you say that when your older son was your younger son's age you had the same "quality time" with him that you're having with the younger boy now. Apparently you feel the younger boy has certain needs that take more time. Naturally enough, your older son feels that his younger brother is getting a lot more attention than he is right now. He is pulling your chain and accusing you of being "unfair." You are probably responding to these charges of "you love Hershel more than me" by saying things like "Honey, why would you say that? You know Mommy loves you so much."

It would be more helpful to try to put your son's feelings into words. Say something like "I'm sorry you feel that way. You believe we spend more time with Hershel than we do with you. You know you are very special to me. You are my one and only Ralphie and there is nobody that could ever take your place. Nobody has your way of saying things and your smile. I'm so glad you're my son."

This approach gets you away from the old problem of having to claim that you love your older boy as much as the younger—

that you "love everyone the same," and so on. Your older son probably won't buy that, but he will buy hearing about why you think he is special and unique. Stress to each child that he is loved uniquely for who he is. This will help him deduce that "Mom really does love me. She spends a lot of time with Hershel, but she does love me too."

In addition, make sure your boys get different bedtimes and different responsibilities according to age. Your older son should get to go to bed later, be able to go places the younger boy can't, what have you. Don't get caught in the trap of trying to work out how you can "spend as much time with your older son as you do with the younger one." You want to spend the amount of time each boy needs; in some cases your younger one may need more time for a while than the older, and in other cases it might be the reverse.

In their fine book, *Siblings Without Rivalry*, Adele Faber and Elaine Mazlish make the wise observation, "To be loved equally is somehow to be loved less. To be loved uniquely—for one's own special self—is to be loved as much as we need to be loved."[2]

Q: I have three children, ages seven, five, and four. They all have difficulty following instructions or obeying my requests. They seem not to be listening and at times it seems I have to tell them at least twenty times to do a task. Finally I get fed up and yell, and then they do it. They get upset when I yell and ask me why. "It's because you don't do it when I ask you nicely," I explain. How can I get out of this rut?

A: Sounds as if your kids have acquired a severe case of "mother deafness." They are controlling you quite nicely with two goals in mind: (1) If they stall long enough, they'll be able to get out of doing something they don't want to do; (2) they know that you don't really "mean it" until your voice reaches a certain decibel level.

Also, they have the additional little lever of making you feel guilty for yelling. What you must do is use Reality Discipline and train your children to understand that you don't want to ask them to do anything more than once. Use the same strategy on all three children. Let them know that (beginning now) you will ask them to do things once and, if it isn't done, they will lose privileges: no playing with friends after school, no TV, no special snacks. Or possibly just sending them to their room for a period of time will do the job. *Whatever consequence really makes a difference to them is what counts.*

The key is to be firm and back up your promise of consequences for mother deafness. For example, say you want to leave for somewhere and you need all three of the children in the car in the next few minutes. They are well aware that you have been preparing to leave and that they had to be ready. Ask them *once* to get into the car. If they fail to comply, invoke consequences: If it's a trip for their enjoyment (to the movies, dance class, Cub Scouts, or the like), cancel it. Make no threats, give no lectures or say "I warned you. . . ." Just smile and say, "I'm sorry, kids, you obviously don't want to make this trip, so we will stay home."

If it's a trip that must happen (for example, a doctor's appointment), let them know, without yelling or lecturing, that there will be penalties. Later, upon returning home, say, "Because you couldn't seem to hear me today when I was trying to get you into the car, I can only think that you aren't very interested in going anywhere to speak of—to your friends' houses to play, for example." Then go ahead and invoke that consequence or another consequence that will "hit them where it hurts." Once your children understand that you mean it and will not tolerate mother deafness, their hearing should improve immeasurably.

Q: Our six-year-old is a very picky eater. My husband says he's on a "power trip" but I don't think it's anything that serious. Our son isn't throwing temper tantrums or anything like that. What is going on and how can we best deal with it?

A: It is hard to say if your son is simply seeking attention in a negative way or is on a power trip. The following are some characteristics that may help you differentiate between the two.

When attention-getting turns negative, we find the show-off, the clown who goes too far or becomes brash, showy, and even aggressive. Other signs of negative attention-getting can be bashfulness (although you need to be careful because some children truly are shy). Negative attention-getting can also turn up in a child's "lack of ability," unstable behavior, a lack of stamina, fearfulness, speech impediment, being untidy or self-indulgent. Another favorite is eating difficulties—just toying with food and never really finishing anything.

When misbehavior by the child moves into the power struggle category, we find the child arguing, contradicting, continuing to do what a parent has forbidden, or having temper tantrums. Some other signs are bad habits and untruthfulness.

On the passive side, children can involve you in a power struggle through laziness, being stubborn, disobeying, or "forgetting."[3]

As for how to deal with your picky eater, try the following:

1. Do your best to divorce yourself emotionally from the situation. All pediatricians agree that missing a few meals will not kill a child.

2. Get rid of all junk food snacks your son may be eating between meals, particularly in the late afternoon. Picky eaters are usually the worst at dinner. One major reason is that they are full of cookies, chips, and the like that they ate just an hour or so earlier.

3. If the child remains picky, try not setting a place for him at the table. When he asks why, say in a friendly manner, "You are usually not hungry, so I thought you didn't want any dinner. I'll fix you a good breakfast in the morning."

4. An alternative to not setting a place for your son is to give him small helpings of what you have fixed. If he picks at food or says things like "I hate spaghetti!" remove his plate immediately —well before dinner is over—and tell him he is excused from the dinner table and there will be no food of any kind until breakfast.

Q: My son lives in two homes. Half of the week he is at his father's house, half of the week he is with me and his stepfather. Because we live in a small community and our homes are just two miles apart, my husband and I tend to run into my ex-husband throughout the week—when attending one of my son's games, for example. When my son is with us and we see his father he will talk to his father, but when he is with his father he hardly will say hi to me because he is afraid his dad will get angry. What can I do about this?

A: Apparently your son is intimidated by his natural father. He undoubtedly wants to speak to you but is afraid of the repercussions. The only way to solve this is to remedy what is really wrong—having a child live "equal time" through the week with each parent. I'm not sure why this arrangement was made during the divorce proceedings, but it is extremely unwise and unworkable, as you are finding out. In a divorce situation, children should be put in the custody of one parent and the other parent allowed visitation privileges. During divorce proceedings, husbands and wives can often become so wrapped up in being sure they "get their fair share" that they even want to split up the children "fifty-fifty." This is no way for a child to have to live.

I suggest that you have your lawyer contact your husband's lawyer and work out a new arrangement. Once the boy is in one home, he will feel more secure. If his father continues to "intimidate him," you will have to sit down with your ex-husband and talk this out as best you can. This may prove difficult, especially if his attitude remains hostile. On the other hand, perhaps your ex-husband simply needs to have this problem pointed out and he will try to correct it himself.

The bottom line here is that your son is in a very unstable situation, which is extremely confusing. In a few words, it is "tearing him apart." He cannot be divided "equally" between the two of you through the week. He is not a thing, he is your son, and you are destroying his self-image with the present situation.

Q: I've tried "active listening" with our daughter who is nine, going on thirteen, but she doesn't buy it. She tells me to "quit playing psychologist" and to "stop repeating what I just said." I believe in acknowledging feelings, but I'm not having much success at it. What do I do?

A: Apparently you are doing a lot of what is called "parroting" instead of really active listening to what your daughter says. For example, if she comes home very upset with a friend and says something like "I hate Jennifer!" don't say "You don't like Jennifer" or something to that effect, which simply repeats exactly (parrots) what she just said. Instead, try to acknowledge her feelings by saying "You sound very upset. Tell me about it." (For many examples of how to listen actively instead of parrot, see Chapter Eight.)

Also, just because active listening doesn't work in certain situations doesn't mean it isn't an excellent technique and that you shouldn't stay with it. Don't get discouraged. Children don't always make the "perfect response" in your attempts to acknowledge their feelings. My children certainly didn't. When our oldest daughter, Holly, was around ten, I can recall telling her, "I'll bet earning those good grades makes you feel great!"

"Not really," she replied. "It probably makes you and Mom feel great, but I could care less."

To be honest, that sort of blew me away and I dropped it for the moment. Later I continued to encourage Holly, however, and let her know that I expected her to always give her best effort in school.

I knew that Holly did care about getting good grades. Just because she wasn't feeling like being "actively listened to" on one occasion did not discourage me.

Q: I heard you suggest in a seminar that allowances can be used as a form of Reality Discipline and teaching responsibility. I want to do this, but how do I keep my kids from seeing dollar signs every time they do something around the house? Whatever became of just helping each other? My children are three and seven years old.

A: It sounds as if you have given your children the idea that their allowances are rewards for work, and whenever they do anything they want more rewards—probably over and above the allowance you have set. Whenever you set up an allowance system, the children must understand that everyone is still required to do certain chores around the house. You are giving your children an allowance to help them learn how to be responsible in handling money that is their part of the family's recreational budget.

The idea behind an allowance is to let your children experience the consequences of "blowing it all" early in the week and not having enough left for a treat or something they want later. Or you also can teach the basic concept that if they save their allowance for several weeks, they can afford something more expensive later.

Another way the allowance is a good teaching tool is that when children do not do their assigned chores around the house, they must pay someone else to do them—out of their allowance. That someone else can be a sibling, or it can even be you or your spouse. It could also be the neighbor kid down the street. Very few children like the idea of paying someone else to do a simple chore that they can do themselves, and the problem usually solves itself.

The key is for the parent to use an allowance as a teaching tool, not as some kind of wage or reward system. Children should never get the idea that every time they do something, they must be paid. In some cases, parents set up "optional jobs" that are over and above regular duties, which children can do to earn extra money if they wish. These optional jobs should be spelled out, and it also should be made clear that every time a child turns a hand he or she isn't necessarily going to be paid. (For more on how to use allowances, see Chapter Six.)

Q: I'm trying to use an allowance as a means of training our seven-year-old daughter, but I'm having a problem. When she doesn't do her chores and I suggest that I'm going to hire her sister to do them and pay the older sister out of her allowance, she says, "That's okay. I really don't care about the money anyway." What can I do?

A: Your problem just goes to show that one strategy doesn't necessarily fit all. Believe me, your seven-year-old daughter will soon arrive at the place where she will no longer be saying "I really don't care about the money." In the meantime, however, perhaps you can deal with her lack of doing her chores by simply telling her, "Honey, I love you, but you aren't going out to play [or any other activity that she truly enjoys] until the chores are done."

As things are, your daughter is acting as if she doesn't really believe you are in loving authority over her in all situations. You may be a bit too permissive and you need to work on being firm but fair. If she really doesn't "care about the allowance money," perhaps she shouldn't get an allowance right now and you can start training her with an allowance in a year or so.

Q: I am a mother of three children, ages ten, eight, and six. My oldest son often flies off the handle when told that it's bedtime or when he doesn't get his way. He says things like "I hate you . . . you're mean . . . you don't love me . . . I'm going to run away from home." This really hurts. What can I do?

A: Try active listening with your son and acknowledging his feelings. I had a client who had the same problem. The client sat down with the older child after one particular outburst and said things like: "You seem to be angry with me—tell me what I'm doing to make you say you hate me. . . . I don't hate you—I love you but I can't let you treat me that way. . . . Tell me what's wrong."

After quite a bit of gentle prodding, she got her oldest son to tell her what was really wrong: "I'm not cute," he cried. "Jennifer is cute, Billy is cute. But *I'm* not cute."

By doing active listening, this mom was able to learn about her son's feelings toward his sister and brother. Jennifer and Billy *were* outstandingly beautiful children, and Mom's adult friends did make a lot of remarks about them, which, obviously, hadn't missed the older boy's ears. Instead of merely trying to tell the older boy, "Oh, you're cute too," Mom was able to say these things: "Jennifer and Billy are cute, but you are handsome. I've always thought you were a very good-looking boy. Besides, you are very special to me, God made you very special, there is no one else like you, and I love you so much. Little kids are called 'cute,' but as boys grow up, they don't want to be cute; but they become handsome and good-looking. . . . Now I know you really don't hate me. Let's talk about better ways to work out your anger."

Q: I am home-schooling my six-year-old son and a lot of things seem to be a little bit hard for him. He often falls back on saying "I'm dumb, I'm stupid," and the other day he even said, "I'm nothing." How can I cope with this? He is my firstborn and I have two other children, four and two.

A: Life can be very hard on a firstborn, especially when you're six and being home-schooled (or schooled anywhere else, for that matter). Firstborns "take the brunt of things." They take the brunt of expectations from their parents, and they also get most of the responsibility around the house. When you have a child who is starting to tell himself at the tender age of six that he's "dumb, stupid, and nothing," you need to back off and take a good look at what's going on. First, find things that your son is good at and let him excel in those things, even if they are very simple and basic. Put the searchlight on what he does well.

Second, take as much pressure off your six-year-old as possible. Back off a little bit and see things "from behind his eyes." He is seeing that life means he has to measure up and, remember, as the firstborn, he measures up the most to the key models in his life who are Mommy and Daddy, very big, powerful, capable people.

Also, when he does something (such as make his own bed), don't come along and do it over or improve on it, saying things like "Honey, that's wonderful, but let's just fix it up a little." All you're telling him is that his efforts have again fallen short of your expectations, and that only reduces his self-image a little more.

Q: How can we get our youngest child—an eight-year-old girl —to work up to her potential? Tests tell us she is very bright, but she gets mostly C's in school and doesn't seem interested in studying. Her older sisters, who are twelve and fifteen, get excellent grades. Any suggestions?

A: Don't panic. Your daughter may be a "late bloomer" who just needs another six months or a year to come alive. In the meantime, you want to encourage her but not put on pressure to perform.

Your youngest daughter is probably a bit intimidated by the older siblings who "get excellent grades." She probably feels she can't measure up to what they have done and she's deliberately hanging back so she won't have that stress and pressure in her life.

Often I see kids like this. Parents say, "Harley isn't working up to his potential." And yet they will go on to tell me that recently Harley's teacher found a paper in his desk that was easily worth an A. The only problem was that Harley hadn't turned it in.

To help your daughter with any inferiority feelings she may have, keep assuring her that you love her for who she is but that you also hope for the best for her and always expect her to do her best. Whatever you do, *never* compare her to her older sisters. Never say things like "Why can't you get good grades the way your sisters do?"

Normally my advice on homework is not to help the child at all, simply let reality do the teaching when the child winds up at school with the homework undone and has to pay the penalty. In this case, however, your daughter is already getting mostly C's and is not interested in studying. You need to take a little different tack, and your best approach is to encourage her to get her homework done, without going ahead and doing it for her. Sit down and talk with her about each assignment to get her started.

Then check back now and then to encourage her to get it finished.

Keep in mind that babies of the family often need a little extra boost when it comes to meeting their responsibilities. Chances are your eight-year-old gives anything she is assigned a "lick and a promise." Don't accept shoddy work, whether it's a simple chore around the house or completing important homework assignments.

Whenever possible, give your eight-year-old a little more responsibility, but don't overload her. Make her stretch a bit, though, and don't accept obviously weak excuses why she doesn't get something done.

Don't overreact when she doesn't complete assignments, but don't let her off the hook either. Keep telling her in every way you can that "We have faith in you. . . . We know you can do it. . . . We expect you to always do your best." (For more ideas on how to encourage rather than praise the child, see Chapter Eight.)

Q: I've heard a lot from friends and people at work about spending "quality time" with my kids. Because I'm a working mom and my husband also works long hours, we don't have great quantities of time. How can we make what time we have count?

A: If you are short of time to spend with your children, you need to carefully plan how to use weekends, vacations, and holidays. If your budget allows it (in fact, even if you have to stretch your budget), hire others to have certain chores done, such as cutting lawns, washing windows, putting up screens, and the like. Consider paying a handyman or a capable teenager money well spent, so you can spend more time with your children. To help yourselves judge the amount of "quality" in the time you spend with the kids, here are some questions developed by Paul Lewis, president of the Family Development Foundation:

> Did you come away confident that you "know" what's really going on in your child's mind—the dreams as well as the disappointments and confusions? . . . Were you appropriately open and vulnerable to your child—thereby modeling the expression you desired from him? . . . Is there a good mix of work, play, service, and investigation, etc., in the ways you've recently spent time together?[4]

In addition to questions like these, Lewis also suggests that you know the answers to very nitty-gritty questions about your child. If you do, it will certainly help your relationship.

- Name your child's best friend.

- Within three pounds, how much does your child weigh?

- What is her greatest disappointment and/or unfulfilled desire?

- If he could change one personal physical characteristic, what would it be?

- Which chore does she hate most?

- What is his favorite TV program, entertainer, song?

- If she could visit anywhere in the world, where would it be?

- What would he say is his best quality?

- What qualities do her friends most admire about your child?

- What does he most enjoy doing with you? Have you done it recently?

- Which are her favorite and worst subjects in school?

- What are his teachers' names?

- If she could set bedtimes and curfews, what would they be?

- What books is he reading now?

- What would she claim to be best at?[5]

While all of these can be helpful, keep in mind that always doing your best to love and unconditionally accept your child is what counts. Then whatever quantities of time you spend will turn into quality moments that build your child's self-image.

Q: Our secondborn nine-year-old son has always been big for his age, very strong and active. His firstborn eleven-year-old brother takes after my husband, who is slightly built and rather passive. My problem is that my secondborn has become somewhat of a bully. He pushes his older brother around, and I've also gotten notes from the school mentioning his bullying behavior with other children. How can we deal with this?

A: It appears you have two problems. Your secondborn son is trying to "take over" from his firstborn brother. In addition, he has learned somewhere that powerful behavior pays off. Your nine-year-old's lifeline tells him: "I count only when I dominate and control—when I'm the *boss!*"

The first thing you might do is check what kind of role model you—his mother—are for your sons. Has your secondborn son possibly learned powerful behavior from you without your ever intending it? What are your sons learning from Mom about how she treats men—especially her husband? Perhaps toning down your own assertiveness might set a better example.

Second, work on what your nine-year-old is doing at home. Leave any bullying he does at school to the school authorities. Let the school authorities know, however, that you are aware of this problem and that you want to cooperate in any way that you can to correct it.

Third, talk to each boy separately. With your smaller, slightly built firstborn, do all you can to encourage him to stand up for himself. Let him know that you are aware of what's going on, and as long as he is not "bugging his bigger but younger brother," you want him to stand up for his rights whenever possible.

Your major work, however, should be with your secondborn son—the "bully" who gets a payoff from dominating and even hurting others, particularly his older brother. Sit down with him and try to actively listen to what he has to say. Try to discover why he feels the need to dominate. For example, you might ask, "How does it make you feel when you beat up on your older brother? Are you angry with him?"

Try to get the secondborn boy to open up and tell you what's on his mind. Also let him know what's on your mind. Send him "I messages" in which you express your own feelings very strongly but never attack his character. Don't label him as "mean" or "a bully." Instead, try to help him see that he can really be nice and get what he wants in life without using force.

Q: I was divorced nearly five years ago and my thirteen-year-old daughter's self-image is still in tatters. How can I help her?

A: First, be sure your daughter doesn't blame herself for the divorce. Assure her that it was not her fault, that she had nothing to do with it. What happened was between you and her father. You simply could not live together and you chose divorce as the lesser of two evils.

Second, work at helping your daughter experience the A-B-C's of self-image: to feel accepted, that she belongs, and that she is capable. At the tender age of thirteen, with all the pressures of adolescence hitting her for the first time, you can be sure the divorce isn't the only thing eating at her self-image. Tell your daughter, "I love you very much. I care about you and I know it hurts but we're together and we're still a family. I expect the best of you. I know you can do it."

Q: How can a newly divorced man who sees his kids only on weekends maintain a close, loving relationship with them?

A: First, realize that you are not going to have as warm and loving and close relationship with your kids as you would like to have. You are going to have to be what they call a "weekend father."

Second, avoid the temptation to let guilt drive you into being a "Disneyland Daddy," which means you give the kids everything they want while they're with you on weekends and seldom discipline them. If possible, talk with your ex-wife about how to discipline the children—the ideal would be that both of you would generally agree on using Reality Discipline and logical consequences.

Third, become involved in your children's lives as best you can. Go to their soccer games, basketball games, plays at school. Whatever they are doing, try to be there. Don't just tell the kids you're interested in them, *show* them. At the same time, realize that the relationship between you and your children is a two-way street. You cannot carry it alone. Trust the children to adapt and carry their end of the relationship. Don't try to do too much.

Fourth, don't just try to "spend time" with your kids. Share yourself with them. Let them know what you have learned about life and what is important to you. Let your kids see you as a person who has hopes, fears—and faults.

Fifth, avoid triangles. In other words, don't make your children some kind of go-between to carry messages to your wife. And, whatever you do, never bad-mouth their mother, no matter how or what you feel. It can only do harm.

Q: I have been divorced for nearly four years. Lately I've been starting to date a man who has some potential, but I haven't brought him to the house yet. I meet him elsewhere. When should I introduce him to my ten-year-old daughter? What if she doesn't accept him?

A: You have shown wisdom by not bringing the man you started to date over to the house just yet. I believe it makes all kinds of sense not to bring any man around until you know that the relationship is serious or could lead to being serious.

I have counseled divorced women who introduce their dates to their children as a matter of course, and this only causes problems and confusion. Sometimes the children get their hopes up that the new date might become "a substitute daddy." And then later, when the relationship ends, they are let down rather hard. On the other hand, sometimes children have a hard time accepting another man in Mother's life, and there is no point in getting them involved unless you feel that the relationship could definitely develop into something long term.

If and when your relationship with this man becomes serious, then you should be brave enough to share your feelings with daughter. Tell her that you like "Bob" a lot. He really has a lot of good qualities and he likes you and that is what is important—to you. If the two of you are thinking of getting married, tell your daughter. Give her the right to her feelings, but do not base your relationship with a man on whether or not your daughter approves. In many cases, a child has a very hard time accepting a stepparent. In some cases, people remarry and the children never fully accept the stepparent but the marriage turns out quite well.

In other words, don't let your daughter dictate what you're going to do with the rest of your life. In a few years your daughter will be out on her own and you will still have a great deal of your life to live.

What is imperative is that you reassure your daughter and let her know that whatever happens, she is very much loved and prized by you. If a man comes into your life, this could be a very big change. Before introducing your new friend to your daughter, caution him to "not come on strong" to make the daughter like him. He should move slowly and respect her feelings. And always reassure your daughter that this man is not there to replace Daddy. No one can replace Daddy. He just lives someplace else.

A Memorandum from Your Child

RE: Me

1. Don't spoil me. I know quite well that I ought not to have all I ask for. I'm only testing you.

2. Don't be afraid to be firm with me. I prefer it. It lets me know where I stand.

3. Don't use force with me. It teaches me that power is all that counts. I will respond more readily to being led.

4. Don't be inconsistent. That confuses me and makes me try harder to get away with everything that I can.

5. Don't make promises; you may not be able to keep them. That will discourage my trust in you.

6. Don't fall for my provocations when I say and do things just to upset you. Then I'll try for more such "victories."

7. Don't be too upset when I say "I hate you." I don't mean it, but I want you to feel sorry for what you have done to me.

8. Don't make me feel smaller than I am. I will make up for it by behaving like a "big shot."

9. Don't do things for me that I can do for myself. It makes me feel like a baby, and I may continue to put you in my service.

10. Don't let my "bad habits" get me a lot of your attention. It only encourages me to continue them.

11. Don't correct me in front of people. I'll take much more notice if you talk quietly with me in private.

12. Don't try to discuss my behavior in the heat of a conflict. For some reason my hearing is not very good at this time and my cooperation is even worse. It is all right to take the action required, but let's not talk about it until later.

13. Don't try to preach to me. You'd be surprised how well I know what's right and wrong.

14. Don't make me feel that my mistakes are sins. I have to learn to make mistakes without feeling that I am no good.

15. Don't nag. If you do, I shall have to protect myself by appearing deaf.

16. Don't demand explanations for my wrong behavior. I really don't know why I did it.

17. Don't tax my honesty too much. I am easily frightened into telling lies.

18. Don't forget that I love and use experimenting. I learn from it, so please put up with it.

19. Don't protect me from consequences. I need to learn from experience.

20. Don't take too much notice of my small ailments. I may learn to enjoy poor health if it gets me much attention.

21. Don't put me off when I ask *honest* questions. If you do, you will find that I stop asking and seek my information elsewhere.

22. Don't answer "silly" or meaningless questions. I just want you to keep busy with me.

23. Don't ever think that it is beneath your dignity to apologize to me. An honest apology makes me feel surprisingly warm toward you.

24. Don't ever suggest that you are perfect or infallible. It gives me too much to live up to.

25. Don't worry about the little amount of time we spend together. It is *how* we spend it that counts.

26. Don't let my fears arouse your anxiety. Then I will become more afraid. Show me courage.

27. Don't forget that I can't thrive without lots of understanding and encouragement, but I don't need to tell you that, do I?

TREAT ME THE WAY YOU TREAT YOUR FRIENDS, THEN I WILL BE YOUR FRIEND TOO.
REMEMBER, I LEARN MORE FROM A MODEL THAN A CRITIC.[6]

TIPS FOR TEACHING RESPONSIBILITY

Teaching six- to twelve-year-olds responsibility may get a little tedious at times, but it's worth it because of what it can do for their self-image. As children learn the benefits of order resulting from cooperation, they begin to see themselves as persons who are capable of making a contribution. They begin telling themselves: "I can do it. . . . I can really help my mom and dad here. . . . I'm not just a little kid anymore." As you assign responsibilities to your child, keep these tips in mind:

- Vary their tasks. Children become bored easily when they have to do the same things over and over. Work at rotating familiar jobs and giving them a new job now and then for the sake of variety.

- Involve your children in setting time limits on the tasks they agree to do. If they play a part in setting the limits, they will be more inclined to meet those limits.

- Always be aware of the power of modeling. Don't expect your children to be orderly or clean if you are not setting a good example.

- If you are inclined to be a perfectionist, work at "lowering your standards" and being willing to accept less than perfect performance by your children. What your children do is not a reflection of your personal worth, but it definitely is a reflection of theirs. Try to keep criticism at a minimum and constructive encouragement at a maximum.

- When teaching responsibility to your children, your goal is to help them grow, develop, and mature. Your motto is: "I will not do anything for my children that they can do for themselves."

Home Responsibilities for First Grade (Six-Year-Olds)

1. Choose own clothing for the day according to the weather or a special event.

2. Shake rug.

3. Water plants and flowers.

4. Peel vegetables.

5. Cook simple foods (hot dogs, boiled eggs, and toast).

6. Prepare own school lunch.

7. Help hang clothes on the clothesline.

8. Hang up own clothes in the closet.

9. Gather wood for the fireplace.

10. Rake leaves and weeds.

11. Take pet for walk.

12. Tie own shoes.

13. Keep the garbage container clean.

14. Clean out inside of car.

15. Straighten or clean out silverware drawer.

Home Responsibilities for Second Grade (Seven-Year-Olds)

1. Oil and care for bike and lock it when unused.

2. Take phone messages and write them down.

3. Run errands for parents.

4. Sweep and wash patio area.

5. Water the lawn.

6. Take proper care of bike and other outside toys or equipment.

7. Wash dog or cat.

8. Train pets.

9. Carry in the grocery sacks.

10. Get self up in the morning and to bed at night on own.

11. Learn to be polite, courteous, and to share; respect others.

12. Carry own lunch money and notes back to school and the like.

13. Leave the bathroom in order; hang up clean towels.

14. Do simple ironing of flat pieces.

15. Wash down walls and scrub floors.

Home Responsibilities for Third Grade
(Eight- to Nine-Year-Olds)

1. Fold napkins properly and set silverware properly.

2. Mop or buff the floor.

3. Clean Venetian blinds.

4. Help rearrange furniture. Help plan the layout.

5. Run own bath water.

6. Help others with their work when asked.

7. Straighten own closet and drawers.

8. Shop for and select own clothing and shoes with parent.

9. Change school clothes without being told.

10. Fold blankets.

11. Sew buttons.

12. Sew rips in seams.

13. Clean storage room.

14. Clean up animal "messes" in the yard and house.

15. Begin to read recipes and cook for the family.

16. Baby-sit for short periods of time.

17. Cut flowers and make a centerpiece.

18. Pick fruit off trees.

19. Build a campfire, get items ready to cook out (charcoal, hamburgers).

20. Paint fence or shelves.

21. Help write simple letter.

22. Write thank-you notes.

23. Help with defrosting and cleaning of the refrigerator.

24. Feed the baby.

25. Bathe younger sister or brother.

26. Polish silverware, copper or brass items.

27. Clean patio furniture.

28. Wax living room furniture.

Home Responsibilities for Fourth Grade
(Nine- to Ten-Year-Olds)

1. Change sheets on the bed and put dirty sheets in the hamper.

2. Operate the washer and/or the dryer.

3. Measure detergent and bleach.

4. Buy groceries using a list and do comparative shopping.

5. Cross streets unassisted.

6. Keep own appointments (dentist, school, etc., if within biking distance) and being on time for them.

7. Prepare a family meal.

8. Prepare pastries from box mixes.

9. Receive and answer own mail.

10. Pour and make tea, coffee, and Kool-Aid.

11. Wait on guests.

12. Plan own birthday or other parties.

13. Use simple first aid.

14. Do neighborhood chores.

15. Sew, knit, or weave (even use a sewing machine).

16. Do chores without a reminder.

17. Learn banking and to be thrifty and trustworthy.

18. Wash the family car.

Home Responsibilities for Fifth Grade
(Ten- to Eleven-Year-Olds)

1. Earn own money (baby-sit).

2. Be alone at home.

3. Handle sums of money up to $5.00 (honesty).

4. Able to take the city bus.

5. Proper conduct when staying overnight with a friend. Pack own suitcase.

6. Responsible for personal hobby.

7. Able to handle self properly when in public places alone or with peers (movies).

Home Responsibilities for Sixth Grade
(Eleven- to Twelve-Year-Olds)

1. Join outside organizations, do assignments and attend. Able to take responsibility as a leader.

2. Dress siblings and put them to bed.

3. Clean pool and pool area.

4. Respect others' property.

5. Run own errands.

6. Mow lawn.

7. Help parent build things and do the family errands.

8. Clean oven and stove.

9. Able to schedule ample time for studies.

10. Buy own sweets or treats.

11. Take care of a paper route.

12. Check and add oil to car.[7]

Chapter Eleven

ROAD-TESTING THE IMAGE

■

Questions and Answers: Parenting Teenagers

For most kids, the teenage years—especially the early teens—are a scary, pulsating, deafening, agonizing, heart-pounding, worrisome trip through what psychologist James Dobson has aptly pegged "the canyon of inferiority."[1]

It's a turbulent time when everything is exaggerated. The little things become big things. A simple zit becomes Mount St. Helens. A certain kind of sweater, shoe, dress, jeans, whatever, becomes *imperative*; they just "have to have it." Tomorrow is "the biggest night of my life," and, of course, the next night after that is even bigger.

Teenagers live for now. Yesterday is ancient history, next week is the far distant future. Coping with being who they are, right now, this minute—unsure, insecure, living in mortal fear of the censure of their peers—is enough of a challenge.

I will never forget one of my own painful moments in that canyon of inferiority. In junior high, I had been one of three seventh graders to make the freshman basketball team. I wasn't very tall but I was a good player (or so I thought). As a fifteen-year-old sophomore, I tried out for the junior varsity and, when it came time for the final cut, the coach gathered us all together and read off the names of those who had made the team. I didn't hear my name and, sure there was some mistake, I went up to the coach and said, "You must have missed my name."

"I didn't miss your name, Leman, you didn't make the team," the coach said rather bluntly and with no sympathy at all in his voice.

Fighting back tears, I turned away and ran down the stairs to the locker room where I grabbed my clothes and ran home through the freezing cold, still dressed in shorts. I never played basketball again.

THEIR SELF-IMAGE GETS RUN OVER

Perhaps no emotion better fits most teens than the gnawing feelings of inferiority and self-doubt. Teenagers' very personality does, indeed, get road-tested, and sooner or later they wind up with two tire tracks right down the middle of their self-image.

Just making the passage into puberty is tough. From the relatively calm years of coltish blundering childhood emerges a moody, irritable, unpredictable being called "a teenager." And it happens practically overnight. Suddenly young Charlie, who never voluntarily used a washrag in his entire life, is now constantly scrubbing his face, frantically trying to get rid of the little black objects that appear in his pores. And young Loretta, who never cared for boys, now spends hours washing, blow-drying, and combing out her hair.

Mixed with these sudden pubescent concerns about personal grooming are other characteristics that bewilder parents. What happened to happy little Charlie and sweet young Loretta? Just yesterday they were good-natured and on occasion even helpful (with a little nudge from Reality Discipline). Today they are moody—way up or way down—as well as feisty, gross, distant, and disrespectful.

Or so a lot of parents tell me. They wonder: Dare you use Reality Discipline on teenagers? What happens when you pull the rug out from under a bundle of uncertain nerves who is your fifteen-year-old daughter? Can you grab a seventeen-year-old buzzard by the beak and come out of it with all your fingers?

I believe you can. In fact, I know you can because I'm doing it right now with three teenagers of my own and it seems to be working. Yes, they have their moods, and they can sometimes be a bit gross, feisty, and disrespectful. But their positives far outweigh the occasional negatives. Holly, Krissy, and Kevin are bright and often ingenious (particularly if they're trying to get around Sande or me). They are also resourceful, lively, spirited, and fun to have around. I'm glad I'm their dad and I'm proud of the way they are handling the hormone years.

And I don't think my kids are unique or even that unusual. I firmly believe that they have a lot of counterparts out there who think and act much as they do. I believe that most teenagers don't want to burn every bastion of adult authority, nor do they want to take over and put all adults in a cage. They simply want to make their way into the ranks of adulthood—at their own speed and with maybe a "little help." They want to break away from their parents and begin to stand on their own, but not completely. In their words, "Give me space, Mom and Dad, but not too much."

As for using Reality Discipline with teenagers, it comes in very handy. In fact, in some ways it is more useful than ever, because now kids are able to see the logic and grasp the full impact of having reality do the teaching. As I said in another book, the rules for using Reality Discipline are the same for teenagers as they are for younger children, as long as you temper them slightly with a little sensitivity—and common sense:

Use action, not just words, but *be sure to think before you act.*

Be consistent, decisive, and respectful—*but remember that teenagers want to be treated like adults, not "little kids."*

299

Hold your teenagers accountable for their actions—*but don't spit in their soup or rub their nose in it.*[2]

WHAT DO TEENAGERS REALLY WANT?

Whenever I think about teenagers and Reality Discipline, I'm reminded of "A Letter to Parents," which appears in the booklet "What Every Teen Should Know," developed by Abigail Van Buren, author of the well-known "Dear Abby" column. Abby researched what sociologists and psychologists have discovered from talking to teenagers on the general subject of "What's bugging you?" Here is what teens themselves said:

LOVE. We want parents who will love us no matter what happens or what we do. We want our dad around more often. We want him home in time for dinner, so we can discuss the day's happenings with him.

UNDERSTANDING. Maybe we don't even understand ourselves. But we want parents who DO, who will listen and at least let us explain.

TRUST. We want to be put on our own. We want our parents to expect the best of us . . . not fear the worst.

JOINT PLANNING. We want parents who will stand BESIDE us, not OVER us. We appreciate guidance in important matters, but after we've proven ourselves to have fairly mature judgment, we don't want to be nagged about every little thing.

PRIVACY. We need a room of our own to retreat to, and a place to pursue our hobbies—and store our junk. We don't want our letters read, or our phone conversations listened in on.

RESPONSIBILITY. We want our share of family tasks. But we'd like to know who's to do what, and why.

FRIENDSHIPS. We want the right to choose our own friends. And unless they have reputations for being "bad" company, such as boozers or dopers, we want them to be welcome in our home.

So ends the Teen-Age Bill of Rights. How much of it applies to your home is for you to decide.[3]

In the following questions and answers, you will find, I hope, suggestions that respond to what teenagers are saying about what they want. Of one thing I am quite sure: All our teenagers aren't going to hell in a handbasket. As usual, a minority is causing enough ruckus and tragedy to make it seem that the vast majority is just as hopeless, hapless, and hedonistic as they are. As the title of one of my books suggests, there are a lot of smart kids out there and some of them are making stupid choices, but there are a lot more kids who want to make the right choices; if they make the wrong ones they need understanding and forgiveness, not sermons and I-told-you-sos.

Q: We have a son who is the middle child of three boys ages fifteen, thirteen, and ten. He's a good kid but seems to have trouble concentrating on tasks, whether they be chores, school work, or whatever. When asked to do something, he seems willing and sets out to do it but later, when I check to see what he's done, you guessed it, he has "forgotten" and is doing something else.

A: Apparently you don't believe he is rebelling or on some kind of power trip, because you say "he's a good kid." The first thing to be sure of is that he has really "forgotten." There is an outside chance that your son has a learning disability. A telltale sign of a child with a learning disability is getting an assignment, setting out to do it, and then never following through.

It might be worthwhile to have your son tested, but do it through a source outside the school system. Contact a reputable psychologist/counselor who does testing of this kind or who can recommend a capable colleague. By going outside the school system, you avoid possible delays, you have immediate access to the results, and, because school psychologists are usually overworked, you usually get a better job of testing. Also, another advantage is that you can choose whether or not you want to share the results with the school.

If your son does not have a learning disability, it is possible that he simply is not a good listener, because he has never been rewarded for paying attention to what you say. Whenever he does anything at all or makes even the slightest accomplishment, do you encourage him? (See Chapter Seven.) It is also possible that he tunes you out because he knows he can always get somebody else to do his work for him. Or he is simply waiting for you to constantly remind him until the job is done.

If you rule out a learning disability, work on the other possibilities I just outlined with the following Reality Discipline techniques:

1. As I mentioned, try encouraging him when he does do anything at all. Say such things as: "Now you're getting it. I'll bet it feels good to get that work done."

2. If he is simply not paying attention because he thinks you'll do the work or at least remind him several times before he has to do it, you may have to make reality a bit more painful. Sit down with your son and point out that "We have a problem. You simply don't follow through when you're assigned anything, whether it's chores, homework, or whatever. What kind of logical consequence do you think would be fair if you don't follow through and get things done?"

Then let your son grapple with two things: First, he knows the jig is up and you're not going to tolerate his "lack of attention" anymore; second, he can think about his own consequence for not doing what he's been assigned to do. This will help him "save face," and you should be able to come out of this by bolstering his self-image and not weakening it.

Q: **My fifteen-year-old daughter wants to hang out at the mall with her friends after school. I don't like the idea. In fact, lately she has been asking me to take her over to the mall *after dinner* and drop her off to spend an hour or two. She assures me she can still "get her homework done."**

A: Teenagers hanging out at a mall is not a good idea—for them or the merchants. If your daughter wants to go to the mall after school, tell her you'll be happy to set up a date to take her shopping, but just going there to hang out is not workable.

As for going to the mall after dinner, that should be totally out on school nights for obvious reasons.

I have always liked the idea of "playing the game on your home court." When your fifteen-year-old gets restless and wants to "get out with her friends," you might try saying, "Honey, we talked about that. You know how I feel. But tell you what. If you want to invite some of the kids over to hang out, pop corn, and watch a video or whatever, that will be great. I'll even ask Dad to spring for pizza."

If you turn into a taxi service that your daughter can call on at any time to run her down to the mall so she can hang out with friends, you give up the healthy authority you have over your child. Teenagers are always testing their parents to see just what their values are, how far they can go, and so on. In many cases, teenagers want parents to say no so they can tell their friends, "My parents won't let me." That gets them off the hook.

In some instances, your daughter may want to do some legitimate shopping at the mall with some friends. Arrange to make it a short trip. Take her (and the friends, for that matter) over to

the mall, drop them off, and arrange to pick them up at a stipulated time and place. Always maintain control and stay in
healthy authority over your teenager.

Q: Our sixteen-year-old son thinks we expect too much by
asking him to keep his room clean. From our point of view,
we're trying to convince him that cleaning his room doesn't
mean "throw everything in a corner." The other day when I
told him that we'd like a little more respect for our wishes, he
retorted, "You and Dad don't respect each other, why should I
respect you?" How can we handle our son?

A: Your son is angry because there isn't much security in his
home. Even at the age of sixteen he feels insecure, threatened,
and afraid. It is much more important for a child to feel that
Mom and Dad love each other than it is for the child to know
that he is loved. I know that's an extreme statement, but I mean
every word of it.

When Dad shows Mom no respect, a male child learns that
women can be dumped on and used, and that is how he is going
to treat his wife when he marries. On the other hand, when Mom
shows Dad no respect, daughters learn that men can be pushed
around and that they aren't worth much. And, of course, that's
how the daughter will treat her husband when she marries.

Coming back to your original sore point—your son's messy
room—I suggest:

1. Talk to your husband and clean up your act together. Start
respecting one another and your son will "sit up and take notice
fast."

2. One approach to the messy room is simply to tell your
son, "Since you don't want to keep your room even moderately
clean, please keep the door closed. Of course, I won't be able to
find any of your dirty clothes in the mess, so you will have to do
your own laundry from here on out."

3. Another approach would be, if your sixteen-year-old wants a filthy room, he can have it, but he forgoes the car keys. This assumes that your son has a license and that he is using your car. If he has his own car, he still forgoes his privilege to drive if he wants to live with you and be irresponsible about his room. Let your son know that how he acts at home is his first priority. If he can't be responsible at home, it follows that he can't be counted on to be responsible while operating a car on public streets and highways.

4. Still another way to deal with your son is to say, "Let's make a deal. Five days a week, you keep your door shut. On Tuesday and Saturday, however, we expect you to shovel out your room and put it in generally good order." Then give your son every opportunity to meet that responsibility.

Q: How can we use Reality Discipline with our fourteen-year-old son who drinks beer at supposedly supervised parties where parents are at home? We try to tell him it's illegal and that we don't approve, but he doesn't listen. He likes the "buzz" he gets from the beer. How can we help our son make better choices?

A: If we could come up with an absolutely foolproof answer to this one, we might bottle and sell it and make enough to put a good dent in the national debt. You have several problems going here:

1. Your fourteen-year-old seems to be in control. Without having further information, I can't make any firm recommendations, but it just could be that "tough love" might really help. Let your fourteen-year-old know that if he goes to any more beer parties (even where parents are supposedly supervising), he will forgo certain privileges that he loves dearly. It's up to you to figure out what those privileges might be. One thing you could tell him is that you will not be too interested in helping him get a driver's license in the future if he's that into drinking alcohol because he "likes the buzz."

2. If confronting your fourteen-year-old with tough love doesn't seem advisable for any number of reasons, try finding other concerned parents who also don't like "supervised drinking" by minors at parties. Not only are these "supervisory parents" stupid, they are asking for a great deal of trouble, including criminal or civil lawsuits.

It is hard to believe that some parents can be so irresponsible that they let underage kids drink in their homes. I know their argument: It's safer for children to drink in a home, supervised by adults, rather than be out in cars drinking or going out to the boondocks to drink and then getting in cars to drive back to town. The argument sounds good, but it doesn't hold water. Allowing a fourteen-year-old to drink in a private home because he "likes the buzz" only encourages him to become more and more addicted to alcohol. Also, it makes getting alcohol, and getting around the law, all the easier.

Don't be afraid to become "street smart" about what your kids are doing. Check with other parents, especially if you hear your son drop an offhand remark while he is on the phone. I'm not saying that you should eavesdrop, go through his mail, or anything like that. I am saying be a good listener and follow through by contacting other parents to see if they know where and when a party might be taking place. Then band together and talk to the parents who will be supervising the party. Tell them, in no uncertain terms, that you do not want alcohol served and, if it is served, your son or daughter simply can't attend. Don't be afraid of offending them. Your kids' lives are at stake!

3. Another possibility is to let your fourteen-year-old get a firsthand look at the devastation that drinking can cause in a person's life. Take your son to an Ala-Teen meeting or a meeting of Alcoholics Anonymous or SADD (Students Against Drunk Drivers). Have him listen to what is said, which will probably include the statistic that the leading cause of death among young people under age twenty-five is driving while intoxicated. Point out to your son that, while he isn't old enough to drive, he really isn't old enough to drink, and by getting into the habit now, he is setting himself up for real problems when he does start operating an automobile.

Another approach would be to make contact with recovered alcoholics you may know and have them talk to your son about what alcohol did to them. Be sure they point out that, while they're not drinking now, they will *always* be alcoholics and will have to fight their addiction until the day they die.

4. It's true that as adults, you and your husband have the legal privilege to drink while your son, who is underage, does not. But if you want to make any inroads with your fourteen-year-old son, your best approach is not to drink yourselves. If you do drink even moderately, you have a choice to make here. By drinking alcohol you are sending your son the message, "It's really okay to drink, you just have to play the wait-until-you're-old-enough game."

Your son has already found a way around the legal age for drinking, or at least he thinks he has. If you do drink alcohol to any degree and want to continue to do so, then you must push hard to convince him that he cannot drink until he is at the legal age, and then in moderation. If he continues drinking at age fourteen "for the buzz," there will be serious consequences with loss of privileges at home. And, later on down the line, he may possibly become addicted to alcohol or find himself in jail for drunken driving.

Q: **My fifteen-year-old daughter is always saying: "But all the other kids are doing it, buying it, wearing it, etc., etc.," and "I'll just die if my friends know about *this*." She's starting to rebel and disobey us. I guess they call this the "power of the peer group." Is there any way we can fight back?**

A: I don't advocate "fighting back" because that will only cause your daughter to be more rebellious. I do, however, suggest taking charge and being in healthy authority over your fifteen-year-old. The peer group is a powerful force. To be honest, the peer group carries more weight and influence with many teenagers than their families do. That doesn't mean, however, you have to simply give up and knuckle under to what the peer group wants your daughter to do.

From their earliest years, my wife and I drummed into our children that "Our family is not like everybody else," and "You don't have to be like everybody else. You can stand for what you really think is right." So far it has worked and we have not been approached by our children with the everybody's-doing-it argument.

The point is, your child does not have to be like everybody else. Your family does not have to be like every other family (or at least an awful lot of families who seem to have lost control). Make your stand quietly, firmly, and with absolute conviction. Do not back off. Stick to your guns and you may be surprised. Your daughter may simply be testing you to see if you have any real values, as she searches desperately for values of her own.

While I had my own problems when I was a high school student (I caused at least one teacher to retire from sheer frustration after having me in class), I did pick up one invaluable trait from my parents. As a teenager I was a nondrinker and at age forty-eight I still have not had even a beer in my entire life.

Interestingly enough, when I was in high school, all the parents of the girls I dated always liked me. They knew I was a safe driver because I didn't drink. That was a rarity, even back in those ancient days.

When I went out with my friends, I was the "designated driver" long before the term came into vogue. They kidded me about never drinking, but when we wound up at a party where they had one too many, they always gave me the keys and asked me to drive home. I didn't lecture them, I just drove. My job was to get them home in one piece. My friends often pressured me to take a drink, but I stood my ground. They accepted me, even though I was different from them. It paid off in many, many ways.

Q: Our thirteen-year-old daughter has become very critical of us. Nothing we say or do is right anymore. How can we keep from taking this personally and lashing back in anger?

A: First, realize you're on the right track but recognize that it won't do a lot of good to lash back at your child, who has now moved into the hormone years in earnest and has suddenly discovered how "dumb" her parents are. I know it doesn't give much comfort, but if you hang in there, in five to ten years your daughter may be amazed at how "smart" you've become. In the meantime, here are some thoughts and responses you can use when your daughter gets critical and disrespectful:

1. A sense of humor is always useful. Be sure you're willing to laugh at yourself, but don't poke fun at her. One reason she's being so critical is that she is very sensitive and vulnerable right now. Her self-image is fragile and making her the butt of any jokes will only do more damage.

When she criticizes you for "antediluvian" thinking, just laugh and say, "Yes, that's true, we were born well before the Flood, but that's how we see it. Why do you see it so differently? We'd really like to understand your views."

With a remark like this, you do two things: First, you disarm your daughter by admitting that you know you're "old and ancient." Second, you invite her to share her honest feelings and ideas. One thing teenagers are fed up with is not being listened to by parents who are sure they are always right, have more experience, and certainly more sense. All of these things are probably true, but throwing them in her face won't help you get your daughter to be more respectful.

2. Build on asking your daughter to share her opinions by inviting her to give input on how things can be different in the family. Let her be involved in some of the rule-making; let her set her own "logical consequences" for failure to do certain tasks, breaking curfew, and the like.

3. One way to diffuse a teenager's criticism is to preface everything you say with "You know, I could be wrong, but . . ." and then give your opinion calmly and logically and offer full opportunity for your daughter to give her side.

4. Call your daughter's bluff when she criticizes you or tells you "get out of my life." The next time she comes to you for help, a loan, or an advance on her allowance, say, "Honey, I'd like to help you but right now I'm out of your life. I'm sure you can handle it."

Whatever you do, it's important not to blow your cool, be sarcastic, or make fun of your daughter. Also, do not pay back her criticism with acid criticism of your own. Always try to point out what she has or hasn't done and then let her deal with it.

Q: How can I convince my fourteen-year-old daughter, who is a Type A perfectionist only child, to loosen up? She must control, organize, and boss every situation she is part of in our home or, I'm told, at school and out among her friends. When she can't be in control, she gets abusive, condescending, and hurtful. I can't understand why she has any friends left, but she is still popular and well liked by her teachers even though she criticizes them too. I worry about her future and her mental health, not to mention mine.

A: I would be worried too. Your daughter is destined to be very unhappy in life. She is setting unrealistic goals for herself and laying that same perfectionist grid on others. If she is finding fault with everyone now, wait until she is an adult and becomes truly adept at flaw-picking. I doubt that your daughter's popularity is going to last much longer. People will figure out that she is not much fun to be around.

One of the best ways you can try to help her is to share your "imperfect self" with her. Admit your own faults and, when the opportunity presents itself, share times that you goofed, made an error, or failed.

Look for subtle ways to point out to her why things don't always go perfectly and are not always well organized. It's time she got acquainted with Murphy's Law.

She is probably very successful in school, but I would not pay undo attention to all her success. Play it down as best you can by encouraging her rather than praising her. Say such things as "Honey, it is nice to see that you enjoy learning," or "So you were elected to the Homecoming Court? I'll bet that makes you feel good."

Don't get caught up in telling her how wonderful she is. She is already trying to run faster and faster so she can be more and more "wonderful."

Another thing you might try is talking about what is really important to you and your daughter. Share with her your values and what you really believe is important. Ask her what she thinks is important. Let her know what you really want for her. Don't make it sound like a demand or some kind of plan to control her life. Simply tell her what you think would be best and why.

Q: Our fifteen-year-old daughter is a secondborn middle child who is eleven months and nine days younger than her older sister. She lives a very organized and planned life, even insists our family book vacations nine months to a year in advance. Our secondborn has to be first everywhere and in everything. Her motto is "If I can't win, I don't compete." She always tries to do more than is required of her and seldom wants to admit she is wrong. Her older sister is much more

quiet and very noncompetitive. What can we do to help our secondborn relax a little? And what can we do to motivate our oldest child, who sees herself as a failure?

A: What you appear to have here is a total role reversal. The secondborn has "taken over" from the firstborn and has developed the usual firstborn characteristics, but in an exaggerated fashion. "If I can't win, I don't compete" isn't your secondborn's only motto. She also has a "lifeline" (a life-style motto) that says "I count only when I control, when I'm right, when I achieve." All of this suggests that, with all of her apparent success, your secondborn has a very fragile self-image. She seems to believe that she will be accepted only if she achieves and performs and, as you put it, "does more than required."

As for the older girl, she is what we call a "discouraged firstborn." Her little sister has outdone her and blown out her candle, so to speak. Her self-image isn't just fragile, it's very weak and unhealthy. Her lifeline motto says "I count only when I can get people to feel sorry for me, when I'm a victim."

Admittedly, at ages fifteen and sixteen it's a little late in the game to change your daughters, but there are strategies you can use to make it easier to live with them and for them to live with themselves.

Concerning your discouraged firstborn daughter, encourage her at every opportunity. Give her special attention and more responsibility. Help her realize attainable goals and with every success encourage but don't praise. (Review Chapter Seven.)

Also, be sure to make a point of giving your sixteen-year-old the larger allowance, later hours—and a driver's license. Even if she says, "Oh, I don't want a license—I don't need to drive," gently insist that she obtain a driver's license because it will be handy—she never knows when she will have to drive you somewhere or pick you up, and so on. Whether she feels she needs the license or not, it will be a big boost for her self-image if she gets one, particularly if she has it ahead of her younger sister, even for a few months.

Concerning your perfectionistic controlling secondborn daughter, try not to be overimpressed with her achievements, particularly when she is very controlling while doing it. Take the payoff out of her perfectionism in every way you can, including "being less than perfect" in front of her. She probably learned her perfectionism from you and/or your husband. Let her know that you believe it's okay to make a mistake, not to have everything just so. Also, try to help her avoid "biting off more than she can chew," a common problem with perfectionists. The best way to do that, of course, is to not bite off more than you can chew yourself.

Q: I have five children, including a twenty-year-old daughter who is unmarried, the mother of a one-year-old and still living at home while she attends a community college. My problem is, I wind up caring for the baby almost all the time while she goes to classes, out with friends, and so on. I'm trying to help my daughter through a tough time in her life. Am I doing the right thing?

A: Your daughter is extremely fortunate to have a mom who is willing to give her and her baby a home. Your loving concern is more than admirable, but at the same time you are being "played for a sucker," as some twenty-year-olds might put it. Your daughter may not be going around behind your back saying "Mom is a sucker for taking care of my kid while I have fun," but she might as well be because that's what's happening.

I suggest that you sit down with your daughter and lay out a much firmer schedule in which she will take a much bigger role in caring for her own child. In other words, back off and give your daughter the responsibility that is truly hers. Tell her you are willing to care for the baby while she is at class or working at a part-time job (which I assume she has or will get soon). When she wants to go out with friends, however, she must hire her own baby-sitter or simply forgo that pleasure and stay home and care for the baby herself.

Another idea is this. If any of your other children are young enough to need care or supervision, your daughter should be asked to baby-sit in exchange for the baby-sitting that you do with her child. Then you can get out now and then yourself, which you should be doing at least once or twice a week for your own sanity.

Because you are apparently a softy, these suggestions may sound "cold and heartless," but they really are not. In fact, it is a rather mild introduction to reality for your daughter, who has been acting irresponsibly. Your long-range goals should include getting your daughter through college and out on her own. Both of these may be several years away, but they are still worthy targets. Good luck!

Q: My teenagers (boy fifteen, girl thirteen) never talk to me. When I ask them, "How was school?" they just grunt. Do you have any tips on how to get kids to carry on a conversation that is more than guttural sounds?

A: I have several suggestions, beginning with: "Don't force it." Teenagers talk when they're ready and willing. The more you pressure them, the more they are likely to clam up.

One of the best strategies for getting a teenager to talk is to "never ask questions." I know that's impossible, but it's a good rule of thumb. For example, don't ask your teenager, "How was school?" Instead, make a declarative statement: "Tell me about your day." The direct invitation or request is much harder to parry with a grunt, a yes or no, or a shrug. "Tell me what you think" is a much better approach than "What are you thinking?" or "What's your opinion?"

Often parents want to convey certain information or ideas to their teenagers, but find it difficult because they won't engage in conversation. One way to get across your message is to let the teenagers "eavesdrop" on conversations that are really for their benefit—between you and your husband, for example. Another way to get information across is to leave books and magazines around, lying open to the right page. If it's a subject that teenagers are really curious about, rest assured they will find a way to read it, usually when you're not around.

Another good approach is to be vulnerable and open. If you do get a child going in a conversation of any kind, beware of preaching, moralizing, or sounding as if you know all the answers. Also, go slow on sounding too definite or dictatorial. This can even carry over to requesting teenagers to catch up on a chore that they haven't done. "I know you don't want to hear this, but the garbage really needs emptying" is a lot better approach than "Hey, you've forgotten the garbage again! Take it out right now!"

If your teenager seems to be inviting your advice (or even your negative reaction) on *any* subject, realize that at this particular juncture, at least, your child does respect what you say. The child would not ask the question or make the comment if, deep down, he or she didn't respect you. This may not happen very often, but when it does happen, it says something for your parenting efforts.

Finally, don't automatically equate your teenager's silence with failure. Just because your teen seems secretive and noncommunicative doesn't mean you've done a bad job. I agree with child psychiatrist Richard Gardner, who points out that healthy adolescents are terrified about growing up and facing the world on their own. They know they're not self-sufficient and they're struggling through that well-known canyon of inferiority. Often teenagers are silent because they feel threatened by adults. They try to protect their fragile self-image by pretending they're invulnerable—shutting you out. Be patient. Do more listening than talking and avoid sounding preachy, critical or judgmental. And, as Gardner says, "Be forthright about your love for them and your desire to help."[4]

Q: **My twelve-year-old son, who just went into seventh grade, is having a very difficult time. The new situation, going to different classrooms, and so on, has sort of thrown him for a loop. He's not getting good grades, he feels nobody likes him, and he hates to go to school. I'm doing my best to praise him, no matter what kind of grades he gets. I tell him that he will make friends eventually and that he must hang in there. But nothing seems to work. He just walks away looking more glum than ever. Do you have any suggestions?**

A: First, stop praising your son. At this time especially, praise is very threatening to him because he doesn't feel he deserves it and he wonders if he can keep measuring up to whatever your praise might be. Instead of praise, use encouragement, which is a much different ballgame. (See Chapter Seven for a lengthy discussion of the difference between praise and encouragement.)

Second, listen carefully to your son and acknowledge his feelings, especially whenever he expresses frustration over being in junior high. Say such things as "Switching classes every hour can be a drag," or "It's hard when everything is changed around."

Let your son know about any struggles you had back in junior high or high school. In one case I was counseling a fifteen-year-old girl who just wasn't interested in sharing anything with me or listening to anything I had to say. I finally broke through to her when I went to my files and got out a letter, written by my high school counselor to my parents, which said, in effect, "Your son will never make it in college." From then on, the girl opened up to me because she knew that I knew what it was like to feel like a failure and to struggle.

Third, help your son learn to "run toward the fear." I have

always told my own children, "You've got to run toward the fear. Whatever you're afraid of, face it or you'll lose in life." Help your son learn to deal with feelings that nobody likes him by giving him some simple tips. No matter how afraid or gloomy he might feel, he should smile and say hello to those he meets at school. He should say "Hi, how are you?" or "Hi, how are you doing?" Remind him that there are a lot of kids in his junior high classes who feel *exactly* the way he does. They too are looking for any shred of friendliness or approval.

Let your son know that when he does make a friend or even begins to strike up a friendly relationship and wants to bring someone over to the house for dinner or just to hang out, you have an open-door policy. Tell him, "Check with me to be sure we'll be home, but, in general, it's okay to have someone over."

Fourth, encourage your son to get into some group activity or organization at school. Join the band, get on a team, join a club—anything to break the massive huge group (the entire junior high school) down into a smaller group where he can cope. Do everything you can to help you son "get good at something," no matter how ordinary that something might be. Right now his self-image is taking a beating, and you need to find a key to helping him build it back up again.

Q: I have an eleven-year-old son and a thirteen-year-old daughter. Being a single parent, I must work away from home right now and there are things the children must do to help. Sometimes they do great, but last night my daughter told me she had done some things around the house, and I believed her. This morning the truth comes out that the things simply were not done. She lied to me.

This isn't the first time that this has happened. I'm not sure how to deal with her. She's too big to spank. I feel guilty about having to carry so much myself and work outside the home. I guess I could just get welfare and food stamps, but I don't want to do that. Very frustrating. I'm working as hard as I can. What in the world can I do? Please help.

A: As you seem to already realize, your worst enemies are guilt and stress. You are carrying a big load right now and you want the children to help—as they should. When they disappoint you, however, you take it very much to heart, and this only increases your stress and your guilt. You're thinking, "If I was a better parent, they would be more obedient and helpful."

Please go back to Chapter One and memorize Image Insurance Principle #1: "Don't take misbehavior personally." That's good advice, to preserve not only your child's self-image but yours as well. Keep in mind that all kids misbehave and disobey and many even lie now and then. All parents struggle at times with feeling inadequate, betrayed, and worthless.

Always expect the best from your kids, but temper those expectations with the realization that they will fail now and then because they are human and far from perfect.

To put all this another way, try to lighten up, step back a little, and be thankful for all those times when "they do great."

As for your daughter lying to you, this should not go unnoticed and unchallenged. Whenever this kind of thing happens, sit down with your daughter, look her in the eye, and let her know that you know she hasn't told the truth. Tell her you are disappointed, but you are willing to forgive and you really want to trust her and give her responsibilities. Point out, "I want you to be happy, but if I can't trust you, all we'll do is butt heads and everyone will suffer."

Tell her you know it's hard to do housework or other chores when she'd rather be talking on the phone or doing something else with friends, but right now you need her help, as well as her younger brother's, and the whole family must pull together.

Also, give her every opportunity to share her feelings. Say, "Tell me how it is. Do you feel you have too much to do around the house? Is there a better way to divide up the chores?" This may open the door to having your daughter let you know that she thinks her little brother doesn't have enough to do and she—the firstborn who always has to carry the big load—has too much.

Whatever you do, don't preach, accuse, interrogate, or carry on in a way that makes your daughter feel guilty. Another thing to explore is how she feels about your divorce. Does she blame herself at all? Is she secretly blaming you? Maybe you need to have a long talk about that, and you need to share why you got the divorce and why you believe that, hard as it is, being a single mom is better than what was going on before.

All of these ideas may not fit your situation exactly, but pick and choose the ones that may start you in the right direction. Your goal here is not simply "Getting my daughter to stop lying and making sure that she helps out around the house." Your real goal is to help her build her self-image at a very crucial time of life—early adolescence. Your question implies that your daughter is quite cooperative a lot of the time. Build on that and don't make her feel as if she has to sneak through life. Make her feel that you trust her and that you know she will be a responsible young woman.

Q: My thirteen-year-old daughter has gone a little crazy. Last year she was sweet and respectful, this year she challenges me on *everything*. What's the best way to handle this?

A: Welcome to the great club called "Parents of Teenagers." The adolescent storm has hit and what you must do is "back off but not back down." Your daughter is going through a very typical stage. She's starting to break away from you in earnest, to think for herself, to get out on her own, and so on. She wants you to know that she is "not a kid anymore."

Right now it appears that your daughter doesn't respect you. Keep in mind that you've already paid your dues as a parent, and, while you can't demand respect, you can be firm but fair and let your daughter decide to respect you. She will do that as you show her respect—as you acknowledge that she is "not a child anymore." Of course, she isn't an adult either, but now you must start to do a little more listening and a little less talking, admonishing, and advising. You must be open to her ideas (even if they're slightly off the wall), less judgmental, and less ready to be there with all the right answers.

What your daughter needs right now is all the help she can get in preserving that fragile self-image that is taking a beating out there in the junior high arena. I know it's hard because the way she's treating you isn't doing your self-image a whole lot of good, but that's a burden a parent has to carry. You can do it if you keep in mind that you are still in healthy authority over your daughter, but now your relationship has changed and will continue to change as she "grows up" in every sense of that term.

What also might help is to read some practical material on teenagers.

Q: They are handing out condoms at my daughter's high school. She thinks it's a good idea. I don't. How can I talk to her about this?

A: You are confronting head-on the "everybody's doing it" phenomenon that has swept our culture, and not just among teenagers. The "sexual revolution" that supposedly began in the 1960s has reaped the whirlwind, and now in the 1990s more and more teenagers are having sex at a younger and younger age. In addition, we have the ghastly specter of AIDS spreading over the earth and threatening literally millions of lives, including yours and the life of your teenager.

Of course most teenagers at your daughter's school think "condoms are a great idea." They want to believe that condoms will protect them from AIDS and other sexually transmitted diseases and that they can go ahead and have sex with anyone they want. According to one recent study, "In 1988, 27 percent of unmarried females age 15 had had intercourse, up by almost half from 19 percent in 1982. (For unmarried males, age 17, it went from 56 percent in 1979 to 72 percent in 1988.) And six out of every ten sexually active females, ages 15 to 19, reported having had two or·more partners."[5]

Boys have always been labeled as being out to get all they could get, but more and more social workers, teachers, school nurses, and the like are reporting that now girls are becoming extremely aggressive and inviting boys to have sex. One left the message "Let's have S-E-X" on a boy's answering machine.[6] The bottom line on all this behavior is not simply that teenage girls or boys are "bad" or "immoral." The bottom line is that girls are inviting boys to have sex because they think this is the way they will find love, affection, and caring. A lot of "sexually active teenagers" come from homes where there isn't a lot of affection, where parents are busy with their own lives and letting their kids "fend for themselves." So, they are fending for themselves, and when the schools start handing out condoms, they welcome the new "equipment."

To deal with your question directly, sit down with your daughter when you are both calm and in a good mood and talk about just how safe condoms really are. Let her know that already the slogan has been changed from "safe sex" to "safer sex." As unemotionally and as objectively as possible, share with her that there is no such thing as absolutely "safe sex." The only safe approach is abstinence—waiting until you are married and marrying someone who has also waited.

That may sound silly or "unreal" to your teenager, but don't back off. Point out that the most conservative estimates predict that 5 percent of all condoms either have holes in them already when manufactured or they will break when used. Some estimates go as high as 10 percent. Also let your daughter know that whenever a girl has sex with a boy, she is having sex with all the other partners that boy had had as well, and vice versa.

Get information to share with your daughter about sexually transmitted diseases, as well as the realities of what it means to get pregnant, consider having an abortion, or having the child and then trying to "raise it on her own." A lot of teenagers think they have all the answers to all these questions. They've seen the film on STDs in health class at school. They think they "know all about" chlamydia, syphilis, gonorrhea, and AIDS. As for getting pregnant, they have heard, "You can always get an abortion." But it is never quite that simple. Even pro-choice advocates admit that having an abortion can be a difficult and even devastating experience for a woman, and it should never be taken lightly.

My personal values tell me that premarital sex is wrong and abstinence is right. My values say abortion is wrong and that a woman's "right to do what she wishes to her body" does not include killing another human being within her womb. You may or may not feel the same way, but as you talk to your daughter, steer away from moralizing and stick with the facts. Telling your daughter that "condoms are immoral" will have little effect. You can be a lot more help to your daughter if you convey the message that you love her very much and you are deeply concerned about the "bill of goods" that she is being sold at her high school and by the entire culture in which she has to grow up.

Condoms are not the answer. They are only a bandage that many leaders, teachers, and authorities who should know better are putting on the problem, which they sum up by saying, "Well, kids are going to do it anyway, so we might as well give them some protection." The only real protection—the only "safe approach to sex"—is abstinence, and having a strong self-image that allows you to respect yourself and not just follow the herd, where you have every real risk of destroying your life.

Q: My fourteen-year-old daughter is very mature and physically developed for her age. She wants to date a boy who is three years older. She has never officially dated before and I think she's too young. How can I best handle this?

A: Initially, sit down with your daughter and say something like this: "Honey, you may not want to hear this, but your father and I agree that you can't go on single dates at fourteen, particularly with a boy who is three years older."

Naturally, your daughter will ask why and you can simply say, "We think that sixteen is a much more realistic age to start single dating. You're only fourteen and it's just too soon, especially with a boy who is a lot older than you are."

Next, your daughter will probably protest, "You don't trust me, I'm not that kind of girl, he's not that kind of boy," and so on.

Tell her, "Honey, we believe you and we trust you. We also have the responsibility to not let you get into situations that put you at risk."

All these are suggestions for taking a stand and doing all you can to discourage this budding relationship between your daughter and someone three years older. When "John" discovers that he can't get your daughter out alone in his car, that may be enough to end the relationship. He may suddenly find it convenient to be interested in someone else. On the other hand, John may not go away that easily. Then you must control the situation as best you can.

Don't hesitate to set up strict rules about what is allowed and not allowed. For one thing, do not let your daughter accept rides home from school in John's car, which can quickly turn into a "date" that could escalate into the very activities you fear. If John wants to see your daughter, he can come over to the house to spend time watching television, studying, and the like, but only when at least one parent is home.

Again, as you suggest rules like this, your daughter will protest and continue to use the argument that you don't trust her, that she is not that kind of girl, and so on. You must stick to your guns and say that you are well aware that she isn't that kind of girl, and that you are simply trying to protect her. If John is, indeed, as gallant and noble as she thinks he is, he will be happy to go along with these rules just so he can spend time with her.

Above all, while being firm, be loving and gentle. Keep in mind that many teenagers want to be parented. Realize that your daughter could be sneaking around, seeing John on the sly, and rebelling against all of your values. Instead, she has come to you and asked your permission to date John. Realize that she is really asking your opinion and your approval. For all you know, she is somewhat fearful of dating John but she is having trouble bucking her peer group who will think she is crazy for turning down a seventeen-year-old stud with a nice car.

One more thing: No matter what ingenious suggestions your daughter and John might make for expanding on whatever rules are laid down, never back off on your original rule: No single dating until age sixteen. Group dates and get-togethers might be okay, but even beware of "double dates." A double date hardly guarantees proper behavior. In fact, the other couple may simply serve as a role model for how to get into serious trouble and a situation your daughter isn't ready for at all.

Also, even though your daughter may cry, carry on, and mope around the house for a while, keep in mind that the interests of fourteen-year-olds can change in anywhere from a week to a few weeks. Your daughter will survive and, in the long run, her self-image will be the better for it.

Q: I have a very open relationship with my son, who is sixteen. He tells me he's getting a lot of pressure to "make out" and "prove he's a man" from both boys and girls in his high school. We have raised him with very high morals and standards and he doesn't want to give in, but he doesn't know how to answer his friends when they tease him. My wife and I were both virgins when we got married, but I know it's a lot tougher now. What can I tell him?

A: Obviously, the first thing to tell your son is that you and his mother waited until marriage to have sex. Let him know that you realize that it is tougher now and the pressure is, in some cases, a hundred times greater, but he doesn't have to follow the herd down a path where he can risk everything—even his life.

Point out that nothing will ever change the reality of guys teasing other guys in the locker room—that sort of thing. Help your son work out some "disarming" replies when he does get teased or asked if "he got a little last night." Give him some ideas for one-liner comebacks that aren't defensive or particularly judgmental of the one doing the teasing. For example:

"Say what you want. Everything is cool."

"C'mon, you seem to worry more about me than my mother does."

And, in some settings, he might even say, "Hey, I'm scared to death of AIDS. Condoms are no guarantee. Maybe you're brave, but I admit it, I'm chicken."

Another entire area to explore with your son is the proper treatment of a girl and proper sexual behavior on a date. If his mother is willing, have her talk to him about how a girl with a healthy self-image views boys. Girls with the same kind of values taught in your family are always attracted to a boy who has manners, who shows respect. For example, he never comes up to her with three or four other guys and tries to mock, put down, or act like a jerk, in general. Also, on a date he doesn't pinch, squeeze, fondle, or maul. A young woman with a healthy self-image appreciates a young man who acts like a gentleman. Manners and respect will never go out of style.

If your son is dating, talk frankly about "how far to go." Holding hands, hugging, and a quick kiss good night can easily be controlled. Necking and heavy petting cannot and may lead to intercourse.

I realize that what I say would cause the typical "studs" who are trying to score as much as possible to laugh hysterically, but they are playing with very real fire that in the end would have a last and final laugh. Be grateful that you have the kind of relationship that you have with your son—it is unusual, if not rare.

Also, you should be aware that the more open parents are about setting strict sexual guidelines, the less sexually active their teenagers become. One study by a sociologist of over 1,100 teenagers revealed that when parents talk to their kids about sex and healthy values, they are far less likely to become sexually involved. In addition, this study also showed that when a teenager's family did a lot of things together, that helped prevent those teenagers from going out to find a cheap substitute for intimacy somewhere else.

The worst extremes are to be permissive and never make any kind of stand at all regarding what is sexually right and wrong or to be very strict but to never talk with your teenager and explain *why* you're strict and help your child understand that you care a great deal about him or her.

Above all, don't brush off the teasing of the peer group by simply telling your son "I know you can handle it." Teasing by the peer group can easily make the strongest teenagers feel inferior and stupid unless they are armed with practical information and the assurance that they are loved, valued, and prized by their family. In the end *that*, above all, is what counts.

Q: My wife and I go round and round with our sixteen-year-old daughter on when to be in from going to her school's football or basketball games, parties, and other events that take her out in the evening. She hates the idea of a curfew and says, "I can't always leave because I'm giving other girls a ride and they want to stay out later." How can we handle this?

A: Stick to your guns on curfew times, but give your daughter reasonable ways to deal with her friends. In some cases, staying out a little later may be justified, and your daughter can simply call home and tell you what's happening. In other cases, your daughter will simply have to bite the bullet and tell her friends, "I'm sorry, but I'm due home by eleven o'clock and if you want to ride with me, let's go."

Remind your daughter that because she has the car and is driving, she is in control. You expect her to be responsible and considerate, and, at the same time, you want to work with her and honor her good judgment.

During her junior year in high school, our daughter, Krissy, went to an out-of-town football game. At eleven-thirty that night she called me from a pizza parlor and wanted to know what time she had to get home. I replied, "Honey, you know what time to be home."

"Well, Dad," she responded, "what time do I have to be home?"

"Just be home at a reasonable time," was all I said.

"But, Dad, we won the game but the team hasn't gotten here yet."

At this point I was getting the picture. The game was over and Krissy and her other friends were waiting for the team to come by the pizza parlor to "celebrate" their victory.

"So, you want to wait for the team—that's why you're there and that's why you're calling."

"Well, yeah, exactly," Krissy said hesitantly.

"Well, honey, I appreciate your calling. Go ahead and wait for the team, enjoy yourself, and be home at a reasonable hour."

Forty-five minutes later Krissy called back a second time to remind me what time it was and I again reminded her to be home at a reasonable time. She finally got home at 12:50 A.M.

Now, all this may sound as if I were a permissive dad, but I don't think so. At the time Krissy was seventeen years old. She had already been driving for over a year and had proved herself very responsible. She called me twice during the evening to be sure that I knew where she was and what was happening. Normally, 12:50 A.M. is a bit late to be getting in, but under the circumstances I think it was acceptable. You see, it's too easy to be prescriptive and lay down hard-and-fast rules. It is much better to put the responsibility on the shoulders of the child and let the child figure it out.

Q: We have two teenagers, a boy fifteen and a girl thirteen, as well as a twelve-year-old who might as well be a teenager herself. All three of our kids complain that their father and I do too much talking or that we "nag too much." I don't want to be a nag, but, frankly, our kids need reminding about some things. What do you think? Should I just be quiet, or should I be a nag if I have to?

A: Be a nag—within reason. You and your husband may talk a little too much (for all I know, you may talk way too much), but your kids are trying to intimidate you and make you back off from giving them any advice. I agree that teenagers do need reminders. They are not infallible and invincible, and they certainly don't know as much as they think they do.

The trick is to preserve their self-image while still making your points. Here are some suggestions:

1. *Don't major in minors.* Pick your priorities and be sure they are the important issues, not superficial stuff that only irritates your kids.

2. *Be specific.* If you're reminding your kids of something you think is important, don't generalize or beat around the bush.

3. *Be brief.* Your kids are right. Adults do tend to go on and on. State your case pleasantly and firmly and *stop.* In a way, this gives you more authority and conveys the feeling that you know you're in charge, but you're trying to be pleasant about it.

Coming back to "being a nag," there are times when a parent feels so strongly about certain issues that repetition is in order. With me, it's "driving rules." I freely confess that I drove Holly and then Krissy a little crazy with my reminders about safe driving practices. Just the other day I started reminding Krissy once again: "And, honey, remember, when you're making a left turn at a stoplight—"

Krissy laughed and interrupted me, "Yeah, yeah, Dad, I know, 'Be sure to never turn left until you know *both* lanes are clear.' "

"Exactly!" I said. "One reason I'm confident about your driving is that I know you make good decisions. I always expect you to make those good decisions."

Q: My fourteen-year-old son, an only child, has very little to do with my husband, who is his stepfather. The divorce happened about four years ago and, while my second husband has no real conflict with my son, there seems to be no closeness or much communication. I've mentioned this to my husband and all he will say is "I try, but I don't seem to get very far." When I talk to my son about it, he just says, "George is okay, I guess, we just don't seem to have much in common."

My son's natural father has moved to the other end of the country, and the last time he saw him was two years ago. I'm

afraid my son is growing up without a good male role model. What can be done about this?

A: Your concern is understandable and even laudable, but you may be making too much of the situation. Keep in mind that your son did have his natural father for a role model until he was ten. The most important time to have a male role model is during those first five to seven years of life when the life-style becomes molded and set.

Keep in mind, too, that your son is fourteen. In four years, possibly less, he will probably not be living with you any longer. Don't try to legislate or force what you want to see happen between your husband and his stepson. Make suggestions about things they might want to do together, stay alert for any like interest they might have, but don't try to manipulate your son or your husband.

If you still are determined to put your son in touch with a wholesome male role model, look for some natural ways to bring your son together with such a person without making a big deal out of it. For example, if you have a brother who likes to fish and your son likes to fish too, ask your brother to invite his nephew to go fishing now and then. As my friend and colleague John Rosemond puts it, don't try to "push the river." Let the river find its own course.

Q: Our seventeen-year-old son got his license last year and he's been careful—until last week. He got two tickets for speeding in four days! My husband is ready to take his keys for "at least six months." I'm not sure that will really help. What's your advice?

A: I would recommend leniency and forgiveness. The Reality Discipline of the situation should be the two tickets (which a careful teenage driver would find totally mortifying). Sit down with the boy, tell him you aren't happy about the tickets, but you are sure neither is he. Of course, he will have to pay all fines and any increases in insurance fees. Nonetheless, you aren't taking away his keys, you are going to trust him, give him another chance to be responsible.

I know something myself about driving as a teenager and feeling the sting of failure for failing to obey traffic laws to the letter. At the age of nineteen while going out on a double date with a friend, I got three tickets in one night!

My first ticket came as I drove out of town a mile or two to pick up my buddy. Then we went to pick up our dates for the evening. As I approached a stoplight in a rather remote area, I saw it turn yellow, but I was sure I could sneak through in time.

I stepped on the gas a little bit but just as I came up to the intersection the light turned red and I went sailing on through doing probably 35 miles an hour. I glanced to my right and there, sitting waiting for the light to turn green, was a patrol car! He turned on another kind of red light and, in less than a minute, I was collecting my first ticket for the evening.

I went on out to my buddy's house, picked him up, and as we headed back into town I told him what happened. He was sympathizing with me when I looked in my rearview mirror and here was another red light! It was different patrol car, and in minutes I had my second ticket of the evening—for going 35 in a 25-mile zone.

We picked up our dates and throughout the evening we all talked about my rotten luck—how I'd gotten two tickets in less than an hour and pretty marginal ones at that. After catching a movie and going to a drive-in, we took our dates home and then I drove my friend out to his house. I kept saying, "Two tickets in one night—my parents are going to kill me."

I dropped my friend off about 1:00 A.M. and headed back into town, anxious to get to bed myself because I had things to do early the next morning. I distinctly remember laughing with him, and his final warning as I dropped him off: "Don't get another ticket!"

Less than five minutes later while driving on the same street where I had gotten my first speeding ticket for the evening, I looked in my rearview mirror and here was my third—perhaps I should say fourth—red light of the evening. It was a different officer, but the same offense, doing 35 in a 25-mile zone.

How does a nineteen-year-old explain to his parents that he's gotten three tickets in one night? Very carefully. I explained to my father about the "yellow-red light" just as I came to the intersection, doing all of 35 miles an hour in a remote area where there wasn't a car in sight. Then I went on to tell him about doing 35 in a 25-mile zone and getting nailed twice by different squad cars. I was thankful he was pretty calm about it. He even seemed to understand, and I recall him saying, "Well, you've probably set some kind of record. I've picked up a few tickets myself. You'll just have to really stick to the speed limit, because the police seem to have their eye on you."

While Dad was willing to forgive, his insurance company was a little different story. Tickets get reported to insurance companies, and not long after my three-ticket evening the insurance company called, wanting an explanation. So I went downtown to talk to my dad's insurance agent and he asked a little incredulously, "Can this be *true*? Three tickets in one *day*?"

"Actually, it was three tickets in one night," I explained, and then I carefully told him what had happened.

The agent listened sympathetically but then said, "The company wants to take you off your parents' policy, or your father will have to pay an exorbitant amount to keep you driving."

I pleaded with the agent. I was working and needed the car to drive to my job or I'd lose it for sure. I was already paying everything I could to allow my father to carry me on his policy. I knew I couldn't afford any more money and neither could he. "Look," I told the agent, "I was wrong, in fact, I was stupid. I got the three tickets, but I wasn't tearing around like some maniac.

From here on out I intend to be extra careful because I know the police have their eye on young guys like me."

The insurance agent listened and told me, "I'll see what I can do." I don't know how he pulled it off, but he was able to write a letter back to the home office in the Midwest saying that he knew me and my family and that he personally vouched for me and my ability to learn my lesson from three tickets in one night. I'm not sure what they thought at the home office, but somehow, "like a good neighbor," they came through. They kept me on my parents' policy without any raise in rates, and in so doing they kept a customer for life.

I believe teenagers, especially, face those moments when they need someone who will believe in them, trust in them, and give them a break. And I'd like to believe that teenagers never forget that.

Q: My seventeen-year-old son and his fifteen-year-old girl-friend are "sexually active." The other night he shocked me by asking if he could bring his girlfriend home to stay with him overnight in his room! I told him I'd have to think about it. What do you think?

A: When faced with this kind of situation, some parents knuckle under, reasoning that their teenagers will go ahead and have sex anyway in places that are unsafe, so they might as well try to make the best of a bad deal. Still other parents refuse to allow their kids to have sex under their roof, but they cop out by tossing all the responsibility on their children. As one woman with a fifteen-year-old son and a fifteen-year-old daughter said: "My son has hinted that he is sexually active, but I don't ask where. If kids are mature enough to have a sexual relationship, they don't need to have their parents there."

While my point of view might seem antediluvian to parents like those just described, I believe the best answer is no sex with the girlfriend under your roof, or anywhere else. Do your best to convince your son to stop having sex with her immediately. Explain that by having sex with her, he is literally risking her health. Any doctor will tell him that the more sexually active a girl her age is, the greater her chance of developing cervical cancer later in life. Also point out that he is risking his own health—possibly his life. How does he know if he is his girlfriend's first partner? Remind him that when you have sex with someone, physiologically you also have sex with everyone else who ever had sex with that person.

This is what the AIDS epidemic is all about—people having sex out of wedlock, playing what amounts to Russian roulette, and hoping they will get away with it.

The truth is, you never get away with it. Sooner or later the piper must be paid. In all likelihood your son will not marry this girl, he is only using her for a short time. On the other hand, he could get her pregnant (condoms are never 100 percent safe) and be forced into an early marriage that can easily lead to unhappiness and an early divorce.

I sympathize with your problem, but it has reached a stage where you don't have a whole lot of choices. You can either draw a line in the dirt and let your son know where you stand, or you can simply sit by and let him continue down a path he seems to have chosen quite a while ago.

Advocates of giving teenagers condoms because they are "going to have sex anyway" believe they are the realists, but I don't think so. The true reality is that premarital sex is always irresponsible and exploitative, always a risk, often the road to disease and unhappiness, and sometimes fatal.

One other possibility is talking to the girl's parents and enlisting their cooperation in a stand against what is going on. But whether they cooperate or not, stick to your abstinence guns without moralizing or hysteria. As bad as the sexual revolution seems to be, a new abstinence revolution is just getting started, fueled in great part by fear of AIDS and other sexually transmitted diseases.

My friend and colleague Dr. James Dobson, founder and president of Focus on the Family, advises teenagers that, even if they have been sexually active, they can, if they determine to do so, become "secondary virgins." They can stop having irresponsible sex and practice abstinence until they are ready for the responsibilities of marriage. Obviously, secondary virginity is an unpopular message, but some young people are beginning to listen. May their tribe increase.

Q: I'm afraid my thirteen-year-old daughter is getting involved with drugs. When I confronted her the other morning, she said, "I tried marijuana once, but that's all." I'm frightened. How can I reach her and explain the terrible danger in drugs?

A: One obvious thing parents can do is make available information about what drugs do to the body. All kinds of materials are available. For example, marijuana was once considered even by the so-called experts to be "quite harmless." Now the experts have done much more extensive research, which reveals that using marijuana leads to what is called the "pot personality." Anyone with a pot personality has impaired short-term memory, emotional flatness, and is very likely to slip into the "drop-out syndrome"—out of sports, out of school, out of family.

In addition, the pot personality is characterized by diminished willpower, inability to concentrate, a shorter attention span, less ability to deal with abstract or complex problems, and less ability to deal with frustration. In addition, there is increased confusion in thinking, impaired judgment, and hostility toward authority.[7]

But providing the "facts" on drugs is only a partial answer and doesn't get to the root of the problem, which, not surprisingly, is a person's self-image and sense of self-worth. According to one study I've seen, the *closer* teenagers are to their parents, the less likely they are to use drugs. The more independent or detached teenagers are from parents, the greater the likelihood that they will use drugs.[8]

I would never be so naive as to say that there is one single answer to drugs, but in a sense this study about how close or detached kids are from parents puts it in a nutshell. Sit down with your daughter whether you feel equipped to do so or not, look her in the eye, and tell her how scared you are for her. Tell her you don't want to preach or lecture, you simply want her to know that you love her very much and that she might as well have told you that she tried Russian roulette or riding along with some idiot who was playing "chicken."

Take heart in the fact that your daughter was willing to tell you that she "tried marijuana just once." There is still a communication connection, and you can take full advantage of it. Get her information, show her articles about what drugs do to young people. Counter the lies and stupidity that her peer group is feeding her with facts and reasonable logic. Do everything you can to give her ammunition that will save her from the jaws of the peer group.

Above all, do everything you can to strengthen your relationship to your daughter and bring yourselves closer together.

If you want to help your daughter, you must do it *now*. If you don't, you may be getting the kind of call I had to make several years ago when I notified a mom and dad that their nineteen-year-old son had overdosed on beer and barbiturates and was dead. Let your daughter know about drugs. Information is everywhere—go to your family doctor, the local health service, the police, or the public library. But more important, let your daughter know how much you care. If she is convinced that you really do love her, the chances are excellent that she will open up and share what's on her mind and deep in her soul.

Q: I was turning over mattresses the other morning and found a stack of *Playboy* plus other even more filthy magazines under my son's bed. I'm still in shock. I haven't said anything to him or his father. What should I do?

A: Tell your husband about the magazines and seek to work together to confront your son in a way that might be constructive. The worst approach, which may well be your husband's first inclination, is to crack down on your son: scream, lecture, ground him, and so on. This will only drive him underground, so to speak, and he will continue ogling *Playboy* and other trash but only be more careful about it. I suggest the following plan, which is based on Reality Discipline:

Don't tell your son what you have found. Instead, leave his copies of *Playboy* and some of the other stuff out on the coffee table with other magazines to which you subscribe. Let him discover his "stuff" is missing. (Chances are he already has and is scared to death wondering who found it.) When he discovers it on the family coffee table, there are two possible scenarios: He may find it while you are present and, if so, you can say with a straight face, "Well, I found these magazines while turning your mattress and I thought I'd just put them out here where the rest of the family could enjoy them."

At this point, your son will be melting with embarrassment as coals of fire are heaped upon his head. He'll be expecting a full-blast lecture on immorality, but, instead, sit him down, look him in the eye, and say, "I am well aware that you're at the time of life when you're very curious about the female body. That's a perfectly natural thing, but what you're getting into here is pornography. I want you to know that I am offended by this kind of material because it is demeaning to all women everywhere. This is just one more example of how women are exploited and used in our present-day society. I want you to take the responsibility of getting rid of all this stuff—get it out of our house and never bring anything like this in again."

That is about all you need to say. Give your son the responsibility of getting rid of the pornographic material. Don't condemn him to the fires of hell for being a sexual pervert. Simply let him know that he's into something that is offensive, demeaning, and that can be addictive if he keeps looking at it.

The alternative to this scenario is that your son will find the material when you're not there. Undoubtedly he will quickly gather it up and quite likely "get rid of the evidence" as soon as he can. Then you need to go and confront him, saying, "I noticed that certain reading material is no longer available on our coffee table. Do you happen to know what happened to it?"

Then you can go into the same scenario just described. Your son will know the jig is up. In all likelihood, he's known it for several days. If he says, "I got rid of it," say, "Good, I'm glad to hear that," and then sit him down and talk to him about how demeaning pornography is to women and how dangerous and addictive it can be. For some people, usually males, pornography can be as addictive as alcohol or drugs. They keep needing material that is more and more explicit and even violent.

Is doing what I describe any guarantee that your son will never look at pornographic pictures again? Of course not, but you must be content with knowing that you've let him know that: (a) it's okay to have a natural curiosity about sex and the female body, but (b) it's not okay to demean women, no matter how air-brushed and "beautiful" the photos are, and (c) you don't want any more of it in your home.

At this point he will have to make his own decisions about how much he wants to look at this kind of stuff in the future, when he's out with friends, and so on. Continue talking with your son openly about sexual matters. Invite his questions. This may be difficult, but it is a far better approach than silently hiding your head in the sand and hoping that somehow he'll get through his teenage years and "outgrow all this dirty thinking."

Home Responsibilities for Teenagers

As your children move through the teenage years, they should be given more and more responsibility, with the ultimate goal of being fully responsible for themselves by age eighteen. Specific home responsibilities for teenagers could be almost too numerous to mention. Two key ones, however, which often lead to tension and even power struggles, include determining how late to stay up on school nights and how late to stay out on weekend dates, games, and gatherings. Parents and teenagers need to negotiate these times, but always put as much of the responsibility on your teenager as possible.

Another key area is money. Teenagers should be fully responsible for any allowances they receive or any money they earn in part- or full-time jobs. Something else you might consider is giving your teenager the responsibility of running the family checkbook. We have done this with our children with excellent results. It is good training for the future, when they will have to take care of checking accounts of their own.

What you hope to see as your teenagers mature is their ability to anticipate the needs of others and initiate the appropriate action. They also need to recognize and accept their capabilities and limitations. Obviously, one of their biggest challenges is to know the difference. Most teenagers think they have great capabilities and few limits.

Your teenagers need to learn to respect others as well as themselves. Above all, they need to learn the full meaning of taking responsibility for their own decisions.[9]

In short, they are becoming adults, just like their parents. The following list can be helpful in guiding them toward their responsibilities.

A Teenager's Ten Commandments to Parents

1. Please don't give me everything I say I want. Saying no shows me you care. I appreciate the guidelines.

2. Don't treat me like a little kid. Even though you know what's "right," I need to discover some things for myself.

3. Respect my need for privacy. Often I need to be alone to sort things out and daydream.

4. Never say, "In my day . . ." That's an immediate turn-off. Besides, the pressures and responsibilities of my world are more complicated.

5. I don't pick your friends or clothes, please don't criticize mine. We can disagree and still respect each other's choices.

6. Refrain from always rescuing me; I learn most from my mistakes. Hold me accountable for the decisions I make in life, it's the only way I'll learn to be responsible.

7. Be brave enough to share your disappointments, thoughts, and feelings with me. I'm never too old to be told I'm loved.

8. Don't talk in volumes. I've had years of good instruction, now trust me with the wisdom you have shared.

9. I respect you when you ask me for forgiveness for a thoughtless deed on your part. It proves that neither of us is perfect.

10. Set a good example for me as God intended you to do; I pay more attention to your actions than your words.[10]

Epilogue

Full Esteem Ahead!

■

It was the summer following Holly's graduation from high school. As we usually do, we had fled the 120-degree heat of Tucson to spend the summer months on cool Chautauqua Lake near my sister's home in Jamestown, New York. We would have had our usual idyllic time, except for Sande's almost constant complaints about having to say good-bye to Holly when she would go off to college in September.

"She's never lived away from home before," Sande kept reminding me. "I just know I'll start crying and I won't be able to stop."

I would just chuckle and reassure my overemotional wife: "All firstborns have to fly the nest sometime. I think it's going to be kind of nice, with one less teenager wanting the car."

Sande would just shrug and give me an empty look, but she didn't stop mentioning Holly's upcoming departure from our home for the first time in her life. It seemed that it would come up at least once a day, sometimes oftener.

As the summer drifted by, I started kidding Sande, saying such things as "Don't worry, honey, when the great moment of parting comes, I'll hold your hand." I started telling friends, "Sande is going to cry all the way home after we drop Holly off at college." The husbands chuckled along with me, but most of the wives gave us that knowing look that only wives can get when husbands aren't too sensitive—or too bright.

The big day finally arrived. We had decided to drive Holly to the school, which was located some 110 miles directly south of our summer home at Chautauqua Lake and almost 2,500 miles east of our permanent home in Tucson, Arizona. We squeezed Sande and Holly and part of her "stuff" into the car Holly would be using while at school. I took the *rest* of Holly's belongings with me in our car. We told Krissy, Kevin, and Hannah, "Have a great day with Aunt Sally!" and drove off.

As I drove along alone, listening to music, I wondered how my wife and firstborn were doing up ahead as they got in some final and important mother/daughter conversation. While we had helped Holly pack for the trip, I had kidded her about how good it would be to get her out of the house. Sande had tried to join in, but her heart wasn't in it. I could see she was already fulfilling her summer-long prophecy. Her eyes were already teary. She had been planning this day of depression for months, and now she was going to have it—in spades!

Poor Sande, I thought to myself. *This kind of thing is so hard on moms. I'll have to remember to take her out to a nice place for dinner tonight to cheer her up.*

The miles rolled by and, in what seemed like excellent time, we pulled onto the campus where a huge sign greeted us:

WELCOME FRESHMEN!

As I looked around at the perfectly manicured grounds, I thought, *Well, this is where Holly is going to spend the next four years. . . . We won't have her around so much anymore. . . .* Suddenly all of my light-hearted machismo started leaking rapidly away and the beginnings of a lump began to form in my throat.

We proceeded up the long drive, obediently following several signs that said:

FRESHMEN WOMEN: THIS WAY

We wound our way to Holly's residence hall and pulled up at the curb to be greeted enthusiastically by ten impeccably dressed young men who were more than happy to help the new student and her parents unload and take all the bags and boxes upstairs to her room. Sande and I didn't have to turn a hand; we just stood and watched, and I quickly noticed our daughter was being watched as well.

As I observed several handsome young males giving Holly the once-over, my first instinct was to punch out two or three of them and send the rest packing with roars of fatherly indignation, but, of course, I knew I had to stay calm. I felt a great deal like Steve Martin in *Father of the Bride* in the scene where he meets his future son-in-law and notices him fondling his daughter's knee as the two of them sit together on the couch, announcing their coming marriage.

And then the thought struck me: *Could it be that one of these ten young men in blue buttoned-down shirts could by my future son-in-law?* I began to realize that this day—the day I thought I would handle with a breeze—was not going to be one of the greatest of my life.

Later we went up to Holly's room and met her roommate and her roommate's parents. Then we dropped by to say hello to the head resident and the "RA" (Resident Assistant, a job I held once myself while in graduate school).

Next we did a quick tour of the campus, sort of finding our way together to the football field, the gymnasium, the auditorium, the library, and some of the classroom buildings. We wound up at the student union where we had lunch. As we ate, I could picture Holly meeting there often in the next four years to grab a bite with friends, to gossip and maybe even simulate studying now and then.

As all this was going on, I would steal an occasional glance at Sande, who was trying to smile and be enthused. Frankly, she wasn't doing a real good job of it. We went back up to Holly's room and, realizing this was her last opportunity to do something motherly, Sande proceeded to make Holly's bed and put away some of her clothes.

Finally we drifted down to the parking lot where we had planned to say good-bye, get in our car, and drive away, all the while smiling at our daughter, letting her know that we shared in her joy over her completely new role: college coed living thousands of miles from us. But by now Sande was crying openly. She and Holly hugged and then my firstborn turned to me. For some strange reason I couldn't see very well. My glasses were foggy or smudged—or something. I had the distinct feeling that I just wanted to get out of there, get clear off that campus, and fast.

Holly's experienced eye detected my want-to-get-going attitude, and she said, "Hey, Dad, what's your hurry? Is there a football game on later?"

"No, honey," I said, swallowing a strange lump in my throat, "it's just a little hard to . . ." and then I was holding my daughter close and the tears were rolling down my face and all over her. I'm not sure how long I held her like that, unable to speak. It could have been five minutes, it was probably less, but I wanted it to last forever.

Holly was crying too, and we didn't say much of anything. Finally I took off my glasses and tried to dry them off a bit. Then, in a strange staccato voice, barely able to get each word out, I barked: "Well, you'd better get going. I love you very much. You're a great daughter. We believe in you. Do a good job."

Getting one of her firstborn I'm-concerned looks, Holly asked, "Dad, are you okay?"

I assured her I was and she hugged me again and kissed me good-bye. I knew I was reaching my limit. I couldn't stand much more of this.

"You'd better go," I said. She nodded and then she was gone, walking away down the steps from the parking lot toward her dorm, just a few yards away. I looked around and saw a lot of other parents and other kids, all wiping away the tears. Then I looked back and saw my daughter still walking toward her dorm. She was still brushing away some tears of her own, but she didn't walk with a slow, dejected gait. In fact, she moved quickly, confidently, her head held high, "walking right out of our lives," or so it seemed to me.

Sande and I drove slowly out of the parking lot, down the long college drive, and onto the highway. That trip back to Chautauqua Lake was the longest of my life. Here I was with the woman I love, but I was feeling terrible, and so was she. My glasses kept fogging up and I couldn't see the road clearly. Sande went through at least one box of tissues and started on another. Off and on we made stabs at talking and we held hands frequently. The rest of the time I just hung on to the wheel and struggled with my thoughts.

I wonder what Holly was thinking when she walked away from us? I'd like to go back and get her, but I can't. I wonder how she is getting along without us? Is she as sad as we are right now? Or is she happy, glad to get out of the house and away from parents for once?

I couldn't stop being amazed at how I had broken down after I was sure I could handle my daughter's leaving home with nary a blink. Right there in the car I vowed to myself that I'd be ready when I had to walk Holly down the aisle to be married. When the preacher said, "Who giveth this woman?" I wouldn't be taking any chances. I'd have my little tape recorder ready and I'd press the button and the prerecorded tape would say "Her mother and I do" in a strong ringing voice. There would be no way I would trust myself at that moment.

I WANTED TO LOVE HER—AND KEEP HER

And then it struck me that some of the catchy little phrases that I like to use in seminars were coming back to haunt me, especially "Love them and let them go." I didn't *want* to let Holly go. Something kept telling me to turn that car around and go back and get her and take her home with us. I wanted to tell her "You're not all grown up yet. We want you back. We *need* you back!"

I knew it was silly, of course. Our daughter *was* grown up, and it was time to get out of the nest and find out what that self-image we had all been working on for eighteen years was made of.

And then I thought back over those eighteen years—all the way back to that first chilly night in November when we brought her home from the hospital. Even in balmy Tucson, the nights are cool in November, and this one was especially so. I turned up the heat to where it must have been around 104 degrees in the house, sure that our little baby would catch pneumonia, or something worse, if I didn't.

And, yes, I literally put a mirror under little Holly's nose one night as I watched her sleep, wanting extra assurance that she was breathing. The awesome responsibility of being father to this twenty-and-one-half-inch little being had hit me hard. I was charged with shaping and molding the kind of young woman she would become some day. Two years away from my doctorate in psychology, I knew something about prevalent theories concerning daddies and daughters. According to the experts, daddies, even more than mommies, shape the resilient part of their daughters.

As I drove along, I remembered one of my favorite pieces of advice to new parents: "Start leaving your child with a baby-sitter as young as two weeks. Be sure to get out with your wife and work on your marriage, and at the same time you're already starting to teach your child healthy Reality Discipline—that you won't always be there."

Yes, that's what I tell them and I'm convinced it's true, but that didn't make it any easier as we drove back to Chautauqua Lake. I remembered how hard it was that first night we left little Holly with a sitter. I suppose I spent ten minutes going over the same instructions that Sande had already given her.

And it hadn't been long until we knew we definitely had a powerful little firstborn on our hands. Holly was walking early, talking early, and into everything. Time and again she tested us with her adventuresome spirit. When she was only eighteen months I was busy in my office with clients. It was my last appointment of the day, around five-thirty, and spring twilight was beginning to fall on the streets of Tucson. As I worked with my clients, a husband and wife, the phone rang and I picked it up, somewhat annoyed, said, "Yes?"

"HOLLY'S GONE! I CAN'T FIND HER. KEVIN, SHE'S GONE. I CAN'T FIND HER!"

It was Sande. I think it would be safe to say she was slightly hysterical.

I tried to calm Sande down, but I was already slightly hysterical myself. I told my clients what had happened and all three of us ran out into the streets to start looking for my child. At the time our home wasn't far from my office, and I knew she had to be somewhere nearby. Later we figured out what had happened. I had been home until late afternoon and then had gone back to work for that early-evening appointment. I hadn't realized that little eighteen-month-old Holly had wanted to go along. She had slipped out the door, and, as I drove away and around the corner, there was my little girl, running down the street, "following her Daddy to work"—but I had no hint of what was happening.

As I dashed up and down the streets and alleys on foot, my mind went back and forth between thinking the worst and muttering, "Please, God, keep Your hand on my little girl." Finally I stopped and used a little cognitive discipline on myself.

Why are you walking? You can cover a lot more ground in a car. Drive around and you'll find her quicker.

I ran back to the office parking lot, got in my car, and started driving up and down the streets near our house. I pulled onto Craycroft, a five-lane boulevard with the middle lane designed for use by traffic from both directions passing and turning left. It was full of rush-hour traffic, and up ahead at a stop light I spotted a car, parked in that middle lane with the driver's door hanging open. Off on the side of the road was a woman, holding a child—*my child*. I screeched to a halt, jumped out of the car, and all I could manage was "Oh, you've got Holly!"

"Are you her father?" the woman said, somewhat incredulously.

"Yes, I am. Where did you find her?"

"I couldn't believe it," the woman told me. "Your little girl was out there in the passing lane and people were speeding by."

Without thinking twice about how a traffic cop might feel about her parking in that middle lane, she had pulled up, jumped out, and grabbed Holly, who was standing there in her diaper and T-shirt, happily watching the cars roar by. Only God really knew how Holly had gotten out there without being killed. Perhaps the stoplight system had caused a long break in traffic. As soon as possible, the woman had dashed for the side of the street where she had waited, holding my eighteen-month-old child and wondering, "Where in the *world* are her parents?"

I thanked the lady profusely (maybe a little more than profusely) and, weeping with joy, I took Holly home, which was only around the corner and up a side street, less than a hundred yards from where she had been found. I handed her to Sande, and we both couldn't stop crying, not even wanting to think about what might have happened to our strong-minded little firstborn who "wanted to follow Daddy to work."

AT FOUR, HOLLY "DROPPED" PRESCHOOL

The memories kept coming as we crossed the New York State line on the interstate and I finally turned onto Highway 17 which would take us to Chautauqua Lake. As Holly had gotten bigger, her strong-mindedness became even more evident. When she was four, we enrolled her in a great little preschool, operated on the campus of the University of Arizona where I was doing my graduate work. Holly was thrilled with her preschool, and especially her teacher, an older lady whom she adored.

But in a few months, disaster struck. The powers that be of the university decided to bring in a Ph.D. to direct the preschool. Full of energy, ambition, and recently learned theories, she replaced the entire preschool staff (including Holly's teacher) with other Ph.D. "specialists" who could help her turn what had been an enjoyable place to learn and play into an "experimental learning center" (that is, kiddie kollege). In just a day or two, Holly was no longer getting little hugs at the door. Instead she was handed photocopied sheets of homework assignments designed to help her with "learning readiness."

Holly lasted a week and then came home one day and said: "I don't like preschool anymore. I don't want to go back!" Because I knew what had happened at the preschool, I had a pretty good idea of why Holly wanted to quit. Always alert for opportunities to use Reality Discipline, however, I said, "Holly, if you don't want to go to preschool, you have to call the teacher and tell her yourself."

My four-year-old firstborn eyed me carefully without blinking and then chirped, "Okay!"

I dialed the number for Holly, handed her the phone, and listened with interest.

As soon as someone came on the line, Holly lisped, "This is Scholly Leman . . . I'm not coming to preschool anymore."

And she didn't. Holly never went back and we honored her

decision, not because we were trying to humor her, but because we agreed with her 100 percent.

But we didn't always agree with her. As Holly got into preadolescence, we clashed frequently. In an earlier chapter I mentioned the time when eleven-year-old Holly let me know that I should "read my own books." And the teenage "thunder years" had their loud moments too. Maybe the loudest was the time Holly wanted a fifth operation on her jaw. Four previous operations to correct a painful problem hadn't worked, and she had wanted to try it again.

Almost the second the words were out of her mouth I roared, *"No, absolutely not! No doctor is touching you again!"*

Holly started to cry and then Sande took me by the hand, calmed me down, and reminded me of the incredible pain our daughter experienced every hour of the day. "Honey," she said, "at least sit down and hear her out."

So, I sat down and heard my daughter out. "Dad," she said earnestly, "this means more to me than anything. I'm going away to college next year and I don't want to be there and have all this pain. I've got to give this one more try."

After much grumbling I finally backed down and let her go ahead with the operation. It turned out that Holly was right. The fifth time was the charm. The operation was a success.

THE UMBILICAL CORD HAD FINALLY BEEN CUT

We were nearing a final turn that would take us home as I realized that my firstborn daughter had often been right and I had often been wrong. The father, psychologist, and counselor had sat at the feet of his child and had learned important lessons of his own. And now she had gone off to school to study and learn —and grow even further away from us, as she should, of course. Things would never be quite the same again. Our relationship to Holly had now changed. The parent/child "umbilical cord" had been cut and she was on her own, totally responsible for everything, from brushing her teeth to paying her bills.

What's the matter with you, Leman? I chided myself. Becoming totally responsible is what it's all about. Isn't that what you tell them at seminars? "We're raising adults, not children!"

My thoughts jumbled on and somehow, despite the "fog" that kept clouding my glasses, I managed to find Chautauqua Lake and our cottage.

Two days later we all flew back to Tucson where the children were due back in school and I was due back in my office to dispense advice to clients as well as worry about the fortunes of the Arizona Wildcat football team.

After getting home, we waited for Holly to call. In fact, we waited and waited and waited—for a total of seven days from the day we dropped her off—but still no call. Every day it got harder. We didn't want to call her because we didn't want to start out being worried parents, hovering over our little girl. Besides, Holly was the one who was out in the world, and she had the responsibility to make contact. I ran all this wonderful Reality Discipline thinking through my mind, but, frankly, it didn't make waiting any easier.

And then one evening, not long after I'd gotten home from the office, the phone rang. It was Holly, and after she chattered with her mom a while, I got on the line and had the chance to ask her a question that had been burning in my brain ever since that day I saw her walk away from us, out of the parking lot, and into her dorm.

"Holly, what were you thinking when we said good-bye in the parking lot and you walked away?" I said, trying to sound casual.

There was a slight pause as Holly tried to remember, and then she finally said, "Well, Dad, I thought, 'Well, they brought me up right and now I'm on my own. I've got to do a good job of it.' "

Suddenly all the grief that I had felt that day when we

dropped her off flooded over me again. I tried to move my mouth, but no sounds came out.

"Dad, are you there?"

Finally I managed an "arrrgh!"

"Dad! Are you all right?" Holly sounded concerned. I guess she thought her father was having a heart attack.

"Y-y-yes, honey, I'm, I'm all r-r-right," I finally managed to quaver. We talked a little longer and then we said good-bye. Holly promised to write and to call, and we told her to study hard and all those other things you say to your daughter when she's almost 2,500 miles away and going to college.

After I hung up I felt like such a jerk for crying on the phone. I hadn't wanted to make my daughter uncomfortable, but I guess I had anyway. I just couldn't help it, the grief had hit me all over again, and I was amazed at the power it still had.

Later I was able to appreciate what Holly had said: "We had raised her right and now she was on her own and had to do a good job of it." Not only was this a beautiful compliment, it was a sort of legacy—a legacy of a strong self-image and healthy self-esteem.

That day in the parking lot our daughter was actually stronger than her parents. All the effort, struggle, nurture, and parenting of our firstborn was really blossoming right there before our eyes. We had changed her diapers, wiped her nose, swatted her on the tail when she had needed it. We had admonished her, told her what was right and wrong, brought her up with godly principles, and, above all, had loved her with all our being.

A few days after that phone call, the greeting card came in the mail addressed to me. If you haven't already guessed, it's the same card that I quoted in the introduction, the one that said, "Thanks, Dad, your strength helped me to grow, and your belief in me allowed me to be myself." I treasure that card, and every time I think of it I'm thankful for a strong-willed daughter who is full of convictions, someone who will always be "herself." Holly is what I like to call a parenting job well done. It isn't a perfect job—Holly's not a perfect child because we aren't perfect parents —but it is a job well done, and now we have to step back and watch her go out and tackle life on her own.

If you're a younger parent who still has younger children— particularly the ankle-biter type who never gives you a moment's peace—you may be wondering "What's wrong with you, Leman? Why all this fuss about a daughter moving out of the house? I can't wait until that day. I wish I could have just one afternoon alone—even an hour's peace."

I understand because Sande and I can remember saying the same thing. But the day will come when those little ones will be "all grown up" and then the bottom line questions will be:

Did we build a strong, loving relationship with our children?

Did we raise adults who are responsible and ready to take on the world?

Did we bring our kids up without tearing them down?

I hope your answer is a big *yes* to all three questions and, above all, I hope you can say, *"Full esteem ahead!"*

Notes

Chapter One

1. Don Dinkmeyer and Gary McKay, *Raising a Responsible Child: Practical Steps in Successful Family Relationships* (New York: Simon and Schuster, 1973), p. 11.

2. Carol Burnett, *One More Time: A Memoir* (New York: Avon, 1986), p. 3.

3. Sally Leman Chall, *Making God Real to Your Children* (Tarrytown, NY: Fleming H. Revell Co., 1991).

4. Dorothy Corkille Briggs, *Your Child's Self-Esteem* (New York: Doubleday/Dolphin Books, 1975), pp. 3, 4.

5. Nathaniel Branden, *The Psychology of Self-Esteem* (New York: Bantam Books, 1971), p. 110.

6. Alfred Adler, *Understanding Human Nature* (London: George Allen & Unwin, Ltd., 1928), p. 19.

7. Dinkmeyer and McKay, *Raising a Responsible Child*, p. 20.

8. Ibid., p. 27.

9. John Bradshaw, *Bradshaw On: The Family* (Deerfield Beach, FL: Health Communications, 1988), p. 31.

10. Kevin Leman, *Making Children Mind Without Losing Yours* (New York: Dell, 1987), p. 9.

Chapter Two

1. Proverbs 13:24.

2. Psalm 23:4.

3. Reported in Julie Szekely, "Child Abuse: How It Happens," *Tucson Citizen,* September 17, 1987, p. F1.

4. From a column by Ginger Hutton, "Overprotection Harms Children," *Arizona Republic,* April 20, 1987, p. B8.

5. See Zig Ziglar, *Raising Positive Kids in a Negative World* (Nashville: Oliver Nelson/Thomas Nelson, 1985), p. 214.

6. See Dr. Lee Salk, "Frustration, Not Hate, Usual Child Abuse Cause," *Arizona Daily Star*, September 25, 1984, p. D1.

7. See Kevin Leman, *Making Children Mind Without Losing Yours* (New York: Dell, 1987), p. 27.

Chapter Three

1. John Bradshaw, *Bradshaw On: The Family* (Deerfield Beach, FL: Health Communications, 1988), p. 6.

2. Karen S. Peterson, "Are Parents the New Scapegoats?" *USA Today*, October 30, 1991, p. D1.

3. Ibid.

4. Don Dinkmeyer and Gary D. McKay, *Raising a Responsible Child: Practical Steps in Successful Family Relationships* (New York: Simon and Schuster, 1973), p. 29.

5. Linda Albert, *Coping with Kids* (New York: E. P. Dutton, 1982), p. 16.

6. Ross Campbell, "How Do I Love Thee? Let Me Show the Ways," *Parents and Children*, ed. Jay Kesler, Ron Beers, and LaVonne Neff (Wheaton, IL: Victor Books, 1986), p. 545.

7. Ibid., p. 546.

8. In his studies, Dr. James Prescott found that violent, aggressive behavior was directly associated to a lack of body touching in childhood. Discussed by Dr. Joyce Brothers, "Childhood Hugs Last a Lifetime," *Los Angeles Times*, Thursday, June 28, 1990, p. E10.

9. Sydney Simon, *Meeting Yourself Halfway* (Niles, IL: Argus Communications, 1974), p. xi.

10. Ibid., p. ix.

11. Quoted by Cal Thomas, "Free Love Is a Free Ride to Destruction," *Los Angeles Times*, November 11, 1991, p. E4.

12. Alan Bloom, *The Closing of the American Mind* (New York: Simon and Schuster, 1987), p. 25.

Chapter Four

1. See Richard I. Evans, *Konrad Lorenz: The Man and His Ideas* (New York: Harcourt Brace Jovanovich, 1975), p. 13.

2. Quoted in ibid.

3. Ibid., pp. 14–16.

4. These studies include the work of Marshall Klaus and John Kennell of Case Western Reserve School of Medicine, Cleveland, Ohio. See Zig Ziglar, *Raising Positive Kids in a Negative World* (Nashville: Oliver-Nelson Books/Thomas Nelson, 1985), p. 110.

5. See Marilyn Elias, "More Kids In Declining Day Care," *USA Today*, November 7, 1991.

6. See Connie Koenenn, "Juggling the Image of Working Mothers," *Los Angeles Times*, October 22, 1991, p. F1.

7. Brenda Hunter, *Home by Choice* (Portland, OR: Multnomah Press, 1991), pp. 32, 33.

8. Ibid., p. 35.

9. John Bowlby, *Attachment*, vol. 1 of *Attachment and Loss*, 2d ed. (New York: Basic Books, 1982), p. 177. Quoted by Hunter, *Home by Choice*, p. 26.

10. Evelyn B. Thoman and Sue Browder, *Born Dancing* (New York: Harper & Row, 1987), p. 5.

11. Hunter, *Home by Choice*, p. 38.

12. Ibid., p. 48.

13. Survey done by Mark Clements Research, Inc., for *Glamour* magazine, August 1987. Reprinted in *Public Opinion* (July/August) 1988, p. 14.

14. See Liz Spayd, "More Women Trading Paychecks for Pay-offs of Full-Time Parenting," *Washington Post*, July 8, 1991, p. D3.

15. See Hunter, *Home by Choice*, pp. 121–122.

16. For a more complete list of home-based kinds of employment, see Paul and Sarah Edwards, *Working From Home* (Los Angeles: Jeremy P Tarcher, 1990). Quoted by Brenda Hunter, *Home by Choice*, p. 130.

17. See Hunter, *Home by Choice*, pp. 124–128.

18. Ziglar, *Raising Positive Kids in a Negative World*, p. 107.

19. Tim Hansel, *What Kids Need Most in a Dad* (Old Tappan, NY: Fleming H. Revell Co., 1984).

20. See Tim Hansel, "Quality Time Versus Quantity Time," in *Parents and Children*, ed. Jay Kesler, Ron Beers, and LaVonne Neff (Wheaton, IL: Victor Books, 1986), p. 90.

21. Ann Landers, "Cherish Those Precious Years," *Los Angeles Times,* August 10, 1990, p. E11.

Chapter Five

1. See Kevin Leman, *Keeping Your Family Together While the World Is Falling Apart* (New York: Delacorte Press, 1992), chapter 9.

2. Rudolf Dreikurs and Vicki Soltz, *Children: The Challenge* (New York: Hawthorne Books, 1964), p. 146.

3. M. L. Bullard, Community Parent-Teachers Education Centers, Eugene and Corvalis, Oregon. Quoted by Vicki Soltz, *Study Group Leaders' Manual* (Chicago: Alfred Adler Institute, 1967), p. 78.

Chapter Six

1. Kevin Leman, *Making Children Mind Without Losing Yours* (New York: Dell, 1987), p. 110.

Chapter Seven

1. Rudolf Dreikurs and Vicki Soltz, *Children: The Challenge* (New York: Hawthorne Books, 1964), p. 36.

2. See John Rosemond, "Offering Rewards Teaches Kids How to Manipulate Their Parents," *Buffalo News,* September 15, 1991, p. E2.

3. See John Rosemond, "Adversity Can Be Opportunity," *Buffalo News,* October 6, 1991, p. E3.

4. See Karen S. Peterson, "Confidence Helps Foster Learning," *USA Today,* October 24, 1991, p. 1D.

5. See ibid., p. 2D.

6. Ibid., p. 2D.

Chapter Eight

1. Rudolf Dreikurs, Raymond Corsini, Raymond Lowe, and Manford Sonstegard, *Adlerian Family Counseling* (Eugene, OR: University of Oregon, 1959), p. 23.

2. Don Dinkmeyer and Rudolf Dreikurs, *Encouraging Children to Learn: The Encouragement Process* (Englewood Cliffs, NJ: Prentice-Hall, 1963), p. 2.

Chapter Nine

1. David Elkind, *The Hurried Child*, rev. ed. (Reading, MA: Addison-Wesley Publishing Co., 1988), pp. xii, 3.
2. Ibid., p. xiii.
3. "When Only Isn't Lonely," The *Buffalo News*, October 14, 1991, p. C1.
4. Ibid., p. C2.
5. Proverbs 13:24.
6. Psalm 23:4.
7. Melanie Kirschner, "Ten Rules to Remember," *Sesame Street Magazine*, p. 4.
8. Taken from "Developing and Sharing Responsibility," monograph by the Community Parent-Teacher-Counselor Education Center, Cooperative Counselor Education Project: Phase II, Counseling and Guidance Department, College of Education, University of Arizona, January 1971. Revised by Rosemary Hooper, December 1976.

Chapter Ten

1. Don Dinkmeyer and Gary McKay, *Raising a Responsible Child: Practical Steps in Successful Family Relationships* (New York: Simon and Schuster, 1973), p. 17.
2. Adele Faber and Elaine Mazlish, *Siblings Without Rivalry* (New York: Avon Books, 1987), p. 89.
3. Adapted from Vicki Soltz, *Study Group Leaders' Manual*, (Chicago: Alfred Adler Institute, 1967), from material contributed by M. L. Bullard, Community Parent-Teacher Education Centers, Eugene and Corvalis, Oregon, pp. 75–77.
4. J. Kesler, Ron Beers, LaVonne Neff, eds., *Parents and Children* (Wheaton, IL: Victor Books, 1986), Paul Lewis, "How Much of Dad's Time Does a Child Need?" pp. 101–102.
5. Ibid.
6. Soltz, Study Group Leaders' Manual, *The Challenge* (Chicago: Alfred), pp. 86–88.
7. Taken from "Developing and Sharing Responsibility," monograph by the Community Parent-Teacher-Counselor Education Center, Cooperative Counselor Education Project: Phase II, Counseling and Guidance Department, College of Education, University of Arizona, January 1971. Revised by Rosemary Hooper, December 1976.

Chapter Eleven

1. James Dobson, *Preparing for Adolescence* (Ventura, CA: Vision House, 1978), pp. 14–17.

2. Kevin Leman, *Keeping Your Family Together While the World Is Falling Apart* (New York: Delacorte Press, 1992), p. 229.

3. Abigail Van Buren, "A Letter to Parents," *Los Angeles Times*, February 26, 1988, Part V, p. 2.

4. Quoted in Marilyn Elias, "Bridging the Teen Communication Gap," *USA Today*, March 13, 1991, p. 4D.

5. Reported by Amy Bach, "Girls Becoming Sexually Active at Younger Age, Defying Traditional Rules," *Arizona Daily Star*, December 31, 1991, p. C1. Statistics quoted were gathered in a study by the Alan Guttmacher Institute, a nonprofit research corporation.

6. Ibid.

7. See Peggy Mann, "Marijuana Alert III: The Devastation of Personality," *Reader's Digest* (December 1981): 81.

8. See Cynthia G. Tudor, David M. Petersen, and Kirk W. Elifson, "An Examination of the Relationship Between Peer and Parental Influences and Adolescent Drug Use," *Adolescence* (Winter 1980): 795.

9. Adapted from "Developing and Sharing Responsibility," monograph by the Community Parent-Teacher-Counselor Education Center, Cooperative Counselor Education Project: Phase II, Counseling and Guidance Department, College of Education, University of Arizona, January 1971. Revised by Rosemary Hooper, December 1976.

10. "A Teenager's Ten Commandments to Parents" from Kevin Leman, *Smart Kids, Stupid Choices* (Ventura, CA: Regal Books, 1987), p. 146.

INDEX

For information regarding
"Bringing Up Kids Without Tearing Them Down"
(an eight-part film series)
Please contact:

Dallas Christian Video
(800) 231-0095

For information regarding speaking engagements
or seminars, please write or call:

Dr. Kevin Leman
7355 N. Oracle Rd. Suite 205
Tucson, Arizona 85704
Phone (520) 797-3830
Fax (520) 797-3809

649.1
L 547
1995

98496